ORGANIZATIONAL CRISIS COMMUNICATION

SAGE was founded in 1965 by Sara Miller McCune to support the dissemination of usable knowledge by publishing innovative and high-quality research and teaching content. Today, we publish over 900 journals, including those of more than 400 learned societies, more than 800 new books per year, and a growing range of library products including archives, data, case studies, reports, and video. SAGE remains majority-owned by our founder, and after Sara's lifetime will become owned by a charitable trust that secures our continued independence.

Los Angeles | London | New Delhi | Singapore | Washington DC | Melbourne

Finn Frandsen & Winni Johansen

ORGANIZATIONAL CRISIS COMMUNICATION

With a Preface by W. Timothy Coombs

SAGE

Los Angeles | London | New Delhi
Singapore | Washington DC | Melbourne

Los Angeles | London | New Delhi
Singapore | Washington DC | Melbourne

SAGE Publications Ltd
1 Oliver's Yard
55 City Road
London EC1Y 1SP

SAGE Publications Inc.
2455 Teller Road
Thousand Oaks, California 91320

SAGE Publications India Pvt Ltd
B 1/I 1 Mohan Cooperative Industrial Area
Mathura Road
New Delhi 110 044

SAGE Publications Asia-Pacific Pte Ltd
3 Church Street
#10-04 Samsung Hub
Singapore 049483

Editor: Matthew Waters
Editorial assistant: Lyndsay Aitken
Production editor: Nicola Marshall
Copyeditor: Neville Hankins
Proofreader: Kate Campbell
Indexer: Gary Kirby
Marketing manager: Catherine Slinn
Cover design: Francis Kenney
Typeset by: C&M Digitals (P) Ltd, Chennai, India
Printed and bound by CPI Group (UK) Ltd,
Croydon, CR0 4YY

Library of Congress Control Number: 2016936129

British Library Cataloguing in Publication data

A catalogue record for this book is available from
the British Library

ISBN 978-1-4462-9705-6
ISBN 978-1-4462-9706-3 (pbk)

At SAGE we take sustainability seriously. Most of our products are printed in the UK using FSC papers and boards.
When we print overseas we ensure sustainable papers are used as measured by the PREPS grading system.
We undertake an annual audit to monitor our sustainability.

BRIEF CONTENTS

CONTENTS

LIST OF FIGURES, TABLES, CASE EXAMPLES, AND CASE STUDIES

FIGURES

TABLES

CASE EXAMPLES

CASE STUDIES

ABOUT THE AUTHORS

Finn Frandsen (mag. art., Aarhus University) is Professor of Corporate Communication and Director of the Centre for Corporate Communication at the Department of Business Communication, Aarhus School of Business and Social Sciences (Aarhus BSS), Aarhus University (Denmark).

Professor Frandsen's research interests include crisis management and crisis communication, environmental communication, public communication, stakeholder theory, and the institutionalization of strategic communication in private and public organizations. Together with Winni Johansen, he originated rhetorical arena theory and the multivocal approach to crisis communication.

His research has been published in international journals, handbooks, and encyclopedias, such as *Corporate Communications: An International Journal*, *International Journal of Strategic Communication*, *Management Communication Quarterly*, *Public Relations Inquiry*, *Public Relations Review*, *Scandinavian Journal of Public Management* and *The Handbook of Crisis Communication*, *Encyclopedia of Public Relations*, *The Routledge Handbook of Strategic Communication*, and the *Handbook of International Crisis Communication Research*.

Professor Frandsen is the Regional Editor (Europe) of *Corporate Communications: An International Journal* and a member of the advisory board of the European Communication Monitor. He has served as a visiting professor at highly ranked universities and business schools in Norway, Sweden, Finland, France, Italy, and Senegal. He has also been a consultant for organizations in the private and public sectors.

Winni Johansen (PhD, Aarhus School of Business) is Professor of Corporate Communication and Director of the Executive Master's Program in Corporate Communication at the Department of Business Communication, Aarhus School of Business and Social Sciences (Aarhus BSS), Aarhus University (Denmark).

Professor Johansen's research interests include crisis management and crisis communication, environmental communication, public communication, social media, and the institutionalization of strategic communication in private and public organizations. Together with Finn Frandsen, she originated rhetorical arena theory and the multivocal approach to crisis communication.

Her research has been published in international journals, handbooks, and encyclopedias, such as *Corporate Communications: An International Journal*, *International Journal of Strategic Communication*, *Management Communication Quarterly*, *Public Relations Inquiry*, *Public Relations Review*, *Scandinavian Journal of Public*

Management, and *The Handbook of Crisis Communication, Encyclopedia of Public Relations, The Routledge Handbook of Strategic Communication*, and the *Handbook of International Crisis Communication Research*. She is co-editor of the *International Encyclopedia of Strategic Communication Vol. I–III*.

Professor Johansen has served as a visiting professor at highly ranked universities and business schools in Norway, Sweden, Finland, France, Italy, and Senegal. She has also been a consultant for organizations in the private and public sectors.

FOREWORD

Steve Vibbert, an important mentor in my career, liked to talk about how writers find their voice. As you are about to learn, voice is an integral part of this book because voice is an essential element in rhetorical arena theory and the multivocal approach it represents. To me, voice is not only how writers express their ideas, but the qualities of those ideas. It is important for writers to demonstrate distinctive voices if they are to capture the ears and imaginations of their readers. Writers are at their best when they contribute new and insightful ideas in a way that helps readers discover, reevaluate, and reconfigure knowledge. The explosion of written works in crisis communication since the formative years in the 1990s attests to researchers' attraction to the topic. I have read the bulk of those writings and most do not provide what I would term a distinctive voice among the crowded literature. Yes, most of the crisis research does contribute to the body of knowledge, if only incrementally. But rare are the cases of the 'big idea' that cause others in the field to listen and forever alter the intellectual landscape of the field. You are about to read a book by two authors who have lent such a voice to crisis communication, namely Finn Frandsen and Winni Johansen. This volume captures some of their keen insights that I believe have altered the vista of crisis management and communication research.

In 2006, Frandsen and Johansen introduced the crisis research world to the multivocal approach. As they note in Chapter 8, earlier researchers had discussed a similar idea but no one had fully articulated the concept. Prior to 2006, crisis research was largely univocal and focused on how organizations in crisis responded to crisis situations. The approach of this early research was natural given that research evolved from a need to address the problems created by a crisis for an organization. The roots and biases of the early perspectives are identified in the reviews of the dominant crisis communication theories provided in Chapters 5 and 6. The multivocal approach is ambitious in its challenge of the myopic focus on the organization in crisis. In some crises, are there not other voices that have a significant effect on the progression and resolution of the crisis management effort? Frandsen and Johansen emphatically state the answer is 'Yes!' Among those potentially influential voices are employees, consumers, citizens, the news media, government officials, and trade associations. Chapters 9–12 explore how these various stakeholders can become relevant voices in the rhetorical arena which forms around a crisis. Along with Chapter 8, these chapters provide a greater appreciation of what a multivocal approach can offer to both the practice and study of crisis communication and crisis management. Of particular note is the information about employees in crises, Chapter 12. Frandsen and Johansen were instrumental in developing the line of crisis research known as internal crisis communication. This line of research reminds researchers and practitioners of the importance of employees during a crisis and the voices they might contribute to the rhetorical arena.

Chapter 8 also provides a detailed explanation of rhetorical arena theory (RAT). Rhetorical arenas are the spaces that open up around the discussion of the crisis. They are the spaces in which a multitude of crisis voices emerge. The multivocal perspective is reflected in the macro-level of RAT that considers the various voices in the arena. The micro-level of RAT explores the various elements of communication that can affect communicative interactions in the rhetorical arena, thereby illuminating potential effects of various crisis voices, which may or may not be in harmony. Of course RAT and its multivocal approach is messy, but messiness is required when you propose a complex view of crises that acknowledges discordant voices. Risk, one of those complicating factors, is integrated into conceptualization and discussion of crisis starting in Chapter 1. Modern thinking on crises must acknowledge the way risk and crisis are intertwined, and this book does so seamlessly.

Applying the book's own metaphor of the arena, crisis communication research is itself an arena populated by various theories and models, all given voice by various researchers. As in the rhetorical arena, the crisis research voices may talk to, past, or against other voices. A voice becomes salient when others in the arena pause to listen to ideas and begin incorporating those ideas into their own voice – a voice is heard and appreciated. This book captures the unique ideas that Frandsen and Johansen have voiced in crisis communication and integrates them with existing insights into the practice and theory of crisis communication. The end product is an ambitious, provocative, and useful book for anyone interested in crisis communication. This book offers a distinctive voice that others in the arena of crisis communication, be they researchers or practitioners, should hear, appreciate, and allow to influence their voices in productive ways.

W. Timothy Coombs
Professor of Crisis Communication
Texas A&M University

PREFACE AND ACKNOWLEDGMENTS

The history of this book, and of our crisis communication research in general, started almost 20 years ago. In mid-October 1997, the German automobile manufacturer Daimler-Benz launched the first generation of its new compact car: the Mercedes A-Class. In Denmark, a large glittering brochure entitled 'The new A-class. Inside there is a big Mercedes' was distributed to households over the weekend of October 18 and 19. A few days later, on October 21, a group of journalists from the Swedish automobile magazine *Teknikens Värld* tested the new car. Among other things, they submitted it to the so-called 'moose test', an evasive maneuver which made the small Mercedes flip over. Daimler-Benz initially denied the problem, and spokesman Hans-Gerd Bode announced resentfully that 'all cars have their physical limits'. However, the German automobile manufacturer soon decided to recall the 2,600 units already sold. Three months later, on February 8, 1998, the manufacturer relaunched the new Mercedes A-Class, which, in the meantime, had been equipped with an electronic stability program (ESP). Daimler-Benz spent DM2.5 billion developing the car, with a further DM300 million to fix it. The whole affair, in particular Daimler-Benz's handling of the crisis, rapidly attracted our attention. How would a large and internationally renowned company such as Daimler-Benz communicate in such a situation? Did it have a crisis management plan? And why did it learn so quickly and change its crisis response strategy? We have studied organizational crisis communication ever since.

In 2000, we published an article entitled 'Rhetoric and crisis communication' in *Rhetorica Scandinavica*. It was one of the very first introductions to organizational crisis communication as a field of research and practice, not only in Denmark, but also in other Scandinavian countries. This article included what was the first outline of the theory of the rhetorical arena (RAT). The theory is based on the assumption that when a crisis breaks out, a multitude of voices, such as the news media, customers, employees, investors, trade associations, citizens, politicians, NGOs, and PR experts, start communicating about, to, with, against, or around each other. In other words, crisis communication is more than just the communication produced by the organization in crisis.

In 2007, our book *Krisekommunikation*, which contained a whole chapter devoted to the multivocal approach, was published. Since then, we have developed the theory in several directions. We have left game theory as a source of inspiration in favor of a new perspective on complexity research. We have made it more evident that the rhetorical arena is neither a new stakeholder theory nor a new theory of the public sphere. We also focus more on the inter-organizational dimension of crises, introducing new concepts such as multi-crisis, second-order crisis response strategy, intermediary and meta-organization. The results of these developments of the theory of the rhetorical arena have recently been published in journal articles, book chapters, and encyclopedia entries, but only in fragments. In other words, there is a need for an updated, comprehensive synthesis. It is our hope that this book will cover at least part of this need.

Along the road we have received help, advice, and encouragement from colleagues around the world. First of all, we would like to thank the many crisis communication scholars with whom we have had the great pleasure to collaborate in writing and presenting research findings, or who have otherwise been instrumental in opening doors to international journals and handbooks: Robert L. Heath, University of Houston; W. Timothy Coombs and Sherry J. Holladay, Texas A&M University; William L. Benoit, Ohio University; Augustine Pang, Nanyang Technological University; Alessandra Mazzei, IULM University (Milan); Heidi Salomonsen, Aalborg University; and Andreas Schwarz, Ilmenau University of Technology.

We would also like to thank the crisis communication scholars at the Centre for Corporate Communication (CCC) at Aarhus University: Helle Kryger Aggerholm, Johan Martin Hjort Jacobsen, Silvia Ravazzani, and Daniel Morten Simonsen.

We would like to thank the many students at the MA, Executive MBA, and PhD levels, from Denmark, Norway, Finland, France, Italy, and Senegal, who have attended our classes on crisis communication and who on several occasions have contributed suggestions on what a textbook on crisis communication should look like. We would also like to thank colleagues who over the years have invited us as visiting professors or plenary speakers: Pål Kraft, Maria Isakson, and Tor Bang, BI Norwegian Business School (Oslo); Martin Nkosi Ndlela, Hedmark University College, Campus Rena; Brigitte Mral and Orla Vigsø, Örebro University; Leena Louhiala-Salminen and Anne Kankaanranta, Aalto University Business School (Helsinki); Alessandra Mazzei, IULM University (Milan); and last, but not least, our colleagues at ICN Business School (Nancy).

We would also like to thank Aarhus University Research Foundation (AUFF) and ICN Business School for having provided us with dwellings at a point in time when we needed a quiet place to read and write. We are very grateful to Matthew Waters, our enthusiastic editor at Sage Publications (London), for believing in the idea and for making it possible, and to Brian Woodward, Støvring Woodward Communications (Copenhagen/Aarhus), for turning our English into something that really is English.

Finally, we would like to thank our families who have supported us and showed interest in our work and writings, both when we have been away and when we have been at home. Finn would like to thank Kirsten, Søren, Gitte, Marianne, and their families for their help and support. Winni would like to thank Bjarne, Jenni, Trine, Britt, and their families for their help and support.

Finn Frandsen and Winni Johansen

GENERAL INTRODUCTION – CRISIS COMMUNICATION AS A FIELD OF RESEARCH AND PRACTICE

This general introduction introduces the aim of this book, its structure, and target audiences. First, we explain how crisis management and crisis communication have developed to become (1) a specific organizational practice or function in private as well as in public organizations and (2) an academic discipline within the social sciences at higher research and educational institutions. Second, we draw a dividing line between crisis management and crisis communication and related practices or disciplines such as disaster and emergency management, risk management, and business continuity management.

It is hard to imagine a better time to publish a textbook on organizational crises, crisis management, and crisis communication than today. The world has suffered from a global financial crisis since the American investment bank Lehmann Brothers declared bankruptcy on September 15, 2008. This crisis, which resulted in wide-ranging consequences for the private and public sectors in many countries, does not seem to be close to its end (despite claims to the contrary). Globalization and the new information and communications technology (the Internet, social media) have only contributed further to the idea that we are living in a crisis society.

On the one hand, this ongoing 'state of crisis' has transformed the very word *crisis* into a fixed component of the vocabulary that organizations and their stakeholders use to describe the world in which they operate. Put simply, crisis is becoming the norm.

On the other hand, crisis management and crisis communication have been institutionalized as an organizational practice or function in many private and public organizations, and as a topic for education and research in many universities and business schools in recent decades. Because of this, our understanding of crisis management and crisis communication has developed substantially. Until recently, we focused almost exclusively on a strategic, proactive, and process-oriented approach to managing organizational crises (cf. Chapters 3 and 4) – an approach symbolized by the formal crisis preparedness of organizations, including having a crisis management team and a crisis management plan. The new normal we speak about, in which crises are an everyday reality and ongoing state of affairs, has brought with it a shift. Today, we have also started focusing on organizational resilience and how organizations can navigate in situations where their crisis management plans are no longer of any use.

This book takes its starting point from this new situation: that crises increasingly are perceived as a distinctive feature of the society and the organizations in which we live and work; and that crisis management and crisis communication have been institutionalized as a field of research and practice.

THE INSTITUTIONALIZATION OF CRISIS MANAGEMENT AND CRISIS COMMUNICATION

Institutionalization is a concept belonging to the sociology of organizations. It designates the process whereby an area of society, a group of organizations, an industry, or an entire sector is penetrated by a new idea due to normative pressure from the environment – an idea that changes the organizations and ends up being adopted and taken for granted by their members. The content of this idea can be a new way to manage and organize companies, or a new research area at universities and business schools (for an introduction to neo-institutional organization theory, see Scott, 2008; Greenwood et al., 2008; Frandsen & Johansen, 2013a).

In this book, we make a distinction between two different, yet closely related, types of institutionalization processes. The first type of process takes place in private and public organizations where crisis management and crisis communication have been recognized as a specific *organizational practice* since the mid-1980s. The second type of process takes place in universities and business schools where crisis management and crisis communication have been recognized as an *academic discipline* per se within the social sciences.

Crisis management and crisis communication defined as an organizational practice and as an academic discipline generate two different types of knowledge: (1) practical knowledge based mainly on personal experience; and (2) theoretical knowledge based mainly on scientific research. However, there is a third knowledge-producing context that we must not forget, namely the *consultancy industry*. Consultants produce insights which are located somewhere between practical and theoretical knowledge and which are highly relevant to a textbook. Consultants also play an important role as disseminators or carriers of new business knowledge (Alvarez, 1998).

It is important to understand how these two institutionalization processes unfold in order to describe and explain how and why crisis management and crisis communication emerged, how they have developed, and how today they form a *field* of research and practice.

As an organizational practice

During the past three decades, more and more private companies have established crisis preparedness. It did not take place at the same time in all countries and different types of organizations have adopted it at different speeds. It started in the United States, whereas countries such as Denmark and Japan did not follow until later. And it was in big corporations that the new idea of crisis management and crisis communication was first adopted (with smaller organizations following suit later).

There are many rational reasons for establishing crisis preparedness. A severe crisis can harm a company in several ways. It can lead to a sudden decrease in revenue or share value. It can make it more difficult to attract the most talented employees. It can reduce the company's political influence. But perhaps most notably, a severe crisis will also often damage the trust or reputation created by the company among its key stakeholders.

Beyond these rational reasons there may also be symbolic reasons for establishing crisis preparedness in an organization. If the majority of organizations within a specific industry or sector, in particular the most progressive and most admired organizations, decide to start practising crisis management and crisis communication, many other organizations belonging to the same industry or sector will automatically follow. This is the phenomenon called *isomorphism* within the sociology of organizations: that is, mechanisms that 'make organizations more similar without necessarily making them more efficient' (DiMaggio & Powell, 1983, p. 147). Isomorphism can explain why a group of organizations adopts a new idea, in our case the idea of crisis management and crisis communication. At the same time, it can also explain why some organizations never succeed in learning to apply the new idea. The reason why they adopted the idea in the first place was not so much the result of an effort to become more effective as the result of a search for legitimacy.

So far, no one has subjected the institutionalization of crisis preparedness in private and public organizations to a longitudinal or point-in-time study. However, based on a series of mutually independent surveys conducted at different points in time and in different countries, it is possible to create a certain overview of the formal adoption of crisis preparedness. In other words, we are able to verify if the organizations have crisis preparedness; we just cannot say anything about how they use it.

One of the very first empirical studies of the crisis preparedness of private companies was conducted by the USC Center for Crisis Management under the guidance of Ian I. Mitroff from 1987 to 1991. The study included interviews with 500 managers from the United States, Canada, and France and a questionnaire sent to executives in Fortune 1000 companies in the United States (Pauchant & Mitroff, 1992). The findings showed among other things that in 1990 only 55 percent of the companies interviewed by Mitroff and his colleagues had established a crisis management team. Nevertheless, about 50 percent of the respondents judged that their company's crisis management plan was sufficient.

From 2002 to 2004, the American Management Association published an annual *Crisis Management and Security Issues Survey*. To the question 'Does your company have a crisis management plan?', 61 percent answered yes in 2004 (against 49 percent in 2002). To the question 'Has your organization designated a crisis management team?', 54 percent answered yes in 2004 (the same as in 2002). The 2004 study only included 174 respondents (www.amanet.org).

Frandsen and Johansen (2004) conducted a survey among private companies and public authorities in Denmark. A total of 750 organizations were contacted, out of which 290 answered the questionnaire (overall response rate: 39.7 percent). Of the 160 private companies that participated, 66 percent answered that they had a crisis management plan and 38 percent that they had a crisis management team. In a survey on internal crisis management and crisis communication in private companies and municipalities conducted almost 10 years later, more than 70 percent of the respondents answered that their organizations had a crisis management plan (Johansen et al., 2012).

Two of the most recent surveys focused on the communicative dimension of organizational crisis preparedness. Cloudman and Hallahan (2006) conducted a survey among 126 public relations professionals in American organizations to measure their crisis communication preparedness. This survey showed that 75 percent of these organizations had a written crisis communication plan.

The 2013 European Communication Monitor, an annual survey published by EUPRERA and EACD, was conducted among 2,710 respondents from 43 different countries. The section devoted to crisis communication included questions concerning the instruments and channels used for crisis communication and the communication strategies used in different crisis situations. Media relations and personal communication came in as the two most used instruments or channels (75 percent), and the information strategy, that is providing stakeholders with facts and figures, explaining next step, etc., was the dominant strategy (82 percent). Another key finding was the evidence that economic and cultural aspects play a role in defining a crisis and communication about it (Verhoeven et al., 2014).

Although the empirical evidence is limited, and although the existence of a crisis management team and a crisis management plan does not tell us everything about the practice of crisis management in an organization, the surveys presented above show that the formal crisis preparedness of private companies has increased during the past two or three decades.

Public organizations represent a special case due to the fact that many of them are ahead of and behind the private companies at one and the same time. They are ahead of private companies because they have been responsible for practising disaster and emergency management for decades, focusing traditionally on extraordinary incidents and citizen safety. They are lagging behind private companies because they have only recently started to look at themselves as 'corporations' that have to protect their reputation among key stakeholders. In certain types of public organizations such as municipalities, this means that crisis preparedness is governed by two variations of the same institutional logic, including the risk of disintegration (Frandsen & Johansen, 2009b; Frandsen et al., 2016).

Finally, a process of specialization has started recently as people within the field have gradually become more and more aware of the specific conditions for practicing crisis management and crisis communication within a specific industry or type of organization. In the United States, where this development is most advanced, one finds both academic books and 'how-to' books on crisis management and crisis communication in areas such as sports (Blaney et al., 2012), tourism (Glaesser, 2006; Henderson, 2006), hospitals (Johnson, 2006), and universities (Zdziarski et al., 2007).

BOX 1

PROFESSIONAL ASSOCIATIONS

The majority of practitioners in charge of the crisis management function of private and public organizations are members of various national and international professional associations, that is organizations seeking to further the interests of the profession and its members – for example, by setting standards and offering professional certification. Here are some of the most important associations within crisis management and crisis communication and related disciplines such as disaster or emergency management, risk management, and business continuity management (cf. the last section of this general introduction):

- The International Emergency Management Society (TIEMS) (1993–)
- Information Systems for Crisis Response and Management (ISCRAM) (2004–)
- International Association of Crisis Management (ICMA) (2006–)
- International Association of Emergency Managers (IAEM) (1952–)
- Public Risk Management Organization (PRIMO) (2007–).

We encourage the reader to visit one of the websites of these professional associations and to take a look at, for example, IAEM's definition of emergency management and its 'Principles of Emergency Management'. Unfortunately, there is no International Association for Crisis Communication.

As an academic discipline

There are also several indicators pointing to the fact that organizational crisis management and crisis communication have become institutionalized as an academic discipline during the past three decades. Again, development has not taken place at the same time in all countries. The United States, France, Sweden, and the Netherlands are among the pioneering countries.[1]

The first and most important indicator comes in the form of the many new insights generated by researchers who are active in this field. These insights are disseminated in research publications which can be subjected to bibliometric reviews (e.g., citation analysis or content analysis) revealing how, when, and where an academic discipline develops and makes progress. Regarding research in crisis management, a computer search on the words 'crisis management' conducted by Pauchant (1988) revealed that 80 percent of materials since 1963, the year in which Charles F. Hermann wrote 'Some consequences of crisis which limit the viability of organizations' and introduced the concept of organizational crisis to the field of management, were published *after 1985*

---

[1] Schwarz et al. (2016a) provide a review of the crisis management and crisis communication research conducted internationally. See also the special issue of *Journal of Contingencies and Crisis Management*, 10(4), 2002, on 'Crisis management in France'.

(Pauchant & Douville, 1993). The book by Fink (1986) is often mentioned as the first one on crisis management. Regarding research in crisis communication, several bibliometric reviews have shown that the number of journal articles on crisis communication have grown considerably in recent years. The first journal article on crisis communication seems to have been published in 1987.[2]

The second indicator is the existence of academic forums where the new insights mentioned above are exchanged. There are international research networks such as the Temporary Working Group on Crisis Communication established by the European Communication Research and Education Association (ECREA) in 2012 and turned into a Thematic Section in 2015. There are also international conferences such as the series of conferences entitled 'Crisis Communication in the 21st Century' which have been held four times so far (at Ilmenau in 2009, Aarhus in 2011, Erfurt in 2013, and Lund in 2015).

The third indicator is the existence of academic journals specializing in crisis management and crisis communication, such as the *International Journal of Mass Emergencies and Disasters* (1983), *Industrial Crisis Quarterly* (1987), *Disaster Prevention and Management* (1992), and the *Journal of Contingencies and Crisis Management* (1992). The majority of these journals were established in the early and mid-1980s or in the early 1990s. Unfortunately, there is still no journal devoted exclusively to the study of crisis communication. Here one has to search for journals with academic labels such as public relations, organizational communication, corporate communication, and strategic communication included in their names. *Public Relations Review* is probably the closest one can get to a 'Journal of Crisis Communication'.

The fourth indicator is the publication of handbooks and collections of 'masterworks'. The purpose of these publications is to define and delimit the field and to provide a systematic account of the core and coherence of the discipline of crisis management and crisis communication. Within crisis management the following books have been published over a short span of years: *International Handbook of Organizational Crisis Management* (Pearson, Roux-Dufort & Clair, 2007), *Handbook of Research on Crisis Leadership in Organizations* (DuBrin, 2013), *Handbuch Krisenmanagement* (Thießen, 2013), and *Encyclopedia of Crisis Management* (Penuel et al., 2013). To these publications one can add *Key Readings in Crisis Management* (Smith & Elliott, 2006). Within crisis communication the following books have been published over a short span of years: *Handbook of Risk and Crisis Communication* (Heath & O'Hair, 2009), *The Handbook of Crisis Communication* (Coombs & Holladay, 2010), and *Handbook of International Crisis Communication Research* (Schwarz et al., 2016a). To these publications one can add *Crisis Communication Vol. I–IV* (Coombs, 2014c).

The final indicator is the publication of textbooks, which often are seen as a sign of discipline formation. Today, crisis management and crisis communication are taught in more and more universities and business schools, and the literature on crisis management education equally is growing.[3] The authoritative textbook on crisis communication is

---

[2] Among the most important bibliometric reviews are An and Cheng (2010) and Avery et al. (2010).

[3] See for example the special issue of *Journal of Management Education*, 37(2), 2013, on 'Crisis management education', including the agenda for educators (and their students) in the epilogue.

Coombs' *Ongoing Crisis Communication* (1999) and its subsequent editions. However, Fearn-Banks (1996) and Ulmer et al. (2007), with their subsequent editions, and Sellnow and Seeger (2013) are also important textbooks.

What can we conclude from this ongoing process of institutionalization? It depends on who you are.

The scholars who have specialized in crisis management tend to be pessimistic in their evaluation of the development of the discipline. Pearson et al. (2007) describe research in crisis management as 'dispersed and noncumulative' (p. viii). It sounds almost like an echo of a similar evaluation published 15 years earlier by Pauchant and Douville (1993), in which research in crisis management is described as suffering from 'fragmentation' and 'the lack of a general paradigm' (p. 59). In return, those scholars who have specialized in crisis communication are more optimistic. Toth (2010) promotes the crisis communication research conducted within the field of public relations as no less than a 'crisis communication paradigm' (p. 714). Coombs and Holladay (2010) take it one step further. In their preface to *The Handbook of Crisis Communication* they write:

> Currently, crisis communication is more of a subdiscipline in public relations and corporate communication. However, as the research in crisis communication continues to grow, it may be able to establish itself as an independent field that is both provocative and exciting. These are lofty goals, but as one popular expression states, 'Go big or stay home' (GOBOSH)'. (pp. xxvi–xxvii)

BOX 2

CRISIS RESEARCHERS

Ian I. Mitroff (born 1938), Professor Emeritus at the Marshall School of Business and the Annenberg School of Communication, University of Southern California, is often considered the founding father of modern crisis management.

Among other important American crisis management and crisis communication researchers, there are (in alphabetical order): William L. Benoit, Glen T. Cameron, W. Timothy Coombs, Robert L. Heath, Keith M. Hearit, Sherry J. Holladay, Matthew W. Seeger, Timothy L. Sellnow, Robert R. Ulmer, and Shari Veil.

Among European researchers we would like to mention: An-Sofie Claeys (Belgium), Patrick Lagadec, Thierry Pauchant, and Christophe Roux-Dufort (France), Martin Löffelholz, Friederike Schultz, and Andreas Schwarz (Germany), Alessandra Mazzei, Silvia Ravazzani, and Chiara Valentini (Italy), Arjen Boin, Paul 't Hart, Uriel Rosenthal, and Marita Vos (the Netherlands), Jesper Falkheimer, Mats Heide, Eva-Karin Olsson, Charlotte Simonsson, and Orla Vigsø (Sweden), and Dominic Elliott and Dennis Smith (United Kingdom).

Among Asian researchers we would like to mention: Yan Jin (China) and Augustine Pang (Singapore).

PURPOSE OF THE BOOK

The overall goal of this book is twofold. First, the purpose of this book is to introduce the reader to organizational crisis management and crisis communication as a field of research and practice, that is as both an organizational practice and an academic discipline. Crisis management and crisis communication are almost as complex as the crises they are expected to handle. They are based on knowledge from many different disciplines within the social sciences and the humanities: anthropology, sociology, psychology, political science, management, organization and communication studies, rhetoric, text and discourse analysis – just to mention the most important of these disciplines. To do justice to this cross-disciplinary complexity we have chosen to apply a *multidimensional* approach to the field. Such an approach entails that the same topic is viewed from two or more dimensions without identifying one of these as the primary dimension. Thus, we present and discuss *five key dimensions* of organizational crises, crisis management, and crisis communication. Each of these dimensions encompasses one or more key questions (see Table I.1).

It is important to keep in mind that none of these five key dimensions exist in isolation. On the contrary, they all form part of specific constellations depending on how you answer the questions related to the individual dimensions. If, for example, you answer no to the question under the societal dimension (Are we living in a crisis society?) you will probably also defend a more functionalistic approach to crisis management and crisis communication. Your main concern will be: How can we handle organizational crises most effectively? In return, if your answer is yes, you will probably apply a more interpretive or critical approach to crisis management and crisis communication. Your main concern will of course still be how to handle crises, but you will also be interested in *understanding* how crises and the way we manage them have an influence on society at large.

Second, the purpose of this book is to introduce the reader to a new theory of crisis communication, that is the theory of the *rhetorical arena* (abbreviated RAT) and the so-called *multivocal* approach. We claim that in a crisis situation it is not only

Table I.1 A multidimensional approach to crisis management and crisis communication

Key dimensions	Key questions
(1) Societal dimension	*Are we living in a crisis society?*
(2) Definitional and typological dimension	*What is an organizational crisis?* *How can organizational crises be categorized into crisis types?*
(3) Managerial dimension	*What are the most important approaches to crisis management?*
(4) Communicative dimension	*What are the most important approaches to crisis communication?*
(5) (Inter)cultural dimension	*Do (inter)cultural differences have an impact on the practice of crisis management and crisis communication?*

Table I.2 A multivocal approach to crisis management and crisis communication

Key voices in the arena	Key questions
(1) Consumers and citizens	*How do consumers interact with an organization in crisis and between each other?*
(2) News media	*How do the news media cover and intervene in a crisis situation?*
(3) Trade associations	*How do trade associations manage the company's reputation, the industry's reputation, and its own reputation in a crisis situation?*
(4) Employees and managers	*How do employees and managers react and communicate when their organization is in crisis?*
(5) The organization in crisis	*How can an organization in crisis manage the many voices in the rhetorical arena?*

important to manage the voice of the organization in crisis (e.g., the crisis response strategies applied by the spokesperson talking on behalf of the organization), but also equally important to understand and to anticipate the many other voices who start communicating as the crisis escalates, such as the news media covering and/or intervening in the course of events leading to a crisis; customers complaining about an organization and the low quality of its products on Twitter and Facebook; employees trying to make sense of a crisis in their organization; experts from PR agencies evaluating and commenting on how an organization manages a crisis; politicians trying to link their personal political agenda to a crisis event; and third parties having a stake, not in the organization as such, but in the crisis (see Table I.2).

STRUCTURE OF THE BOOK

The book consists of this general introduction, 12 chapters, and an epilogue. The chapters are divided into two parts in accordance with the two purposes of the book. Part 1 (Chapters 1–7) provides an advanced, up-to-date introduction to crisis management and crisis communication which is based on the most recent research within the field, while Part 2 (Chapters 8–12) introduces the reader to the theory of the rhetorical arena and the multivocal approach to crisis communication. Most of the chapters are structured in the same way. They contain a chapter overview, at least one case example and/or one major case study, one or more thematic boxes, and a chapter summary. At the end of each chapter, there are suggestions for further reading.

TARGET AUDIENCES

The primary audience for the book is composed of graduate students (and their teachers) in corporate communication, public relations, organizational communication, strategic communication, and management and organization studies in universities and business schools. Executive MBA students and PhD students can also benefit from reading the book. The secondary audience consists of practitioners in charge of the crisis management and crisis communication function in their organization. Consultants from communication and management agencies will also find the book relevant and useful. Practitioners just have to read the book differently. Whereas graduate students will benefit most by reading it right from the beginning, chapter by chapter, we recommend that practitioners read the book backwards, starting with the epilogue and Chapter 8 (in particular case study 8.1). Depending on the level of knowledge and/or experience of the reader, he or she can then continue reading either Part 1 or the rest of Part 2.

DELIMITATION

What is an organizational crisis?

The topic of this book is organizational crises, crisis management, and crisis communication. What does this mean? First of all, it means that our focal point will always be a crisis *for an organization*, and not, for example, a social, political, and religious crisis or a personal crisis. An organizational crisis is a crisis that is caused by an organization and/or a crisis that has negative consequences for an organization. It can damage the economic capital, political capital (influence), social capital (trust), and symbolic capital (image and reputation) of the organization. Our understanding of what an organization is will remain broad throughout the book. Most of the time, we will refer to private and public organizations, such as companies and municipalities, but we also define, for example, trade associations, political parties, sport associations, and NGOs as organizations. Second, this means that crisis management and crisis communication will be seen as *embedded in an organizational context*. This context includes not only the formal organization of the crisis preparedness (cf. Chapter 1), but also important factors such as type of organization and organizational culture. We assume that this 'embeddedness' will influence how the organization manages and communicates in crisis situations.

Crisis management and crisis communication – one or two disciplines?

Now and then we will refer to crisis management and crisis communication as if we were talking about two different disciplines. It is most evident in Part 1 where two chapters have been devoted to each of the two disciplines. However, it must be emphasized that we see crisis management and crisis communication as one and only one discipline based on the following principle: *no crisis management without communication, and no crisis communication without management, when a crisis breaks out*. Crisis communication cannot be reduced to an operational or tactical activity (e.g., the production of a press release) which is not activated until the crisis management team of the organization has decided which strategy it will pursue in order to handle the crisis. The decision-making process is also a communicative process. We will return to this principle in Chapter 4.

Related disciplines

Occasionally we will also refer to disciplines other than crisis management and crisis communication, such as disaster and emergency management, risk management, and business continuity management. Each of these disciplines has its own history, area of activity, terminology, and theoretical traditions.

Disaster management (or *emergency management*) is the oldest of these disciplines. As indicated by the name, the rationale of disaster management is to handle disasters (from the Latin word for 'bad star', *dis* + *astro*), that is a severe disruption of the functioning of a society or a community. It is common to make a distinction between *natural disasters* (earthquakes, floods, hurricanes, etc.) and *human-made disasters* (oil spills, fires, nuclear accidents, etc.). The most common disasters are natural disasters, but the line between natural and human-made is often blurred (cf. Hurricane Katrina).

Disasters are mostly handled by public emergency response organizations such as the police, fire departments, emergency medical services, home guards, and agencies at the local and/or national level (e.g., FEMA in the United States and DEMA in Denmark). However, private disaster relief organizations such as the Red Cross also often play a key role. The terminology of disaster and emergency management includes: citizen, disaster, emergency, extraordinary incident, information, public safety, etc.

The Center for Disaster Research (CDR), the first social science research center in the world devoted to the study of disasters, was founded in 1962 by Enrico L. Quarantelli, a pioneer within the sociology of disasters. Quarantelli is the author and (co-)editor of a series of important books, including two anthologies, both entitled *What is a Disaster?* (1998, 2005), and, most recently, *Handbook of Disaster Research* (2007).

Disaster and emergency management differ from crisis management by focusing on specific types of negative events without necessarily including an organizational dimension (although this is often the case).

Risk management is another important discipline practised within areas such as health, security, the environment, and finance. As the new risk society emerges, risk management is introduced in a growing number of private and public organizations. Power (2004, 2007) has examined the consequences of this 'risk management of everything' (cf. Chapter 1). In its simplest form, risk is defined as the multiplication of the probability of a negative or dangerous object by the consequences or severity. It is common to make a distinction between *pure* or *absolute risks* (such as safety, fire, major hazards, security lapses, environmental hazards, etc.) and *speculative risks* (such as financial investment, marketing, human resources, IT strategy, commercial and business risks, etc.) (Waring & Glendon, 1998).

The objective of risk management is to eliminate, reduce, or control pure risks, and to gain enhanced utility or benefit and avoid detriment from speculative risks. Risk management consists of a series of iterative processes such as risk identification, risk analysis and profiling, risk decisions and actions.

The terminology of risk management is based on keywords such as: risk, hazard, threat, probability, consequence, assessment.

Risk management differs from crisis management by focusing exclusively on the pre-crisis stage.

Business continuity management (BCM) is the youngest of the disciplines mentioned above. Business continuity can be defined as the capability of an organization to continue delivery of products or services at acceptable predefined levels following a disruptive incident (ISO 22300, 2012).

The historical roots of BCM lie in information systems (IS) management and protection, but the discipline has moved far beyond this narrow approach since the 1990s (for a historical overview, see Elliott et al., 2002; Herbane, 2010a). BCM started out in the 1970s as an IT-focused discipline in the financial services sector. The main objective was to protect hard systems such as corporate mainframe systems. At that time, BCM was known as disaster recovery planning. In the 1990s, the technology mindset of this approach was gradually replaced by a holistic and value-based mindset where organizations are defined as socio-technical systems, and where the focus is on protecting the entire organization, not just specific core functions. This development is reflected in the ISO definition of BCM as a

> holistic management process that identifies potential threats to an organization and the impacts to business operations those threats, if realized, might cause, and which provides a framework for building organizational resilience with the capability of an effective response that safeguards the interests of its key stakeholders, reputation, brand and value-creating activities. (ISO 22301, 2012)

The terminology of BCM is based on keywords such as: continuity, disruption, hard and soft, and information system.

BCM differs from crisis management by focusing on specific types of negative events and situations. However, since the 1990s, BCM has moved closer to crisis management. A good example of this is Elliott et al.'s (2002) *crisis management approach to business continuity*.

Toward convergence?

Organizational crisis management, disaster or emergency management, risk management, and BCM are disciplines in their own right, with their own history, areas of activity, terminology, and theoretical traditions. These differences have from time to time triggered controversies between scholars representing the disciplines.

Risk management has been criticized by crisis management researchers for taking a perspective on risk and crises that is too narrow and cost–benefit oriented. Perrow (1984) claimed that risk management is 'a narrow field, cramped by the monetarization of social good' (p. 308). Similarly, Pauchant and Mitroff (1992) claimed that risk management 'involves evaluating the cost of a risk after multiplying by its probability of occurrence. A disaster with a high cost but low probability of occurrence will not be taken into consideration. In contrast, *crisis* management involves focusing not only on the most probable events but also on the event with the greatest impact' (p. 93). More recently, Mitroff (2005) has started warning against risk management as well as BCM: 'CM is in danger of a "hostile takeover" by risk management (RM) ... RM and BCP threaten to reduce CM to a series of structured exercises and checklists ... RM and BCP are not comprehensive and systemic enough' (pp. xv–xvi).

However, there are also signs of convergence between the disciplines involved. Two good examples of this can be found within disaster management and BCM. In *Business Continuity Management* (2002), Elliott et al. take a 'crisis management approach' to business continuity. By this they understand a broader approach than the one presented in the early BCM literature, where business interruptions are seen as systematic in nature, comprising both social and technical elements. Similarly, in their chapter to *Handbook of Disaster Research* (2005), Boin and t' Hart apply a 'crisis approach' to disaster management. By this they too understand a broader approach providing a framework for managing and studying the dynamic evolution of disasters (cf. the staged approaches presented in Chapter 4).

INTRODUCTION SUMMARY

This general introduction has demonstrated how organizational crisis management and crisis communication have been institutionalized, over the past two or three decades, as organizational practice in private and public organizations as well as an academic discipline in universities and business schools. The chapter also describes the main differences between crisis management and related disciplines such as disaster management, emergency management, risk management, and business continuity management.

 Further reading

Coombs, W. T. (2014). Crisis communication: A developing field. In W. T. Coombs (Ed.), *Crisis Communication I–IV, Vol. 1, Origins of Crisis Communication*. London: Sage Benchmarks in Communication.

DIMENSIONS OF ORGANIZATIONAL CRISES, CRISIS MANAGEMENT, AND CRISIS COMMUNICATION

Organizational crises can be studied from many different perspectives. In this part we apply a multidimensional approach exploring the five key dimensions of the field: (1) the societal dimension, (2) the definitional and typological dimension, (3) the managerial dimension, (4) the communicative dimension, and (5) the (inter)cultural dimension. After reading Part 1, the reader should be able to provide answers to the following questions:

- Are we living in a crisis society?
- How can organizational crises be defined and categorized?
- What are the most important approaches to crisis management and crisis communication, and how can they be applied in practice?
- Do national and organizational cultures have an impact on how private and public organizations communicate in a crisis situation?

LIVING IN A CRISIS SOCIETY

CHAPTER OVERVIEW

This chapter explores the societal dimension of organizational crises, crisis management, and crisis communication. In examining the question 'Are we living in a crisis society?', the chapter provides an introduction to risk sociology, claiming that we can apply Ulrich Beck's theory of the risk society as the overall explanatory framework in our study of organizational crises. The consequences of the development toward a risk society are discussed.

INTRODUCTION

It is very likely that crisis is an anthropological universal: that is, a feature which characterizes human life across all historical eras. In all known societies – from the hunter–gatherer society to the agricultural and industrial society to the post-industrial and post-modern society – human beings and their communities have been hit on a regular basis by negative events that correspond to what we would today call a crisis. However, until now, no society in history has felt it more urgent to identify, to prepare for, to handle, and, last but not least, to *talk* about crises than our society. This observation leads us directly to this chapter's key question: Are we living in a crisis society? If yes, which concepts do we need in order to be able to describe such a society? And how does this affect the crisis management and crisis communication activities of private and public organizations?

SIGNS OF A CRISIS SOCIETY

A first sign of the emergence of a crisis society is the fact that we have started using the word *crisis* much more frequently than before. One way to verify this is to examine the appearance and frequency of keywords from the crisis terminology as reflected in the news media. While concepts such as crisis management and crisis communication have been in use for a long time in pioneering countries such as the United States and France, this is not the case in, for example, Denmark and Japan (West, 2006). We carried out an analysis of the frequency of the words *crisis*, *crisis management*, and *crisis communication* in three Danish newspapers (*Jyllands-Posten*, *Politiken*, and *Børsen*) from 1990 to 2010, that is until the effects of the global financial crisis were being felt everywhere and where we expected that the word *crisis* would become omnipresent. The results of this analysis showed that there is a clear increase in the use of words such as *crisis* starting in the mid-1990s. From 1990 to 1995, *crisis* is used only 14 times in *Jyllands-Posten*, the largest newspaper in Denmark. However, from 1996 to 2000, it is used 7,281 times. From 2001 to 2005, it appears 7,043 times, and from 2006 to 2010, it is used 17,888 times (in the same newspaper). Regarding more technical terms such as *crisis management plan (CMP)*, *crisis management team (CMT)*, *crisis management*, and *crisis communication*, these do not appear until the late 1990s and early 2000s (see Figure 1.1). In *Jyllands-Posten*, *crisis management* is used for the first time in 1997, and *crisis communication* in 2002.

In the two other Danish newspapers, *Politiken* and *Børsen*, we found similar patterns in the frequency of these terms.

In *Discourse and Social Change* (1992), British critical discourse analyst Norman Fairclough explains how social changes are reflected in our use of language. According to Fairclough, important areas of our society such as higher education have been subjected to *marketization*, which is reflected in our discourse on higher education when we refer to educational programs as 'products' and to students as 'clients' (Fairclough, 1993). Similarly, our use of terms such as *crisis management* and *crisis communication* reflects new and important developments in society.

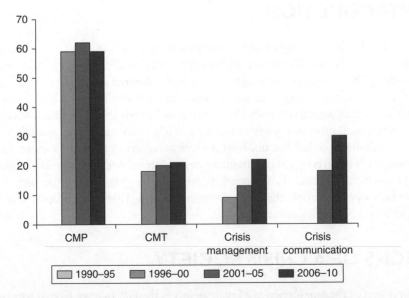

Figure 1.1   Frequency of crisis terminology in *Jyllands-Posten* (1990-2010)

A second sign that we are living in a crisis society is the importance we ascribe to crises. Seeger et al. (2003) claim that crises such as the *Titanic* disaster, the *Exxon Valdez* oil spill, the Chernobyl nuclear disaster, the Space Shuttle *Challenger* explosion, and the 9/11 terrorist attacks are life-changing occurrences that have become archetypical events for both individuals and communities. These crises have transformed into 'social icons, around which broader meaning is constructed, maintained, symbolized and conveyed' (p. 6).

Once again we can bring in the news media if we want to verify that certain crises have become social icons. Every time we remember a crisis that has acquired the status of a social icon in society at large – a year, 5 years, 10 years, 20 years, or more after the crisis took place – the media cover the event. This may be to illustrate that the aftermath of the crisis has still not reached its final conclusion (an investigation, a trial in the courts, etc.). It may be in order to tell the personal stories of the people who survived a disaster, or of those who were left behind. Or it may be in order to evaluate the consequences of the crisis from a larger historical perspective (see case example 1.1 on the MS *Estonia* disaster).

A third sign that we are living in a crisis society is the widespread idea (or should we say feeling?) that the number of crises is constantly increasing and that we must handle and investigate these crises. In 2003, we conducted a survey among private companies and public authorities in Denmark (cf. the general introduction). Our aim was to study how the two populations perceived and defined crises, how many crises they had experienced, how they practised crisis management and crisis communication, and how they evaluated their learning needs (Frandsen & Johansen, 2004). As part of the study, 18 follow-up interviews were conducted in which the interviewees were asked the question: Are there more crises today than before? The majority answered yes. However, those who answered yes justified their answer in two different ways. Some gave an 'objective' explanation claiming that society has developed in such a way that there are in fact more crises today than before. Others gave a more 'subjective' explanation claiming that we have become more aware or conscious of crises, but without postulating that this also meant that there are more crises today than before.

So how can we explain – using social changes as our starting point – that we talk more and more about crises, that we define them as social icons, and that we imagine that there are more crises today than ever before?

 Case example 1.1 ————————————————

The MS *Estonia* disaster as a social icon

On September 28, 1994, the MS *Estonia*, a 155 meter long and 24 meter broad cruise ferry with a capacity of 2,000 passengers, sank in the Baltic Sea on its way from Tallinn to Stockholm. In all, 852 people lost their lives, including more than 500 Swedes. Only 137 survived. The investigation following the disaster revealed that the locks on the bow door had failed from the strain of the waves and that the door had separated from the rest of the vessel.

The day of the wreck of MS *Estonia*, a maritime disaster described as the worst ever in Scandinavia, has over time become a day of commemoration that is covered by the news

(Continued)

(Continued)

media in many of the countries affected. From 1994 to 2014, for example, *Dagens Nyheter* (DN), one of Sweden's largest newspapers, wrote 257 articles about the disaster. The majority were published after the fatal night in September 1994.

Ten years after the disaster, DN released seven articles during the days immediately before and after September 28. The headlines of the articles read: 'Create clarity about MS Estonia' (September 29, 2004), 'Estonia commemorates the victims of MS Estonia' (September 29, 2004), 'Evocative commemoration of the victims of MS Estonia' (September 28, 2004), 'Survivors talk about ferry disaster' (September 27, 2004), 'Swedish parliament releases report on MS Estonia', 'Risk of a new disaster' (September 19, 2004) and 'MS Estonia archive opens today' (August 31, 2004).

Twenty years after the disaster, DN released two further articles. The first one, entitled 'The unthinkable is not impossible' (September 28, 2014), was about how new equipment had turned the Baltic Sea into a safer workplace for emergency crews, but that it has been difficult to draw a more general lesson from the disaster. The second article, 'About MS Estonia. Commemorative music that will not settle down' (September 29, 2014), was about a memorial concert at the Baltic Festival where Finnish composer Jaakko Mäntyjärvi's choral work 'Canticum Calamitatis Maritimae' from 1997 was performed.

Several Danish and Norwegian newspapers also covered the disaster at that time. One of the Danish newspapers contained the article 'MS Estonia comes back to haunt us' (BT, September 29, 2014). Another Danish newspaper's headline read: 'The disaster that changed Sweden' (*Jyllands-Posten*, September 29, 2014). In the latter article, a Swedish professor of political science claimed that the MS *Estonia* disaster had changed the Swedish national character.

This case example demonstrates how history not only belongs to the past, but also is remembered in the present (Connerton, 1989), and how the MS *Estonia* disaster has become a social icon in the media. There is a big difference in media coverage in 2004 when attention is focused on the victims, the survivors, and the investigation, and that in 2014 when attention is focused on how this tragic event has changed the Swedish national character.

RISK SOCIOLOGY

The societal dimension of organizational crises, crisis management, and crisis communication is the least researched of the five key dimensions forming the multidimensional approach which gives structure to Part 1 of this book. The majority of scholars in this field have not been interested in studying the development toward a crisis society. Some scholars are satisfied with claiming that the number of crises has increased or that a new type of crisis has emerged. This applies to Mitroff (2004), who in his history of crises talks about the 'rise of abnormal accidents'. Other scholars provide very brief sociological explanations. This applies to Ogrizek and Guillery (1997) who identify three sets of factors that can explain why we are experiencing more crises today: (1) the influence of the media, (2) the products and production procedures of the industrial society, and (3) a lower psychological and ethical level of tolerance among citizens.

It is not just interesting but necessary to include the societal dimension in the study of organizational crises, crisis management, and crisis communication. The fact that the number of crises has increased – or the belief that this is the case – does not come about by chance or coincidence. Neither is the case that business managers are less competent or fortunate when handling crises today. That the number of crises seems to have increased is the result of a series of important transformations that have taken place, and still are taking place, at various levels in society. A theoretical understanding of these transformations and the new type of society they produce will help illustrate why we are living in a crisis society.

We claim that it is within *risk sociology*, that is the study of how society organizes in response to risk, that we will find an explanatory framework for the development in society described at the beginning of this chapter. Risk society and crisis society are two sides of the same coin. As is often emphasized by both risk and crisis scholars, crises occur when risk is manifested (Heath & O'Hair, 2009).

We can understand risk sociology by taking a look at how researchers conceptualize and talk about risk in other social science disciplines (for an overview of risk sociology, see Peretti-Watel, 2000, 2001). Below, we present six different approaches to risk (see Table 1.1).

Table 1.1 Overview of approaches to risk

Discipline	Representatives	Approach to risk
The techno-scientific approach		The objective risk
The psychological approach	Paul Slovic, Baruch Fischhoff	The experienced risk
The organizational approach	Michael Power	The organized risk
The politological approach	Patrick Lagadec	The technological risk
The anthropological approach	Mary Douglas	The selected risk
The sociological approach	Ulrich Beck, Anthony Giddens, Niklas Luhmann	The constructed risk

The techno-scientific approach

The techno-scientific approach to risk is rooted in the positivist worldview of the natural sciences. According to this approach, researchable characteristics of our world determine what is dangerous and how dangerous it actually is. The probability and consequences of unwanted events can be assessed by objective methods. A risk is defined as the probability of an event A multiplied by the consequences of A. To the extent that one has reliable knowledge about the probability and the consequences, it is possible to balance different risks against each other objectively in a risk–benefit analysis. The techno-scientific approach is an expert approach, the purpose of which is to eliminate false ideas made up by lay people concerning how dangerous an object, a situation, or an event is.

The psychological approach

The psychological or psychometric approach, which appeared in the 1970s and 1980s, is based on the assumption that a risk will always be experienced subjectively.

This applies not only to the objective risks 'out there', but also to how human beings perceive certain things as more dangerous than other things, the so-called *risk perception*. Research has demonstrated that people's assessment of risk depends on various factors without any immediate correlation to the objective risks. The perception of something as dangerous is thus reduced if the phenomenon is well known, visible, controllable, and does not have immediate consequences. Paul Slovic and Baruch Fischhoff are the leading theorists in the risk perception field. The Social Amplification of Risk Framework (SARF) was developed in the late 1980s in an attempt to explain why relatively minor risks, as assessed by experts, often elicit strong public concerns. The idea behind this conceptual framework is that hazards interact with psychological, social, institutional, and cultural processes in ways that may amplify (or attenuate) public reactions to the risk (Kasperson et al., 1988).

The organizational approach

The organizational approach does not take part in the debate on whether risks are objective or subjective. It focuses on what happens to an organization when its members start thinking in terms of risks. In books such as *The Risk Management of Everything* (2004) and *Organized Uncertainty: Designing a World of Risk Management* (2007), British professor of accounting Michael Power has investigated how the idea of risk management has spread to more and more organizations and has transformed from being a type of managerial control to being a benchmark for good corporate governance. Power claims that this development is not so much caused by a need to handle real risks as by a need for accountability and legitimacy.

The politological approach

The politological approach is first and foremost represented by the French political scientist Patrick Lagadec and his theory of the risk civilization (1980, 1981). Furthermore, he is the only scholar mentioned in this overview who has contributed actively to the study of crisis management and crisis communication. The cornerstone of Lagadec's conceptual framework is the concept of *major technological hazard*. This concept was coined under the impression of a series of large industrial accidents such as Seveso (1976), *Amoco-Cadiz* (1978), and Three Mile Island (1979), all of which took place in the late 1970s. Major technological hazards differ from hazards of the past both in quantity and in quality. In terms of quantity, major technological hazards are bigger and involve more people and larger geographical areas. In terms of quantity, major technological hazards are different in nature. The consequences of a major nuclear accident would not only affect people living today, but have an impact far beyond the current generation.

The anthropological approach

British social anthropologist Mary Douglas connects our ideas about what is risky and what is not risky to a fundamental distinction in human cultures: the distinction between *pure* and *impure* (Douglas, 1966; Douglas & Wildavsky, 1983). According to her, the ideas about what is considered pure and impure in a specific society must be seen not just as rules and concepts of what is hygienic and contagious. Such ideas are also linked to fundamental ideas of social order as such. Purity is order, and impurity is disorder. We applied this approach in our study of a rumor crisis which led to the recall of an 'impure' product that was disturbing the social order of many consumers: namely, the Wash & Go two-in-one shampoo launched by Procter & Gamble in the Danish market in 1990 (Frandsen & Johansen, 2009a). According to the rumor, the use of Wash & Go made it difficult to perm and color your hair, and could even cause hair loss, due to the amount of silicone in the shampoo.

The sociological approach

How does the sociological approach to risk differ from the other approaches presented above? First, the sociological approach does not conceptualize risks as objective phenomena – as in the case with the techno-scientific approach. Here risks are defined as *social constructions*. Second, the sociological approach is not concerned – as in the case of the psychological approach – with how risks are experienced subjectively. The key question here is instead: Where do risks come from? The sociological approach claims that risks must be studied in their social and cultural context. The risk assessments made by human beings are connected with their life conditions in general. The sociological approach also claims that there are certain values incorporated in the so-called objective methods and risk evaluations conducted by experts. These values will either collapse or be different from the values of lay people.

In the remainder of this chapter, we will detail one of the most influential representatives of risk sociology, German sociologist Ulrich Beck, and his theory of the risk society. First, we will introduce the reader to his theory of the risk society, and what he calls the 'age of uncertainty'. Then we will demonstrate how there is a link between the rise of the risk society and the emergence of crisis management and crisis communication as a field of research and practice.

ULRICH BECK AND THE RISK SOCIETY

In 1986, Ulrich Beck published *Risk Society: Towards a New Modernity*, a book which over the last 30 years has become a classic within sociology in general and risk sociology in particular. The book's key point – that we are on our way to a risk society where uncertainty will be the fundamental condition for social life – was emphasized by the fact that the book was published in the same year as the worst nuclear disaster in history in terms of costs and casualties.

On April 26, 1986, a catastrophic accident occurred at the Chernobyl Nuclear Power Plant in the former Soviet Union (Ukraine today). The disaster began during a systems test at reactor number four of the plant. There was a sudden and unexpected power surge, and when an emergency shutdown was attempted, an exponentially large spike in power output occurred. This led to the rupture of a reactor vessel and a series of steam explosions. These events exposed the graphite moderator of the reactor to air, causing it to ignite. The resulting fire sent a plume of highly radioactive fallout into the atmosphere and over an extensive geographical area, including the nearby city of Pripyat. The plume drifted over large parts of the western Soviet Union and Europe.

The general population of the Soviet Union was first informed about the disaster on April 28, two days after the explosion, with a 20 second announcement in a TV news program. During that time, all radio broadcasts run by the state were replaced with classical music, which was a common method of preparing the public for the announcement of a tragedy. Only after radiation levels set off alarms at the Forsmark Nuclear Power Plant in Sweden, over 1,000 kilometres from the Chernobyl Plant, did the Soviet Union admit that an accident had occurred. Nevertheless, the authorities attempted to conceal the scale of the disaster.

Radioactive radiation is perhaps the best illustration of what Beck understands by new risks. In the very first pages of his book he describes how Chernobyl has provided his projective theory of the risk society with a 'bitter taste of truth'.

Surprisingly enough, Beck's theory of the risk society has not been used to any large extent within the fields of crisis management and crisis communication; and, in contrast to Lagadec, Beck himself has not contributed to these fields. However, what is interesting about Beck, and what makes him relevant to this book, is that based on a single characteristic of late modern society – the logic of risk production – he has been able to establish a general theory of the risk society that can explain why it has become so urgent for us and our societies to identify, prepare for, and handle crises.

Before we take a closer look at Beck's theory of the risk society, we had better say a few words about his methodology, given that his approach differs from main stream social science research on several points. He describes his theory as an 'empirically oriented, projective social theory' (Beck, 1992, p. 9); that is to say, a kind of futurology. Consequently, Beck does not invoke any representativity. He wants to 'move the future which is just beginning to *take shape* into view against the *still* predominant past'. He even criticizes the concept of representativity for entering an alliance with the past and for blocking our view of the peaks of the future. Today, 30 years after the publication of *Risk Society*, we are in the privileged position of *looking back* on the development and observing the extent to which Beck was right.

CLASSICAL AND REFLEXIVE MODERNIZATION

Risk Society is a book about the history of modernity – that is, how pre-modern society develops into modern society and, then again, how modern society develops into post-modern society.[1] To describe this evolution in greater detail, Beck introduces a distinction between *classical modernization* and *reflexive modernization*. The former refers to the historical transformation process leading to the replacement of

---

[1] There is a rich literature on Ulrich Beck, including several introductions to his theory of the risk society. See for example *Ulrich Beck: A Critical Introduction to the Risk Society* (Mythen, 2004) and *Ulrich Beck: An Introduction to the Theory of Second Modernity and the Risk Society* (Sørensen & Christiansen, 2014). More general introductions to the concept of risk also often include a chapter devoted to Ulrick Beck and his theory of the risk society. See for example Lupton (1999).

the traditional agricultural society by an industrial society. The latter refers to the successive historical transformation process during which the industrial society itself is modernized, giving rise to the new risk society.

Beck focuses on two key aspects of risk society and reflexive attention. The first aspect is the detraditionalization of industrial ways of life. The second aspect is the emergence of a social production of risks which in the new risk society will dominate the social production of wealth that was the underlying driver of industrial society. Beck identifies two conditions that must be fulfilled in order for this evolution to take place: (1) reduction of material need; and (2) exponential growth or overdevelopment of productive forces. It is in the first of these two conditions that we find the roots of the paradox of today's society: on the one hand, we have never lived in a society that is wealthier and safer; on the other hand, we have never been more preoccupied and conscious about the risks which are part of this society. One might say that the amount of material need is in inverse proportion to the amount of risk awareness. The bigger the need, the less the focus on risks that lay waiting in the future. As French risk sociologist Patrick Peretti-Watel expresses it:

> Our relationship with risks depends on our time horizon. Poverty reduces this horizon installing the most helpless people in a precarious situation embedding them in the present and forbidding them to take a look at the future ... You are more concerned with risks, as soon as a certain material security in the present secures our presence in the future. (2000, p. 17)

 Case example 1.2

The swine flu pandemic and the risk society

In April 2009, an outbreak of swine flu began in the state of Veracruz, Mexico. The virus spread rapidly to the rest of the world, and on June 11 the World Health Organization (WHO) declared the outbreak a pandemic. The last update made by the WHO a few days before the declaration showed 94,512 confirmed cases in 122 countries and 429 deaths. The pandemic began to taper off in November 2009, and on August 10, 2010, the Director-General of the WHO announced the end of the pandemic. According to WHO statistics, the virus killed more than 18,000 people.

What at first sight seemed to be a straightforward and objective thing – most people have had the flu at least once – turned out to be something much more complex and constructed.

The reactions to the swine flu pandemic were very different from country to country, and from experts to lay people. In some countries, the public authorities perceived the pandemic as very dangerous and recommended vaccination. In other countries such as Denmark, the public authorities did not perceive the pandemic as any more dangerous than an 'ordinary' flu epidemic and did not recommend vaccination to the same extent.

In Russia, the government prohibited the import of pork from Mexico, even though the virus cannot be spread by eating pork or pork products. Stock exchanges all over the world reacted negatively. The share price of British Airways, Air France-KLM, and Lufthansa decreased by 7 to 20 percent.

(Continued)

(Continued)

A 'flu naming war' involving the WHO, the European Union, politicians, and a diverse group of organizations broke out (Vigsø, 2010). *The Mexican flu* was the first name that emerged. Mexican officials immediately protested, claiming the name would stigmatize Mexico and the Mexican people. In China, the Mexican Ambassador, Jorge Guajardo, went so far as to apply a shifting-the-blame strategy (cf. Chapter 5), claiming that the flu was brought to his country by an infected person from 'Eurasia': 'This did not happen in Mexico. It was a human who brought this to Mexico.'

But it was the *swine flu* name that sparked the greatest controversy. First, it became a cultural and religious controversy that concerned the fact that pigs and pork products are considered impure by both Jews and Muslims. Second, an economic controversy arose involving the pork meat industry, which argued that the relation between the flu pandemic and pigs was of a dubious nature, and that there was no risk that the flu could be transmitted to people through pork products. The last two names were *the new flu* and *N1H1*, of which the latter especially was seen as more scientific and less loaded with connotations.

In his study of the 'flu naming war', Vigsø (2010) concludes that the naming of the pandemic was, in fact, a case of crisis communication, as the choice of name for the disease could damage the reputation and economic interests of the social actors involved. The 'flu naming war' is a particularly interesting case viewed from the perspective of terminological control theory (cf. Chapter 5).

Source: Vigsø (2010).

OLD AND NEW RISKS

One of the points where Beck clearly differentiates himself from Lagadec's theory of the risk civilization, taking us a step further in our understanding of the risk society, is his distinction between old and new risks. By risk, Beck means *techno-scientifically produced* risk first and foremost. Simplifying Beck's exposé of his own theory a little, we can describe the difference between old and new risks on the basis of four characteristics, as follows (see Table 1.2).

The new risks are *global*. In the industrial society, risks were local, which is to say that they were attached to a specific place, to a specific point in time, and to a specific group of people. In the new risk society, risks cross geographical borders (nation-states), social borders (social classes), and professional borders (specializations):

Table 1.2   Characteristics of old and new risks

Old risks	New risks
• Local	• Global
• Actual	• Potential
• Visible	• Invisible
• Evident	• Not evident or knowledge dependent

> Objectively, … risks display an equalizing effect within their scope and among those affected by them. It is precisely therein that their novel political power resides. In this sense risk societies are *not* class societies; their risk positions cannot be understood as class positions, or their conflicts as class conflicts. (Beck, 1992, p. 36)

The new risks are *potential*. In the industrial society, risks were actual. We first spotted them when they had transformed into something other and more than risks, namely into real incidents. In the new risk society, risks form what Beck calls *not yet events*. Risks contain a component referring to a future that has to be prevented. This is reflected in a new risk mentality:

> In the risk society, the past loses its power to determine the present. Its place is taken by the future, thus something non-existent, invented, fictitious as the 'cause' of current experiences and actions. We become active today in order to prevent, alleviate or take precautions against the problems and crises of tomorrow and the day after tomorrow – or not to do so. (Beck, 1992, p. 34)

The new risks are *invisible*. In the industrial society, risks were visible, they 'assaulted the nose or the eyes and were thus perceptible to the senses'. In the new risk society, risks have lost their visibility. They 'escape perception and are localized in the sphere of physical and chemical formulas' (Beck, 1992, p. 21). This leads us directly to the fourth and final characteristic.

The new risks are *knowledge dependent* or non-evident. In the industrial society, there was a consensus about risks. You knew when something was a risk; it was evident. In the new risk society, as mentioned above, risks are invisible, they can only be sensed by the 'sensory system' of the sciences (theories, experiments, measuring instruments) and are, therefore, based on 'causal interpretations, and thus initially only exist in terms of the (scientific or alternative scientific) *knowledge* about them' (Beck, 1992, p. 23). The risks attached not only to the use of nuclear power, but also to toxins and pollutants in the air, to water and foodstuffs, to genetically modified organisms, to mobile telephone communications, to diseases such as avian flue, and so forth, thus become open 'to definitional processes in society' (ibid.). At the same time, science is losing its monopoly on rationality in the risk society, and the consequence is a series of definitional struggles in the media and between experts. When is something dangerous? When is something not dangerous? The questions are brought up again and again by consumers and citizens, and each time they receive a different answer.

MICHAEL POWER AND THE RISK ORGANIZATION

Beck's theory of the risk society represents what sociologists define as a macro-level theory: a theory of how a new type of society is emerging and how this will change political and economic life, culture, everyday life, power relations, and legitimacy. In a book on organizational crisis communication, however, we are of course also interested in knowing how this large-scale societal transformation will change organizations in general and their efforts at preventing, preparing for, and managing crises in particular. So what is taking place at this meso-level? Will the risk society turn private and public organizations into risk organizations?

According to Beck and Holzer (2007), organizations play a crucial role in the shift from the industrial society to the risk society; from a safety culture with calculable risks or dangers to a culture of uncertainty and non-calculable risks; from 'objective' probabilities to 'subjective' expectations of possible damage related to decision making. In this understanding, organizations are considered *sources of risk* due to their use of more and more advanced technologies. The risks that exist in the risk society are based on decisions and considerations of utility (profit, economic growth), which in most cases are made by corporate and political organizations and institutions.

British professor of accounting Michael Power attacks the question from a somewhat different angle. According to Power (2004, 2007), risk has become an *organizing concept* like never before. More and more organizations, not only private companies, but also public sector organizations, hospitals, universities, etc., redefine and redescribe themselves in risk terms. Power investigates how the ideas of risk and risk management have emerged from their positions within specific fields to become implicated in new visions and discourses about organizing and managing in general: 'Risk management, in an abstracted sense, is constitutive of organization' (Power, 2007, p. 8).

Two of his ideas are of particular interest to crisis management and crisis communication as organizational practice. The first is his idea that the concept of stakeholder is emptied of moral content and any kind of rights in risk management. In the risk management thinking about stakeholders, the key question is: Who might blame and thereby damage the organization? We shall return to this viewpoint in Chapter 4. The second is Power's idea of *secondary risk management*. He claims that the growth of reputation surveys and rankings since the mid-1990s (i.e., the rankings made by the Reputation Institute) has created a new class of risk: the so-called 'secondary risk' (Power, 2007, p. 142). This new class of risk is accompanied by the institutionalization of *reputation* as a new management paradigm across the sub-fields of finance, marketing, human resources, and communication. It is difficult not to see some kind of connection between this development and the focus on crisis, response, and reputation in the very first articles on crisis communication (see, e.g., Coombs, 1995).

AN EXPLANATORY FRAMEWORK

The theory of the risk society developed by Ulrich Beck will serve as the explanatory framework for the study of the societal dimension of crises, crisis management, and crisis communication in this book. We realize that we could have made other relevant theoretical choices – both within sociology in general and within risk sociology. Within sociology in general, for instance, we could have opted for Niklas Luhmann and his theory of social systems. Within risk sociology, we could have opted for Anthony Giddens and his theory of late modernity. Both Luhmann and Giddens have contributed substantially to the study of risk in society: Luhmann in *Risk: A Sociological Theory* (1993) and Giddens in, among others, *The Consequences of Modernity* (1990). In our opinion, however, Beck provides us with by far the most complete sociological explanation of why we today find it so urgent to identify, to prepare for, and to talk about crises in our society.[2]

Our application of Beck in this book is based on two assumptions that take his theory a small step further.

First, we assume that as a consequence of the emerging risk society, a new risk awareness has been born, and that this new awareness is reflected in various types of *anticipative risk behavior* at the personal, the organizational and the societal level. Beck himself touches upon the topic of anticipation and risk behavior several times in his book: 'We become active today in order to prevent, alleviate or take precautions against the problems and crises of tomorrow and the day after tomorrow – or not to do so' (Beck, 1992, p. 34). That he assigns a key role to this future-oriented risk awareness becomes only more evident if we look at his social-constructivist philosophy of science: in the modern industrial society, being (reality) determined consciousness; in the postmodern risk society, '*consciousness (knowledge) determines being*' (p. 53).

Second, we also assume that risk awareness – and the anticipative risk behavior in which it is reflected – is not merely related to what Beck defines as techno-scientifically produced risks. Risk awareness has been *generalized*, and now multiple other areas of society, if not all, are understood as potential risk areas. Here we are inspired by Power's theory of the 'risk management of everything'. One sign that such generalization has taken place is the transformation of management disciplines like risk management, which has shifted from a narrow to a broad perspective including reputation as a risk area (cf. the previous section). Judy Larkin's book *Strategic Reputation Risk Management* (2003) illustrates how reputation management is also secondary risk management: 'Reputation risk management involves anticipating, acknowledging and responding to changing values and behaviours on the part of a range of stakeholders' (p. 38).

Based on these two assumptions we claim that crisis management and crisis communication, in particular in the strategic, proactive, and process-oriented version (cf. Chapter 3), is a distinct type of anticipative risk behavior which has become a widespread organizational practice that began in the 1980s.

REACTIONS TO THE RISK SOCIETY

We would like to conclude this chapter on the societal dimension of organizational crises, crisis management, and crisis communication by asking one last question: How does a society – its individuals and organizations – react to being transformed into a risk society? If we remain within the field of crises, crisis management, and crisis communication, it seems possible to identify at least four important reactions:

---

[2] We are hardly the first nor the only crisis researchers to introduce Ulrich Beck's theory of the risk society. In her criticism of the sociology of disasters for its lack of theoretical innovation, Tierney (2007) refers to Beck and risk sociology as a new field within mainstream sociology which is highly relevant to disaster research. Her book *The Social Roots of Risk: Producing Disaster, Promoting Resilience* (2014) is a good example of how she herself has applied Beck in her study of how the consequences of all types of disasters arise from decision making by organizations, political groups, and other powerful actors.

(1) the new practice of crisis management and crisis communication in private and public organizations; (2) the emergence of consulting firms counseling organizations in crisis management and crisis communication; (3) the emergence of crisis journalism as a subdiscipline; and (4) crises as a new field of study.

Crisis management and crisis communication in private and public organizations

More and more organizations in the private and public sectors have started allocating resources to prevent, prepare for, and handle various types of crisis situations (cf. the general introduction). The business world had of course been hit by crises and scandals long before we started talking about the risk society, but it was not until the 1980s that crisis management and crisis communication entered the corporate agenda as a specific organizational practice.

The Johnson & Johnson Tylenol crisis in 1982 has often been described as the first example of modern crisis management (Mitroff, 2005).[3] During the fall of 1982, seven people in the Chicago area were reported dead from taking Tylenol, the leading pain-killer medicine in the United States at the time. It was soon discovered that an unknown person or group of persons had replaced Tylenol capsules with cyanide capsules, resealed the packages, and deposited them on the shelves of pharmacies and food stores. Once the connection was made between the Tylenol capsules and the reported deaths, and the news media became interested in the story, Johnson & Johnson started handling the crisis. What did the company do?

First, CEO and Chairman of the Board James E. Burke took on the leadership role. To assist him, Burke formed and headed a seven-member strategy team, which also included Corporate Vice President of Public Relations Lawrence G. Foster. Second, consumer safety was placed ahead of all other considerations. All the Tylenol products suspected of poisoning were immediately recalled from the market. Every type of advertising for the products was suspended, and a hotline was established. Third, all relevant stakeholders were informed: the customers, the employees, the public authorities, and especially the press. Finally, in its crisis management activities, Johnson & Johnson was driven by its Credo, a document written in the mid-1940s by Chairman Robert Wood Johnson that describes the company's everyday business and social responsibilities: 'We believe our first responsibility is to the doctors, nurses and patients, to mothers and fathers and all others who use our products and services.'

During the first month of the crisis, Tylenol's market share fell from 35 percent to less than 12 percent. However, Johnson & Johnson's handling of the Tylenol crisis proved to be effective. In January 1984, Tylenol had won back its market share.

Although Johnson & Johnson was hit by a similar poisoning crisis in 1986, its handling of the 1982 crisis has for many years served as a model for how to practise good crisis management. Several of the elements in Johnson & Johnson's crisis management

---

[3] For a description of the Johnson & Johnson Tylenol crisis, see Fink (1986), Andrews (2005), www.jnj.com and www.tylenol.com. For studies of the crisis, see Benoit and Lindsey (1987) and Mitroff and Kilmann (1984).

correspond to what are today considered obligatory elements in the strategic, proactive, and process-oriented approach to crisis management. Burke's strategy team, Johnson & Johnson's Credo, and the focus on customer safety, internal communication, and interaction with the press represent what we today would call a crisis management team, a crisis management plan, and stakeholder management.

Crisis consulting firms

When private and public organizations start focusing on preventing, preparing for, and handling crises, a new *risk market* appears. Beck describes this new market in the following way:

> Hunger can be assuaged, needs can be satisfied; risks are a 'bottomless barrel of demands', unsatisfiable, infinite. Unlike demands, risks can be more than just called forth (by advertising and the like), prolonged in conformity to sales needs, and in short: manipulated. Demands, and thus markets, of a completely new type can be *created* by varying the definition of risk, especially demand for the avoidance of risk. (Beck, 1992, p. 56)

One of the products promoted on the new risk market to satisfy the organizational demand for avoidance of risk is crisis consulting.

The crisis management firms that started to emerge in the 1980s were typically based on the knowledge and personal experience of just one person. Steven Fink, author of the first book with the words 'crisis management' in its title, *Crisis Management: Planning for the Inevitable* (1986), is a good example. He wrote his book on the basis of what he learned from the Three Mile Island accident.

The Three Mile Island accident was a partial nuclear meltdown that took place on March 28, 1979, in the Three Mile Island nuclear plant in Pennsylvania, United States. The partial meltdown, which resulted in the release of unknown amounts of radioactive gases into the atmosphere, was rated five on the seven-point International Nuclear Event Scale. It crystallized anti-nuclear safety concerns in the American civil society and resulted in new regulations for the nuclear industry. Thus, it was a crisis that led to an issue. At the time, Fink had a position in the administration of Pennsylvania Governor Dick Thornburgh and was involved in handling the accident as a member of the crisis management team established by the governor.

Today, Steven Fink is President and CEO of Lexicon Communications Corp., which presents itself as the oldest crisis management firm in the United States, and which offers a comprehensive range of crisis management and crisis communication services, including: issues management, risk assessments, crisis management plans, crisis management teams, vulnerability audits, pre-crisis review teams, and crisis management awareness seminars (www.crisismanagement.com). Fink makes a clear distinction between crisis management and crisis communication. Crisis management deals with the *reality* of the crisis. Crisis communication deals with the *perception* of the reality. We shall return to these services and this distinction in Chapters 5 and 6.

Steven Fink is also the author of *Crisis Communications: The Definitive Guide to Managing Message* (2013) (cf. Chapter 12).

Crisis journalism

The news media play a key role in the risk society. It is in the newspapers and on radio and television that the new risks are visualized and symbolized. It is here that the 'definitional struggles' between experts take place. The continuous process of *mediatization*, that is the diffusion of the media logic both within specific sectors as well as throughout society as a whole, only makes the impact of the media more powerful (cf. Chapter 10).

In parallel with the organizations and the crisis consultants and their efforts to establish a crisis preparedness system and gain practical competencies regarding crisis management and crisis communication, schools of journalism started to develop a new discipline with a new curriculum: *crisis journalism*. After 9/11, the American Press Institute published a comprehensive handbook edited by Warren Watson and entitled *Crisis Journalism: A Handbook for Media Response* (2001). In 2001, Art Botterell, a well-known American disaster and crisis journalist, published *The Life Cycle of a Disaster: A Field Guide for Journalists*. According to this field guide, a typical disaster or crisis can be divided into six stages: (1) Preparation, (2) Alert, (3) Impact, (4) Heroic, (5) Disillusionment, and (6) Recovery. As we will see in Chapter 10, this model has a lot in common with the staged approaches within the strategic, proactive, and process-oriented perspective on crisis management.

Crises as a field of research

In the 1980s, researchers from many different scientific disciplines started to define organizational crises, crisis management, and crisis communication as a field of study (cf. the general introduction). The first large international research project within this field was conducted between 1987 and 1991 by Ian I. Mitroff and Thierry Pauchant and their colleagues from the University of Southern California Center for Crisis Management (CCM). The project was divided into two parts: (1) a qualitative study consisting of more than 500 personal interviews with managers, professionals, and senior executives responsible for crisis management in the United States, Canada, and France; and (2) a survey based on questionnaires sent to Fortune 1000 companies in the United States. The findings of this project form the empirical basis of Pauchant and Mitroff's seminal book *Transforming the Crisis-Prone Organization* (1992).

The first academic publications and conferences also saw the light of day in the 1980s. The first issue of *Industrial Crisis Quarterly* was published in 1987. The First International Conference on Industrial Crisis Management, organized by Paul Shrivastava, author of *Bhopal: Anatomy of a Crisis* (1987), took place in 1986 in New York at the Industrial Crisis Institute. From 1991 onwards, Larry Barton organized a series of international annual conferences at the University of Nevada, Las Vegas, under the heading *New Avenues in Risk and Crisis Management*.

BEYOND THE RISK SOCIETY? CRITICISMS AND ELABORATIONS

Since the publication of *Risk Society* in 1986, Beck's theory has been subjected to criticisms and further elaborations from various quarters. Mythen (2004) criticized

Beck for being too universalistic in his conceptualization of the risk society, refuting the claim that the dispersal of risk engenders a new type of society. According to Mythen, Beck's risk society thesis suffers from both theoretical and empirical deficiencies. With regard to empirical weaknesses, Mythen refers first of all to Beck's unwillingness to engage in empirical validation. Nevertheless, Mythen is convinced that Beck is right in many of his assumptions about the risk society and that these assumptions are supported by empirical evidence, For example, there *has* in fact been a relative rise in public risk consciousness. With regard to theoretical weaknesses, Mythen has identified no less than seven key areas where the risk society thesis seems to be problematic. One of these areas is Beck's unconditionally negative conception of risk as harm neglecting the positive risks.

Tierney (2014) criticized Beck for focusing too narrowly on techno-scientifically produced risks and for overlooking the importance of non-technological risks such as epidemics, financial risks, terrorism, and climate change.

Nohrstedt (2010) elaborated further on Beck by claiming that the late modern society in which we live today should be regarded as a new emergent phase: a threat society. The threat society differs from the risk society by focusing on politicized risk and by adding an active subject who directs a danger toward someone else. However, the concept of threat society is not to be seen as an alternative, but rather as an addition to the theory of the risk society made necessary by the expansion of a culture of fear.

CHAPTER SUMMARY

This chapter started with the question: Are we living in a crisis society? The chapter continued by providing an overview of various theories of risk and by introducing German sociologist Ulrich Beck and his theory of the risk society, which serves as the explanatory framework for the study of the societal dimension of organizational crises, crisis management, and crisis communication in this book. Finally, the chapter identified four reactions to the emergence of the risk society.

 Further reading

Beck, U., & Holzer, B. (2007). Organizations in world risk society. In C. M. Pearson, C. Roux-Dufort, & J. A. Clair (Eds.), *International Handbook of Organizational Crisis Management* (pp. 3–24). Thousand Oaks, CA: Sage.

Power, M. (2004). *The Risk Management of Everything: Rethinking the Politics of Uncertainty*. London: Demos.

WHAT IS A CRISIS? DEFINITIONS AND TYPOLOGIES

2

CHAPTER OVERVIEW

This chapter examines the definitional and typological dimensions of organizational crises. First, the chapter describes how the concept of crisis has developed, from the early 1960s until today, by means of six important crisis definitions. Second, the chapter briefly presents some of the most recent concepts such as *double crisis*, *the crisis after the crisis*, and *multi-crisis*. Finally, the chapter introduces the reader to some of the most important crisis typologies, including the standard version as well as the extended version of the crisis portfolio model.

INTRODUCTION

Crises are complex processes that can be examined at various levels and from various perspectives, depending on the purpose of the study (Rosenthal et al., 2001b). Most people will agree that a crisis represents some kind of *negative discontinuity*. However, this does not necessarily mean that they always agree about when to call something a crisis.

Why is it important to define crisis and establish crisis typologies?

For the practitioner, crisis definitions are important to the crisis management process. If an organization and its members do not know *what* a crisis is, they cannot know *when* they are experiencing one. They cannot be sure when their organization must activate its crisis preparedness system (crisis management team, crisis management plan, etc.). By defining what is meant by the word *crisis*, crisis-related risks are identified and the members of a given organization will have the opportunity to discuss the likelihood for various types of crises that may affect their organization.

For the researcher, crisis definitions are also important. The researcher has to be aware of the many crisis definitions that are available, their history, the language in which they are formulated, and the metaphors upon which they are based (for an introduction, see Millar & Beck, 2004). Like the practitioner, the researcher will always have a pre-understanding of what constitutes a crisis. He or she does not start from scratch.

In this book, we take a social constructivist perspective on organizational crises. Crises are not just 'out there'. They are social constructions. Crises are something that are interpreted as crises. Sometimes there is more than one interpretation, sometimes the interpretations are negotiated. This happens, for example, when it is not the organization itself but the news media that use the word *crisis* about an event in which the organization is involved – and especially when the organization itself would have preferred to use a different word (for an explanation of the frequent use of the word *crisis* in today's society, see Chapter 1).

CRISIS DEFINITIONS

It is impossible to give a complete overview of the many different definitions of organizational crises. There are simply too many. Instead, in this section, we will present some of the most important definitions in an attempt to demonstrate how they have developed over time and how they have explored different dimensions.

More than 50 years ago, American political scientist Charles F. Hermann provided us with one of the very first definitions of organizational crises. Based on his experience from the military, the political field, and the business world, he established the following definition: 'An organizational crisis (1) threatens the high-priority values of the organization, (2) presents a restricted amount of time in which a response can be made, and (3) is unexpected or unanticipated by the organization' (Hermann, 1963, p. 64). As it appears, he identified three characteristics of a crisis: *threat*, *short response time*, and *surprise*. Despite the fact that it is one of the oldest crisis definitions, Hermann's definition is still popular among crisis communication researchers. See for example Seeger et al. (2003), Ulmer et al. (2007), and Sellnow and Seeger (2013) who consider these three characteristics 'general attributes' (p. 6).

BOX 2.1

WHAT IS A DEFINITION?

A definition is a statement of the meaning of a term. Fearn-Banks (2011) writes that:

> A crisis is a major occurrence with a potentially negative outcome affecting the organization, company, or industry, as well as its publics, products, services, or good name. A crisis interrupts normal business transactions and sometimes threatens the existence of the organization. A crisis can be a strike, terrorism, a fire, a boycott, product tampering, a product failure, or numerous other things [reference to a list of different crises]. The size of the organization is irrelevant. (p. 3)

(Continued)

(Continued)

In doing so she is stating the meaning of the term *crisis* (as she understands it).

Definitions can be divided into two major categories: (1) intensional definitions (which try to give the essence of a term) and (2) extensional definitions
(which list every single object covered by the term). Fearn-Banks' definition is
both intensional (the definition cited above) and extensional (the list of crises
she refers to and which gets longer and longer for each edition of her book
Crisis Communications: A Casebook Approach).

A term may have multiple meanings and thus require multiple definitions. To
fully understand Fearn-Banks' definition of crisis, for example, you also have to
know her definition of *publics* and *good name*. How do these two terms differ
from *stakeholder* and *reputation*?

Further reading: Jaques (2009).

Twenty-five years ago, crisis management researchers Thierry Pauchant and Ian I. Mitroff applied a systemic approach to organizational crises in *Transforming the Crisis-Prone Organization* (1992). In a systemic approach, the focus is not on how one variable can cause a crisis (simple causality), but on how several variables can trigger certain interactions in a system. Pauchant and Mitroff defined a crisis as 'a disruption that physically affects a system as a whole and threatens its basic assumptions, its subjective sense of self, its existential core' (p. 12). This definition is more radical than Hermann's definition. A crisis affects the whole system, and it has both *physical* and *psychological* consequences: 'the basic assumptions of the members of that system need to be chal-lenged to the point where they are forced either to realize the faulty foundation of these assumptions, or to develop defense mechanisms against these assumptions' (ibid.).

Another important crisis definition with a similar focus on the psychological dimension has been established by organizational psychologist Karl E. Weick. His approach, however, is not a systemic approach, but rooted in retrospective sense-making theory. Weick (1993) defines a crisis as a cosmology episode: 'A cosmology episode occurs when people suddenly and deeply feel that the universe is no longer a rational, orderly system. What makes such an episode so shattering is that both the sense of what is occurring and the means to rebuild that sense collapse together' (p. 633).

The most widespread definition of organizational crises within the crisis man-agement literature we examined is probably the definition established by Pearson and Clair (1998). They define a crisis as a 'low-probability, high-impact event that threatens the viability of the organization, and is characterized by ambiguity of cause, effects and means of resolution, as well as by a belief that decisions must be made swiftly' (p. 60). In contrast to Pauchant and Mitroff, Pearson and Clair go a little deeper into the description of the crisis situation itself: a crisis is *ambiguous*. Pearson and Clair's (1998) definition of crisis has been criticized for overly focusing on major organizational crises: 'A problem with such a definition is that it excludes many situ-ations which lack clarity when they occur' (Acquier et al., 2008, p. 103).

If we shift to the corresponding literature on crisis communication, Timothy W. Coombs has produced an extended definition. In the first edition of *Ongoing*

Crisis Communication (1999), he defined a crisis as an 'event that is an unpredictable major threat that can have a negative impact on the organization, industry or stakeholders if handled improperly' (p. 2). As it appears, a crisis is not only viewed as something that is important to the organization, but also important to the *industry* and the *stakeholders*. Most interesting, however, is the addition 'if handled improperly'. This may be interpreted in the following way: if an event considered a crisis is handled in a proper manner, the event does not necessarily lead to a crisis for the organization. In other words, the handling of the crisis becomes central to whether or not a crisis is perceived as a crisis.

In the fourth edition of *Ongoing Crisis Communication* (2015) Coombs elaborated on his first definition: 'A crisis is the perception of an unpredictable event that threatens important expectancies of stakeholders related to health, safety, environmental, and economic issues, and can seriously impact an organization's performance and generate negative outcomes' (p. 3). This time, Coombs added the word *perception*. In doing so, he emphasized that the event may be interpreted differently. This definition is also much more specific regarding the stakeholders' stakes.

Today, a complex, broad perspective on crisis management is in the making (cf. Chapter 3). This evolution has already had an impact on crisis definitions. Alpaslan and Mitroff (2011) find that 'all crises are complex systems of multiple, interacting and interdependent crises, all of which can and will be viewed differently by different stakeholders' (p. 38). To them, crises are 'messy' for three reasons: first, because affected stakeholders perceive crises differently and disagree about what is going on and how a crisis is to be understood; second, because crises contain a series of interdependent 'issues, problems, and assumptions' that cannot be handled independently from one another; and finally, because 'an initial crisis always and quickly triggers a chain reaction of other crises' (pp. 37–38). This definition is congenial to the complexity approach in this book.

BOX 2.2

CRISIS PERCEPTION

Crisis perception, or how we 'see' a crisis, is an important factor for our ability to define crises as well as for crisis planning and decision making in an organization. However, different organization members may perceive crises in different ways.

Billings et al. (1980) established a model for crisis perception based on the assumption that accurate models of crisis perception will make it possible to better understand human reactions to crises. Their study showed that individual differences such as personal degree of anxiety (to threats), self-esteem factors (self-assured, self-confident, resilience), and internal locus of control (outcomes caused by their own actions) are antecedents of crisis perception. This means that some organization members 'see' more than others. Some see too much, some see too little. It depends on personal as well as organizational factors.

(Continued)

(Continued)

Penrose (2000) investigated the role of perception in crisis planning. He studied how the perception of a crisis as either a (positive) opportunity or as a (negative) threat for the organization may have an impact on the crisis preparedness of the organization.

Based on these investigations, we understand crisis perception as the ability of managers or employees to identify 'something' as a crisis, or as something that can develop into a crisis. We assume that such an identification, or the lack of such an identification, depends both on specific physical aspects of what is identified and on specific interpretation schemes activated by manager(s) or employee(s).

In 2003, we conducted the first nation-wide crisis preparedness study among private and public organizations in Denmark by means of an online survey among 750 respondents (all of whom were responsible for the crisis preparedness of their own organization) (response rate: 39 percent). The study demonstrated that there was no clear correlation between crisis perception (which crises do the respondents 'see'?) and crisis experiences, but that it was the crisis perception – and surprisingly not the crisis experiences – that made the organizations optimize their crisis preparedness.

The study also showed that private and public organizations have different crisis perceptions and experiences. In terms of crisis perception, the public organizations first and foremost focused on *terrorism, bomb threats, accidents involving person injuries*, and *environmental pollution*, whereas the private organizations also included *information technology breakdowns, product recalls*, and *negative media coverage* among the most salient threats. In terms of crisis experience, the public organizations primarily reported on experiences with *information technology breakdowns, environmental pollution, interruptions*, and *large restructurings*. Thus, except for environmental pollution, their crisis perception interestingly did not correspond to their crisis experiences.

Source: Frandsen and Johansen (2004).

NEW CONCEPTS OF CRISIS

Recently, a series of new crisis concepts have emerged within the field of crisis management and crisis communication. These concepts share the same ambition: to highlight a specific and hitherto under-researched aspect of organizational crises.

Double crisis

The concept of double crisis was originally established by Johansen and Frandsen (2007). A double crisis is 'a crisis where a communication crisis overlaps the original crisis in so far as the organization in crisis is not able to manage the communication processes that should contribute to the handling of the original crisis' (p. 79). Any kind of crisis can transform into a double crisis if the handling of the crisis goes wrong. In this case, the organization has to deal with two crises at the same time, although the second crisis often seems to attract more attention than the original crisis. Very often the second crisis is a *communication crisis*, that is a crisis caused by poorly executed communication, a lack of communication, or even wrongful communication (such as lying).

Grebe (2013) uses the concept of double crisis as well as the concept of *secondary crisis* in her article 'Things can get worse: How mismanagement of a crisis response strategy can cause a secondary or double crisis: the example of the AWB corporate scandal'. The corporate scandal investigated by Grebe started in 2005 when it was discovered that AWB Limited, a grain marketing organization based in Australia, had been paying kickbacks to the regime of Saddam Hussein in Iraq in exchange for lucrative contracts, which was a violation of the UN Oil-for-Food Program. AWB Limited's attempt to 'cover up' the problem triggered a double crisis and caused additional damage to the company.

In some cases, a double crisis can even be extended to a triple crisis where several crisis-handling problems overlap the original crisis. During the Toyota recall crisis in 2010, for instance, the Japanese automobile manufacturer was accused not only of having problems with the accelerator in some of its cars, but also for blaming the drivers instead of apologizing to them, for loaning out cars without disclosing or fixing its problems, and for allowing its VPs to communicate arrogantly (Alpaslan & Mitroff, 2011).

The concept of double crisis must not be confused with Thompson's (2000) concept of *second-order transgression* where attention is 'shifted from the original offence to a series of subsequent actions which are aimed at concealing the offence' (p. 17).

The crisis after the crisis

Sometimes it can be difficult to determine when a crisis is over. The *crisis after the crisis* concept was originally developed by Rosenthal et al. (1994) in a study of a plane crash in the Netherlands on October 4, 1992. A Boeing 747 from the Israeli airline El Al crashed in Biljmer, a densely populated residential area in Amsterdam. The cargo plane hit two nine-storey apartment buildings, destroyed 266 apartments, and killed 43 people. According to Rosenthal et al. (2001a) this crisis changed its form or identity at least five times. It started as (1) a disaster due to the plane crash, but it moved and turned into an example of (2) urban crisis management, and (3) a 'loose ends' crisis, because the Biljmer area was a multi-ethnic area with both legal as well as illegal immigrants. This meant that it was very difficult to distinguish between the real victims of the crash and so-called pseudo-victims – that is, illegal immigrants who claimed that they lived in the area although they did not. In 1996, the crisis turned into (4) a public health issue when many of the surviving residents suffered from post-traumatic stress disorder. In the end, following the formation of a 1998 parliamentary commission of inquiry looking into the rights and treatment of the surviving residents, the crisis turned into (5) a national political crisis in the Netherlands.

The crisis after the crisis challenges our understanding of a crisis as an event with a clear beginning and a clear end. The Biljmer case highlights one of Rosenthal et al.'s (2001a) main points, namely 'that crises should be viewed as processes rather than concrete, time- and space-specific events. As the process unfolds, a crisis often takes on different identities' (p. 201). Some of the world's worst industrial disasters, Bhopal (1984) and Chernobyl (1986), are still not over.

Crisis by association

A crisis by association can be defined as

> a situation where a crisis to an individual, an organization or a group of individuals or organizations – through association – is perceived as a crisis (a threat, an attack or an insult) to another individual(s) or organization(s) who in different ways and for different reasons are related to or are affected by the crisis of the focal organization(s) or individual(s). (Johansen et al., 2016)

When an organization representing a specific industry experiences a crisis, it often has a spillover effect on other members of the same industry. When VW faced the 'Dieselgate' scandal in September 2015, due to improperly installed engine control unit (ECU) software that gamed emissions control testing, other automobile manufacturers ran the risk of being suspected to have the same kind of problems (cf. case study 8.1). The spillover effect can also take place between organizations within complementary industries. For instance, a company that produces packaging for liquids such as milk or juice risks a crisis by association if the contents of the packages are contaminated or tampered.

Multi-crisis

A multi-crisis is a crisis involving two or more organizations. Thus, in a multi-crisis, the focus is on the *inter-organizational* dimension of a crisis. Two basic types of multi-crisis can be identified: (1) *horizontal* multi-crises involving organizations located at the same level of operation (e.g., reputation commons problems, cf. Chapter 11); and (2) *vertical* multi-crises involving organizations located at different levels of operation (e.g., supply chain crises). Ham et al. (2012) have investigated how a series of companies within the same industry handled electronics explosion incidents (rice-cookers in Korea in 2004 and laptop batteries in the United States in 2006). They found that response strategies were influenced by the amount of competition within the specific industry. Previous research has primarily been intra-organizational in its approach. The study of multi-crises brings about a change of direction in favor of a multi-vocal approach (cf. case study 11.1).

Paracrisis

The Internet and social media are triggers – as well as accelerators – of organizational crises (cf. Gonzáles-Herrero & Smith, 2008). They have made it very easy for customers or activists who want to promote a specific cause to publicly voice their opinions online. This often leads to what Coombs (2015) has chosen to call a *paracrisis* (see also Coombs, 2012). Coombs describes a paracrisis as 'a specific type of crisis warning sign' that 'mimics a crisis itself' and 'appears in full view of stakeholders' (p. 27). As the crisis threat is typically triggered online, it calls for online crisis management.

This means that the organization has to publicly deal with the crisis, showing all of its key stakeholders how it reacts to the problem. Previously, most crisis prevention was enacted internally, or at least the managing actions were hidden from public scrutiny.

However, the concept of paracrisis can be problematic. On the one hand, the definition of a paracrisis is close to the concept of an issue (cf. Chapter 4). On the other hand, it is also close to the definition of crisis as such, because it corresponds to a triggering event leading to some sort of crisis management activity, even though Coombs claims that a paracrisis seldom calls for the activation of the crisis management team. Thus, one could wonder how to identify the tipping point where a paracrisis turns into a real crisis. It mostly has to do with intensity, dynamics, and interpretation, topics that we are going to study in more detail in the next section.

CRISIS TYPOLOGIES

Crises come in many shapes and sizes. Some are small, some are big. Some are sudden, some are smoldering. Some are intentional, some are unintentional. Some are human made, some are 'acts of God'. In order to manage organizational crises it is not only important to know what a crisis is, but also important to know what kind of crises the organization will be confronted with.

Some practitioners and researchers have tried to establish more or less systematic lists to capture the many different crisis types that, for example, private companies risk facing. Gerald M. Meyers' book *When It Hits the Fan: Managing the Nine Crises of Business* (1986) is a good example. The nine forms of crises referred to in the book's title are: public perception, sudden market shift, product failure, top management succession, cash crises, industrial relations, hostile takeover, adverse international events, and regulation–deregulation. These lists are only useful if the crises appearing on them are either typical (for a specific organization or industry) or new (compared to already-known crises). They are typically not based on any explicitly formulated categorization criteria.

Some companies also include lists of crisis types in their crisis management plans. However, these lists are not general, but only contain the crises that are relevant to the specific company. Such a list could look like the one in case example 2.1.

 Case example 2.1

Lists and clusters of crisis types in crisis management plans

The local crisis management plan of an international manufacturing company with subsidiaries located in different countries may include the following list of crisis types:

- Product recalls
- Accidents related to the use of the company's products
- Natural disasters

(Continued)

(Continued)

- Staff (accidents or mental problems)
- CEO or other key figures (death/illness)
- Loss of important customers
- Patents that expire
- Downsizing and cutbacks
- Competitors having technological breakthroughs
- Political changes or regulations
- Lawsuits that threaten the company's financial situation
- Industrial espionage
- IT breakdowns
- Cybercrime (hackers, virus, theft)
- Plant accidents (fire, power cuts, accidents, explosions, etc.)
- Rumors or misleading media coverage
- Firestorms on social media (angry customers)
- Kidnapping of staff
- Internal working environment

Some companies prefer to work with clusters or families of crises, such as:

1. Product-related crises (e.g., death/illness associated with product, accidental contamination, deliberate tampering, litigation, product recall);
2. Site-related crises (e.g., fire, industrial accident, machinery breakdown, production or distribution problems, labor disputes, plant closures, IT breakdown),
3. People-related crises (e.g., redundancies, accidents, criminal activities); and
4. Corporate level crises (e.g., financial problems, loss of key-contract or important customer, political regulations, anti-competitive behaviour, branding/trade mark issues, competitor problems, partnership problems, etc.).

Source: Based on information and documents received from international manufacturing companies.

Are there any alternatives to these lists? If we turn to the academic literature, several researchers have tried to establish crisis typologies based on categorization criteria that reflect specific aspects of a crisis. These can be criteria such as the nature or 'content' of crises (Shrivastava & Mitroff, 1987; Coombs, 1999; Alpaslan & Mitroff, 2011), causes (Rosenthal et al., 2001b), consequences (Drennan & McConnell, 2007), a combination of causes and consequences (Marcus & Goodman, 1991), speed or timescale (Moore & Seymore, 2005; Drennan & McConnell, 2007), nature of direct vs. indirect involved actors (Perrow, 1984), degree of intentionality (Ulmer, et al., 2007), or possibility of handling the crisis according to predictability and influence possibilities (Gundel, 2005). On top of this, some researchers have also tried to include atypical crises or to draw attention to crises never before seen. To illustrate, Mitroff (2004) makes a distinction between normal vs. abnormal crises, and Rosenthal et al. (1989) introduce the following unusual typology: not imaginable crises, neglected crises, almost avoidable crises, and crises everybody or some actors would like to see happen.

BOX 2.3

WHAT IS A TYPOLOGY?

A typology is an attempt to divide, classify, or categorize a field or an area into *genus* and *species*. There are two approaches to categorization. The first approach is based on Aristotle's theory of categories, in which things are categorized according to their commonalities. The result is a classification in which members of a specific category are all equally valid members; that is, they all live up to the same criteria (defined as necessary and sufficient membership conditions). The second approach is based on Wittgenstein's concept of *family resemblance* and Rosch's theory of *prototypes*. The result is a classification in which some members of a specific category are more valid than other members. Some members are *central* while others are *peripheral*.

Coombs has made several contributions to the study of crisis typologies. In his situational crisis communication theory, Coombs (2015) divides crisis types into three clusters corresponding to the level of responsibility attributed by the stakeholders to an organization in crisis: (1) a victim cluster, (2) an accident cluster, and (3) a preventable cluster. In a *victim crisis*, the organization has not caused the crisis but is itself a victim. The level of crisis responsibility is low. In an *accident crisis*, the organization has unintentionally caused the crisis, and the level of crisis responsibility is moderate. Finally, in a *preventable crisis*, the stakeholders strongly believe that the organization has deliberately engaged in wrongdoing. The level of crisis responsibility is high. However, mitigating or intensifying factors such as prior reputation or crisis history may influence the level of responsibility attributed to an organization in a specific crisis situation (cf. Chapter 6).

Coombs (2015) has also established a typology of *social media crises* where he distinguishes between three types of crises based on two sources (organizational or stakeholder actions) and the nature of crises: (1) misuse of social media (organizational actions), (2) customer complaints (stakeholder actions), and (3) challenges (stakeholder actions).

Misuse of social media is a crisis type triggered by the organization and its misuse of social media. In 2009, the Danish tourism organization Visit Denmark launched the social media campaign 'Karen 24' in hopes of attracting younger tourists to Denmark. The goal was to show another side of Denmark that went beyond the traditional, iconic image of Tivoli Gardens and Hans Christian Andersen. In a YouTube video testimonial, Karen (a Danish actress playing the role of a young mother) explains that she is trying to find a foreign man whom she met in Copenhagen and spent the night with about a year earlier. She wants to tell him that he is the father of August, her little son. The video was meant to be humorous and create awareness of the independence of women and free-spirited nature of the Danish people, but instead it lead to the resignation of the CEO of Visit Denmark, who was criticized for having portrayed a bad image of young women in Denmark.

Customer complaints crises are a crisis type triggered not by the organization, but by its customers, due to dissatisfaction with products or services – including customer service (cf. Chapter 9). Finally, a *challenge* is a crisis type that breaks out when different stakeholders find that a company's behavior and/or policies are inappropriate or unethical. Challenges can be difficult to manage because they are often based on differing socio-cultural norms and values. The killing and dissection in public of a giraffe named Marius in Copenhagen Zoo, on February 9, 2014, is one example. The zoo euthanized the giraffe for genetic reasons in accordance with the European Breeding Programme. When zookeepers decided to turn the dissection of the giraffe into a public educational session for zoo guests, however, citizens from all over the world criticized Copenhagen Zoo on Facebook (cf. Chapter 9).

Alpaslan and Mitroff (2011) claim that the number of different crisis clusters remains relatively small. Based on a study of the health-care sector, they have established a typology of eight clusters, or families, of major crisis types. Importantly they state that 'no crisis has been found to be a single, well-defined crisis that is contained solely within one and only one cluster or family' (p. 49). Thus, no matter how well a typology is executed, it is difficult to establish crisis typologies that cannot be problematized.

THE STANDARD CRISIS PORTFOLIO MODEL

It is neither practical nor cost efficient for an organization to develop a crisis management plan for each individual crisis type. But how can we reduce the number of crisis types and crisis management plans and still have a well-functioning crisis preparedness system?

One of the tools that could solve this problem is Shrivastava and Mitroff's (1987) crisis portfolio model. It is a framework for classifying crisis-triggering events according to *where* the crisis is triggered and *which* systems are the primary cause. *Where* refers to whether the crisis-triggering event is located inside or outside the organization. *Which* refers to whether the crisis-triggering event takes place in a technical/economic system or in a human/organizational/social system.

If we combine these two sets of dimensions, the result is a model with four cells (Figure 2.1). Cell 1 represents technical and economic failures in internal organizational

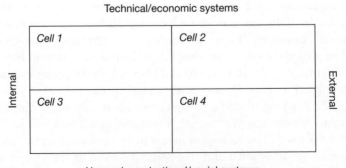

Figure 2.1 The standard version of the crisis portfolio model

systems (e.g., a defective product or a computer breakdown). Cell 2 represents primarily technical and economic failures in the organization's environment, causing crises within the organization (e.g., a hostile takeover). However, this cell also includes natural disasters. Cell 3 represents failures in social processes and systems (e.g., failure to adapt to change or mismanagement). Finally, cell 4 represents failures in the social environment of the organization (e.g., a boycott).

The idea behind the model is that organizations do not have to prepare for just one kind of crisis (or for all kinds of crises). Instead, they compile a crisis portfolio, preparing for a 'family' or a cluster of crises. Each organization, each industry, and each sector will fill out the four cells differently – with different crisis-triggering events depending on the specific conditions in each organization, industry, or sector and the crisis perception of managers and employees.

Figure 2.2 represents the crisis portfolio of a fictitious university. But how would the model look if it was the portfolio of a manufacturing company? Some crisis types would be the same for the company as well as the university, while other crisis types (such as examination fraud and plagiarism and work accidents and production errors) would be specific for either the university or the company. This also means that, to be able to fill out the crisis portfolio of a specific (type of) organization, such as the Dutch diary cooperative FrieslandCampina in case study 2.1 at the end of this chapter, you must possess or have access to detailed knowledge about the history of this organization, its corporate governance, its policies, its stakeholders, its products and services, the (inter)national markets in which it operates, and so forth.

Technical/economic systems

Cell 1 Fire Safety conditions issues IT breakdown Data loss (during electronic exam)	**Cell 2** Political regulation Smaller cohort sizes Natural disasters Applicants Tuition Financial crisis Mergers and acquisitions
Cell 3 Plagiarism Exam cheating Cheating with research findings Labor disputes Fraud Mismanagement Discrimination	**Cell 4** Boycott Terrorism Shootings Rumors Dissatisfied students Lack of qualified faculty Reputation problems

Internal (left side) — External (right side)

Human/organizational/social systems

Figure 2.2 Crisis portfolio of a university

The crisis portfolio model is a useful tool because it identifies clusters of crises instead of long, detailed lists of the potential crises an organization may face. The crisis portfolio model also ensures that organizations establish specific crisis management plans for crisis types in each of the four cells, preventing them from ignoring one or more of the cells, especially cell 3, which includes, for example, mismanagement – a topic that can be notoriously difficult to manage in a strategic and proactive manner. It seems easier to identify crisis types belonging to one of the two external cells (cells 2 and 4).

However, the crisis portfolio model can also be challenging. First, it is crucial that the four cells are filled out with *triggering events*, and not the *causes* or the *consequences* of these events. If you replace the triggering events with their causes, you quickly end up with an *infinite regress*, because behind the cause there is the cause of the cause, and behind this there is the cause of the cause of the cause, and so on. And if you replace the triggering events with their consequences, you quickly end up with one and the same type of consequence – negative media coverage and reputational damage – in all four cells. Second, some triggering events, such as strikes, can be placed in two different cells, namely an internal cell (a local strike) and an external cell (a general strike), depending on whether you apply an Aristotelian model (all representatives of a category are equally valid members of this category) or a prototype model (some representatives of a category are more central or peripheral than others).

THE EXTENDED CRISIS PORTFOLIO MODEL

To do justice to the complexity of crises, we have transformed Shrivastava and Mitroff's (1987) standard crisis portfolio model into an *extended crisis portfolio model*. This extended model takes as its starting point the fact that as a crisis manager you must always be prepared to provide answers to four questions that are important in the handling of a crisis:

- What is the nature or 'content' of the crisis?
- How high is the intensity of the crisis?
- How dynamic is the crisis?
- How do the stakeholders interpret the crisis?

The answers to the first question correspond to the standard crisis portfolio model.

Crisis intensity

Organizational crises differ not only in terms of their nature or 'content', but also in terms of their intensity. By intensity we mean the force with which a crisis affects the 'field' inside which it occurs and develops. Small crises differ from big crises, but even within these two categories there are differences regarding how severe a crisis is. Few people will disagree when we say that the tsunami in South East Asia in 2004 which claimed 230,000 lives, the earthquake in Sendai, and the Fukushima nuclear disaster in Japan in 2011 were crises with a huge impact. But what about the VW diesel emissions scandal in 2015? Compared to the Fukushima nuclear plant disaster it is smaller, but undoubtedly a severe crisis for VW. Then again, was it bigger than the Toyota floor mat/accelerator crisis in 2009–2010 that ended with the recall of approximately 9 million vehicles? In fact, all crises can be considered 'corporate tragedies' for the individual company, but they differ in intensity.

Intensity typologies are well known within the field of emergency management in relation to natural disasters, such as hurricanes and earthquakes, but also in relation to (inter)national terrorist attacks. One of these intensity typologies is the International Nuclear Event Scale (INES). It was introduced in 1990 by the International Atomic Energy Agency (IAEA) to enable prompt communication of safety significance information in the case of nuclear accidents such as the Fukushima disaster. The nuclear event scale consists of seven levels, from anomaly to major accident and is often represented using a color scale (Figure 2.3). Each increasing level represents an accident approximately 10 times more severe than the previous level. INES has been criticized for not being an objective scientific scale and for conflating magnitude with intensity.

Color coding is often used in intensity typologies as a shorthand reference for level of risk or danger (Sellnow & Seeger, 2013, Chapter 3). Inspired by emergency management, many private companies have adopted color coding (e.g., green, yellow, orange, and red) in their attempt to express different levels of crisis intensity (cf. the title of Coombs' book *Code Red in the Boardroom*, 2006c).

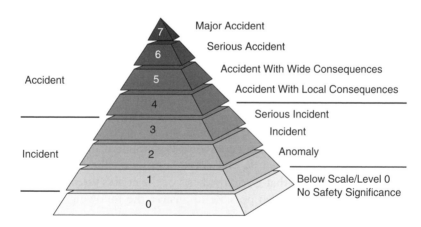

Figure 2.3 International Nuclear Event Scale (INES)

Crisis dynamics

The third question on which the extended crisis portfolio model is based concerns an aspect often neglected by researchers as well as practitioners, namely the dynamics of a crisis. How does a crisis develop over time? We have actually already touched upon this aspect in the previous section when we discussed how to measure the intensity of a crisis. But the dynamics we shall focus on in this section is of a different nature. Shrivastava and Mitroff's (1987) standard model is a typology of crisis-triggering events that have been divided into four categories or 'families'. Unfortunately, however, many crises do not remain within the categories in which they originally were triggered.

As mentioned previously, Alpaslan and Mitroff (2011) claim that

> *every* crisis is a *system* of multiple crises. *Every* crisis literally is in at least two or more families simultaneously. This happens because either the initial crisis consists of multiple crises in two or more families to begin with, or because the initial crisis sets off a chain reaction of crises. Any particular type of crisis, or crises, is (are) capable of serving as the cause, the effect, or both of any crisis or crises. (p. 49)

Thus, a crisis can move from one category to another; it can be replaced by another crisis or, even worse, it can be overlaid by another crisis creating a situation where the organization has to face not just one crisis, but a complex of crises. A double crisis may serve as an illustrative example of such a situation. A double crisis, which is very often a communication crisis, is triggered by poor handling of what we could call the original crisis. This might be because the organization in crisis remains silent, it takes too much time before it starts communicating, it withholds important information, etc. Often the news media are more interested in how the organization handles the double crisis than in what happened in the first place.

Further, we must add that most crisis management researchers concentrate on studying one organizational crisis at a time.

Crisis interpretations

The last, but not least, important question concerns the interpretation of crises. How is a crisis interpreted, and by whom? Before we go into detail on this question, we will briefly introduce a distinction between two meta-theoretical approaches to the study of crisis management and crisis communication.

The first approach is the essentialist approach. Proponents claim that this approach makes it possible to always identify and define a crisis on the basis of a range of objective traits or features – that is, on the basis of the crisis's *essence*. According to this approach, it is therefore also possible to answer the following questions in an unambiguous way: What is a crisis? And are we as an organization currently in crisis? Accordingly we can then activate or not activate the crisis preparedness system of our organization.

The second approach is the social constructivist approach. The proponents of this approach claim that it is impossible to identify and define a crisis on the basis of a range of objective traits or features. The question is not 'What is a crisis?' but 'What is interpreted as a crisis?' Crises are considered *social constructions*, something that can be interpreted and negotiated by multiple stakeholders. This does not mean, however, that crises do not really exist. They do! But it is how they are interpreted by human beings that turns them into crises. And interpretations are real.

Crisis interpretations may vary from top management to employees, from stakeholder group to stakeholder group, from organization to organization, and from sector to sector. Sometimes it is difficult for a CEO to accept that his or her company is in crisis. If this is the case, the CEO or his or her advisors (the crisis management team of the organization, cf. Chapter 4) can apply what we would call the 'stakeholder test'. As Coombs (2015) explains: 'If stakeholders believe an organization is in crisis, a crisis does exist, and stakeholders will react to the organization as if it is in crisis' (p. 3).

To sum up, when a crisis breaks out and develops over time, it is important to closely follow how the crisis is interpreted by different external and internal stakeholders and how their interpretations develop – or do not develop – over time. Research has demonstrated that personal and organizational factors such as educational background, function, seniority, the crisis history of the organization, etc., may influence how people perceive and understand crises (cf. Chapter 12). Different interpretations may have different impacts on how people think, behave, and communicate in a crisis situation.

Both the standard version and the extended version of Shrivastava and Mitroff's (1987) crisis portfolio model can be used by private and public organizations to discuss the following questions at a pre-crisis stage: How do we interpret crises in our organization? Which crises do we 'see' and 'remember'? And how do our stakeholders interpret (our) crises? Are there important differences, not only externally among different stakeholder groups, or between us and them, but also internally among different stakeholder groups? However, the two models, and especially the extended crisis portfolio model, can also be used at both the crisis stage and the post-crisis stage: to analyze, measure, and create awareness about the intensity, dynamics, and interpretations of the crisis situation; and to collect information about and learn from the results of this part of the crisis management process.

As shown in Figure 2.4, the four components of the model are interdependent. The arrows point in both directions. In so doing, the arrows indicate that each of

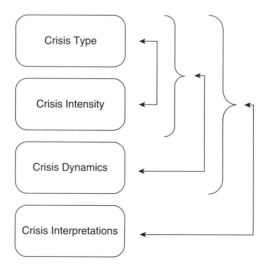

Figure 2.4 The extended crisis portfolio model

our four questions must be answered individually, but also that the answers influence each other. To illustrate, the answer given to the first question (What is the nature or 'content' of the crisis?) depends on the answer given to the fourth question (How is the crisis interpreted, and by whom?).

Unlike the standard crisis portfolio model which remains event oriented and relatively static, the extended crisis portfolio model is a process model which captures changes in intensity, dynamics, and interpretations. It is not a typology of events, but a typology of processes. The best way to apply the extended crisis portfolio model in practice is, therefore, to turn the typology into scenarios (cf. Chapter 4).

We will let the French crisis management researcher Christophe Roux-Dufort, who has studied the standard crisis portfolio model in detail, conclude:

> The weakness of typologies in general, and of crisis typologies in particular, resides in the temptation to believe in the partitioning of the established categories. However, what characterizes a crisis is precisely that it activates and brings together elements, actors, debates, and issues which do not belong to the same field of transactions. That is the reason why we have to read this typology in a dynamic way. (Roux-Dufort, 2000, p. 35)

CASE STUDY 2.1

THE CRISIS PORTFOLIO MODEL OF FRIESLANDCAMPINA

FrieslandCampina is a Dutch dairy cooperative. It is the result of a merger between Royal Friesland Foods and Campina in 2008. Like so many other dairies in the Netherlands, it has grown through mergers and takeovers. Today, FrieslandCampina is the world's largest dairy cooperative with annual revenues of €11.4 billion. It employs more than 20,000 people and its products are sold in more than 100 countries.

FrieslandCampina supplies consumer products like dairy-based beverages, cheese, and desserts across Europe, Asia, and Africa. A growing global demand for healthy, sustainably produced food offers FrieslandCampina a number of opportunities as well. Products are also supplied to professional customers, including cream and butter products to bakeries and catering companies. FrieslandCampina supplies ingredients and half-finished products to manufacturers of infant nutrition, the food industry, and the pharmaceutical sector around the world.

The company's stated ambition is to create the most successful, professional, and attractive dairy company for its member dairy farmers, employees, customers and consumers, and for society. To fulfil this ambition, FrieslandCampina formulated the *route2020* strategy for the period 2010–2020. The keywords behind the strategy are sustainable growth and value creation: the sustainable growth of the company and maximizing the value of all the milk produced by the cooperative's member dairy farmers.

Headquarters: Amersvoort, the Netherlands

Try to imagine that you have been employed by the issues and crisis manager of FrieslandCampina and that your first task is to revise the list of crises that the Dutch dairy cooperative risks facing today and in the future. The revised list will form part of the general crisis management plan applied by FrieslandCampina in real crisis situations as well as in drills and simulations.

Identify at least five crises types in each of the four cells of the standard crisis portfolio model. Avoid being too general in your selection of crisis types – that is, only identifying crises that every other organization could be hit by. Be as specific as possible.

After you have filled out the four cells, answer the following questions:

- What would constitute a major crisis for FrieslandCampina? Try to find out if you can use one of the crisis definitions introduced in the first part of the chapter.
- In each of the four cells of the standard portfolio model, how would you prioritize which of the crises you have identified is/are the most important?
- Try to imagine a scenario for one of the crises that you have prioritized. How will it develop over time (intensity, dynamics)? How will it be interpreted by key stakeholders?

Source: www.frieslandcampina.com.

CHAPTER SUMMARY

In the first part of this chapter we introduced and compared six important, but very different, definitions of organizational crises: one from the early 1960s, three from the 1990s, and two after the year 2000. A presentation of some more recent concepts followed: double crisis, the crisis after the crisis, crisis by association, multi-crisis, and paracrisis. The second part of the chapter was devoted to crisis typologies focusing on the crisis portfolio model, a crisis management tool invented by Paul Shrivastava and Ian I. Mitroff and developed further by the authors of this book. In the standard version, it is a typology of crisis-triggering events divided into four 'families'. In the extended version, it is a dynamic and complex reading of crises, involving not only their nature or content, but also their intensity, dynamics, and interpretation by various groups of stakeholders.

 Further reading

Gundel, S. (2005). Towards a new typology of crises. *Journal of Contingencies and Crisis Management*, 13(3), 106–115.

Mitroff, I. I., Pauchant, T., & Shrivastava, P. (1988). The structure of man-made organizational crises: Conceptual and empirical issues in the development of a general theory of crisis management. In D. Smith & D. Elliott (Eds.) (2006), *Key Readings in Crisis Management: Systems and Structures for Prevention and Recovery* (pp. 47–74). London: Routledge.

CRISIS MANAGEMENT (I): GENERAL PERSPECTIVES – FROM ANTICIPATION TO RESILIENCE

3

┐ **CHAPTER OVERVIEW** ┌

This chapter describes how the discipline of crisis management has developed from a tactical, reactive, and event-oriented perspective toward a strategic, proactive, and process-oriented perspective. Where the former perspective is limited to situations in which a crisis is already manifest, focusing on how to mitigate the negative consequences of the crisis, the latter also focuses attention on what happens before and after the crisis breaks out. The chapter also introduces some of the most recent trends in crisis management, including the debate on anticipation vs. resilience.

INTRODUCTION

Many organizations are hit by a crisis at one point or another. There are even senior communication and management consultants who claim that the question is not *if* a crisis will hit an organization, but *when* a crisis will hit.[1] While such a claim could be interpreted as purely wishful thinking, formulated as it is by consultancies that make a living from advising organizations on crisis management, there is still a grain of truth in it (cf. Chapter 1).

If it is no longer possible for organizations to completely avoid crises, they can at least strive to handle them in the best possible way, by introducing some kind of crisis preparedness system and by practising crisis management. Empirical studies show that private companies that have prepared for crises recover better, and faster, from

---

[1] As early as the late 1980s, Mitroff et al. (1987) made the following claim: '[I]t is no longer the question of whether a major disaster will strike any organization, but only a question of *when, how, what form it will take, and who and how many will be affected*' (p. 291).

a crisis than companies that are unprepared. Knight and Pretty (1999) examined how the financial markets reacted when listed companies experienced a 'corporate catastrophe'. The companies fell into two relatively distinct groups: recoverers and non-recoverers. Where the initial loss of stock value was approximately 5 percent on average for recoverers, it was about 11 percent for non-recoverers. If we look at the situation 12 months after the crisis, the average cumulative impact on stock returns was 7 percent on average *above* the pre-crisis level for recoverers, but 15 percent on average *under* the pre-crisis level for non-recoverers. Knight and Pretty (1999) suggested two explanations for this remarkable difference between recoverers and non-recoverers. The first explanation concerned the immediate estimate of the associated economic loss. The second explanation concerned how good the companies were at handling the crisis: 'Although all catastrophes have an initial negative impact on price, paradoxically they offer an opportunity for management to demonstrate their talent in dealing with difficult circumstances' (p. 369).

The purpose of this chapter is twofold. First, it describes how the discipline of crisis management has developed since the mid-1980s from a narrow tactical, reactive, and event-oriented perspective to a broad strategic, proactive, and process-oriented perspective. Second, the chapter briefly introduces some of the new perspectives on crisis management, including mindful crisis management, organizational improvisation, and the debate on anticipation vs. resilience. The question is whether these new perspectives will force us to rethink our understanding of crisis management.

WHAT IS CRISIS MANAGEMENT?

We define crisis management as the conceptualization, implementation, maintenance, and activation of the crisis preparedness (systems) of a private or public organization – that is, the resources allocated by the organization to be able: (1) to identify, analyze, and evaluate signs indicating that a crisis is building up; (2) to prevent a crisis from breaking out; (3) to prepare to handle the crisis if it breaks out anyway; (4) to bring the crisis to an end and reduce as much as possible the damage caused by the crisis to the organization, the industry, and external and internal stakeholders; and (5) to learn from the crises experienced by the organization and other organizations and to implement the changes made necessary by this organizational learning process. As it appears, our definition of crisis management includes all the three stages of the crisis life cycle. Or, to put it another way: the crisis management team is also at work when there is no actual crisis.

The crisis preparedness of an organization is composed of one or more of the following types of resources: actors (e.g., the members of a first response team or an external or internal spokesperson), structures (e.g., the organization of a crisis management team or an internal whistleblower arrangement), processes (e.g., the activities linked to the use of specific disciplines or tools) and documents (e.g., a crisis management plan).

The tradition and conditions for practising crisis management, including the type and size of crisis preparedness, vary by organization, industry, and sector. Large companies, for example, have more resources than small companies, and therefore it is often easier for them to establish a specifically designed, comprehensive crisis preparedness system. In general, large companies also get more attention from crisis management researchers, and therefore we know more about how they perceive and handle crises. Recently, however, a new research agenda promoting a crisis-based view of small-business research has seen the light of day (Herbane, 2010b, 2013).

In the private sector, there are industries such as the aviation industry in which crisis preparedness of the individual companies is subject to regulation at both the national and international levels. The aim of the International Civil Aviation Organization (ICAO), which is a specialized agency of the United Nations, is to work with the Chicago Convention's 191 Member States and global aviation organizations to develop international Standards and Recommended Practices (SARPs). States reference these SARPs when developing their legally enforceable national civil aviation regulations. ICAO also defines the protocols for air accident investigation followed by transport safety authorities in countries that have signed the Convention on International Civil Aviation.

In the public sector, there are also organizations such as municipalities where crisis preparedness is subject to regulation. This is the case, for example, in Denmark where municipalities have been in charge of municipal rescue preparedness since the beginning of the 1990s. This is perhaps no surprise given that one can find something similar in many other countries. But what is surprising is that this kind of public crisis preparedness (taken on by emergency/public safety officers) is being overlaid by a second type of public crisis preparedness – one undertaken by chief communication officers. In 2009, we examined how the two institutional logics behind this transformation – an older emergency management logic and a new crisis management logic – have co-existed and interacted to shape the institutionalization of the crisis communication function in the Danish public sector (Frandsen & Johansen, 2009b).

BOX 3.1

CRISIS MANAGEMENT OR CRISIS LEADERSHIP?

Some scholars make a distinction between *crisis management* (crisis managers) and *crisis leadership* (crisis leaders) inspired by the debate on management vs. leadership that started in the late 1970s. According to popular understanding, leadership is about setting a direction, formulating a vision or strategy, motivating and inspiring employees, and achieving large-scale changes, whereas management is about implementing action plans, setting up budgets, solving problems, controlling employees, and creating order in the organization (for an overview, see Bolden, 2004).

Mitroff (2004) is one of the scholars who started to make a distinction between crisis management and crisis leadership. Whereas the former is based on a centralized and bureaucratic design of an organization's crisis preparedness, the latter is based on an integrated design and what Mitroff calls the 'Big Picture'.

DuBrin (2013) has edited a handbook about the process of crisis leadership and the crisis leader's characteristics. Among the most important *personal attributes* of crisis leaders we find charisma, strategic thinking, the ability to inspire and to show sadness and compassion. Among the most important *behaviors* of crisis leaders we find directive leadership, extensive communication, and managing the flow of information. According to Jaques (2014), a good leader provides the crisis management team with focus, direction, decisions, support, humanity, drive, clarity, and accountability.

For further reading, see DuBrin (2013).

GENERAL PERSPECTIVES ON CRISIS MANAGEMENT

The discipline of crisis management has developed significantly since the mid-1980s. The easiest way to explain this development is to describe it as two shifts in perspective, where by 'perspective' we mean a cluster of shared conceptualizations of crises, (crisis) management, and (crisis) communication. The first shift that took place was the development from a *narrow* tactical, reactive, and event-oriented perspective toward a *broad* strategic, proactive, and process-oriented perspective (see Tables 3.1 and 3.2). Today, this process-oriented perspective is described as the dominant paradigm in crisis management: 'Organizations are urged to prepare as much as possible during non-crisis times so that they will be able to act swiftly and effectively to prevent and manage any untoward situations that arise' (Gilpin & Murphy, 2008, p. 4). The second shift has only just begun and is taking place before our eyes. It can be described as a shift from a *simple* broad perspective toward a *complex* broad perspective (see Table 3.3).

Table 3.1 Overview of the narrow tactical perspective on crisis management

The narrow tactical perspective

Crisis	An isolated event
Crisis management	Reactive management Focus on tactics Operational preparedness
Crisis communication	Focus on instructions, information, and crisis intervention
Key actors	Public emergency response organizations Citizens
Vocabulary	Community resilience, crash management, damage control, extraordinary incidents, public safety, vulnerability

Table 3.2   Overview of the broad strategic perspective on crisis management

The broad strategic perspective

Crisis	A dynamic process
Crisis management	Proactive (interactive) management Focus on strategy Organizational preparedness Opportunity management
Crisis communication	Focus on instructions, information, crisis intervention *and* reputation
Key actors	Private companies Stakeholders
Vocabulary	Crisis, image, legitimacy, renewal, reputation, symbolic capital

Table 3.3   New trends – toward a complexity perspective in crisis management

New trends

Crisis	A complexity A social construction
Crisis management	Focus on emergent management Contingency approach Mindful management Resilience Improvisation
Crisis communication	Focus on multivocality
Key actors	Interdependent organizations
Vocabulary	Complexity, contingency, emergent

The tactical, reactive, and event-oriented perspective

Within the narrow tactical perspective, crises are conceptualized as isolated, unexpected, and sudden *events*. These might include accidents, fires, or floods, where the focus is on reacting as fast as possible in order to regain control (Roux-Dufort, 2000; Jaques, 2014). One does not start handling the crisis until it breaks out. Thus, there is a strong focus on the *crisis stage*. Pauchant and Mitroff (1992) describe this perspective with words such as *crash management* and *damage control*.

Regarding the understanding of crisis management, this perspective is inspired by the idea of *command and control* that originated with the military. According to the *US Department of Defense Dictionary of Military and Associated Terms* (2012), *command and control* is defined as: 'The exercise of authority and direction by a properly designated commander over assigned and attached forces in the accomplishment of the mission. Also called C2'. Over time, the idea of *command and control* has developed from C2 to, for example, C3 (Command, Control & Communication(s)) and C4 (Command, Control, Communication & Intelligence). This idea is well established within public sector disaster and emergency management (cf. the general introduction).

Regarding the understanding of crisis communication, it is first and foremost a matter of information, instructions, and crisis intervention.[2] The fact that communication follows command and control, instead of being placed right at the beginning (how can you command and be in control without communicating?), reveals the kind of functionalist communication theory on which this perspective is based.

From this perspective, crises are viewed as something negative and the primary objective is to return to *business as usual* as quickly as possible.

The narrow perspective has developed significantly in recent years. Inspired by the broad perspective, practitioners have started understanding disasters and emergencies as dynamic processes that evolve through a progression of phases, as well as incorporating the Internet and social media in their communication with citizens in disaster and emergency situations.

Finally, practitioners have also started incorporating the new community resilience perspective, as well as developing advanced assessments instruments. The Crisis Communication Scorecard is a good example of the latter (Vos et al., 2011). It is inspired by the Balanced Scorecard approach developed by Kaplan and Norton (1996). It is structured according to a staged approach to emergency management (like the Crisis & Emergency Risk Communication (CERC) approach developed by the Centers for Disease Control and Prevention in the United States) including a selection of key stakeholders (citizens, news media, response organizations, and networks), a set of performance indicators for each stage describing the communication actions taken, and finally an evaluation scale.

The strategic, proactive, and process-oriented perspective

Within the broad strategic perspective, crises are not conceptualized as isolated events but as dynamic processes evolving through a progression of stages or phases as in a life cycle (Roux-Dufort, 2000; Jaques, 2014). Therefore, you do not wait until the crisis breaks out before you start handling it – as in the narrow perspective on crisis management – but focus attention on what is going on in the pre-crisis and post-crisis stages, on the opportunities for preventing and/or learning from a crisis. The terminology and number of stages may vary. The most common is to make a distinction between three stages: (1) the pre-crisis stage; (2) the crisis stage (sometimes called the focal incident stage or the trans-crisis stage); and (3) the post-crisis stage (Coombs, 2015). Fink (1986), however, who was among the first to introduce a process perspective, made a distinction between four stages all entitled something completely different (cf. Chapter 4 on staged approaches).

---

[2] Crisis intervention or psychological first aid is emergency psychological care given to individuals who are the direct and indirect victims of a crisis. For an overview, see James and Gilliland (2008).

Regarding the understanding of crisis management, this perspective is very much inspired by strategic management. This means, first of all, that the crisis prepared-ness of an organization must be fully *anchored*, not only in top management, but also among employees. The crisis management team cannot do its work properly without the support of the CEO and/or the board of directors, or if the employees are unin-formed about the scope and nature of the crisis preparedness of their organization.

Second, it also means that crisis preparedness must be *integrated*. A crisis can damage the reputation, trust, or ethical position that a company has built up among its stakehold-ers. There is every reason to check that there is coherence between the promises made by the company to its stakeholders in the shape of written values, policies, programs, codes of conduct, *and* its crisis preparedness. When a crisis hits, will the company be able to fulfill what it has promised? Or have the promises created false expectations among stakeholders on how professional the company will behave when handling a crisis?

Finally, this also means that the crisis preparedness of the organization must be defined as a specific practice or function that will be developed continually.

Schannon (2006) introduced a distinction between *operational preparedness* and *organizational preparedness*. The former is about managing disasters, that is events that are dramatic, but in most cases also manageable. The latter is about managing crises, that is processes which are often the result of mismanagement. Therefore, organizational preparedness is first and foremost about the creation of a *crisis mind-set* among the members of the crisis management team.

Regarding crisis communication, it is no longer just a matter of information, instruc-tions, and crisis intervention. It is also a matter of protecting and repairing the image and reputation, trust and credibility, of the organization vis-à-vis its stakeholders. There is a focus not only on the economic, human, and material capital of the organization, but also on its symbolic and social capital.

From a broad strategic perspective, crises are no longer viewed as something exclusively negative, but also as something which can contribute to positive thinking. Organizations may in fact emerge stronger from a crisis (cf. the introduction to this chapter). Some researchers even talk about *opportunity management* and crisis as inspiring renewal to a new normal (Ulmer et al., 2007). This places new demands on the discipline of crisis management.

BOX 3.2

IMAGE, REPUTATION, STATUS, AND LEGITIMACY

A crisis can harm an organization and its stakeholders in numerous ways. For a private company, for example, a crisis often leads to a hit on sales of products and services (key stakeholder: customers) and a fall in share price (key stakeholder: investors). A crisis often affects employer branding and makes recruiting and keeping the most talented members of the workforce more difficult (key stakeholder: employees). Practising public affairs and maintaining a level of political influence (key stakeholder: government) can also be affected by a crisis. The company will lose some, if not all, of the trust that it has built up among its stakeholders (social capital).

However, when we speak about the negative consequences of a crisis, we often, and perhaps even primarily, refer to how the *symbolic capital* of an organization, that is its image and/or reputation, is threatened. Here are some definitions of the key concepts.

Image

Image has been defined in several ways. Some researchers define it as the *projected* image (how insiders want outsiders to see the organization), other researchers define it as the *perceived* image (how outsiders actually view the organization). There are others still who define image as the *reflected* image (insiders' perceptions about how outsiders view the organization) (Foreman et al., 2012). Scholars in favor of the concept of perceived image will have to explain the difference between image and reputation, unless they consider the two concepts synonymous. The concept of image plays a key role in image repair theory where it is applied with similar, yet different, concepts like ethos, face, and reputation (cf. Chapter 5 on crisis communication theory).

Reputation

Fombrun (2012) defines reputation as 'a collective assessment of a company's attractiveness to a specific group of stakeholders relative to a reference group of companies with which the company competes for resources' (p. 100). In their mapping of the definitional landscape, Barnett et al. (2006) identified three clusters of meanings: (1) reputation as awareness, (2) reputation as assessment, and (3) reputation as asset. The concept of reputation plays a key role in situational crisis communication theory (cf. Chapter 6 on crisis communication theory).

Status

Status can be defined as a type of evaluation that influences the stakeholders of an organization independently of their evaluation of reputation. Thus, we can imagine organizations that are high on status but low on reputation, which may protect them in a crisis situation, other things being equal. Status is an organization's position in a hierarchical order and is generated by relations and affiliations to other actors. None of the four crisis communication theories introduced in Chapters 5 and 6 has exploited the potential of this concept.

Legitimacy

Suchman (1995) defines legitimacy as 'the generalized perception or assumption that the actions of an entity [an organization] are desirable, proper, or appropriate within some socially constructed system of norms, values, beliefs, and definitions' (p. 574). Legitimacy represents an evaluation regarding the *appropriateness* of an organization, while reputation represents the *effectiveness* of an organization. The concept of legitimacy plays a key role in terminological control theory (cf. Chapter 5 on crisis communication theory).

(Continued)

(Continued)

This strong focus on protecting the symbolic capital of an organization in crisis must not make us forget that a crisis can also harm the stakeholders, not only before the negative event becomes a crisis for the organization, but also after it has stopped being a crisis for the organization. A defective product may put customers' lives and health at risk a long time before the company finally decides to recall the product. A bad investment may have consequences for investors long after the company has gone bankrupt. We will return to the concept of reputation – corporate reputation, industry-level reputation, and trade association-level reputation – in Chapter 11.

For further reading, see Barnett and Pollock (2012) and Carroll (2013).

New trends in crisis management

Today, the contrast between the narrow, tactical and the broad, strategic perspectives of crisis management is not as noticeable as it may appear from the presentation given above. Public sector organizations are fully aware of the fact that natural disasters can easily develop into political crises, and that crisis communication can transform into political communication (Boin et al., 2005). Public sector organizations are also fully aware that the reputations of national and local government and emergency response organizations are on the line when they are called upon to take action (cf. Sturges' (1994) definition of crisis communication in Chapter 5). A good example is the political crisis triggered by the Scandinavian Ministries of Foreign Affairs' poor handling of the tsunami disaster in South East Asia in late December 2004 (Kivikuru & Nord, 2009; Frandsen & Johansen, 2016b).

Furthermore, the contrast between the narrow, tactical and the broad, strategic perspective of crisis management is being overlaid by a new contrast between two perspectives which we have decided to call the *simple* broad perspective and the *complex* broad perspective. The former corresponds *grosso modo* to the broad perspective, as presented hitherto, whereas the latter is an attempt to identify some of the most recent trends in the field of crisis management. Among these trends we would like to highlight the following.

A more complex understanding of crises. This new understanding comes in two variations: (1) the understanding of crises as such (conceptual models) and (2) the understanding of how crises have developed historically, in organizations and in society at large (empirical complexity). Let us begin with the first variation. At first, it seems obvious to understand crises as processes that go through a progression of stages or phases corresponding to the beginning, middle, and end of a life cycle. But how obvious is this conceptual model in reality? When does a crisis *actually* begin? When the first signs of weakness are identified, or when you suddenly find yourself at the epicenter of the perfect media storm? When an event has been defined as a crisis by the organization itself, or when it has been defined as a crisis by outsiders? And when does it end? Is the Chernobyl crisis (1986) over? And what about the Cartoon affair (2005–2006)? New concepts such as *the crisis after the crisis*, introduced by Dutch crisis management researcher Uriel Rosenthal and his colleagues and illustrated by the plane crash in

Bijlmer in the Netherlands in 1992 (cf. Chapter 2), may prove useful in our attempt to grasp the complexity of crises. If we then continue with the second variation, we can observe that crises have become more mediatized, more international or global, and more filled with dilemmas. According to Rosenthal et al. (2001b), this empirical complexity makes it harder for crisis managers to 'determine the exact nature of the crisis: Is it type X or type Y?' (p. 18). This problem is also reflected in Alpaslan and Mitroff's (2011) claim that every crisis is a system of multiple crises (cf. Chapter 2).

The last issue under this heading that we will briefly touch upon concerns the ontology of crises. Organizational crises are no longer (without any initial discussion) identified as objective phenomena. Organizational crises are increasingly understood as social constructions. Tierney (2014) defines social constructivism as follows:

> The key insights of social constructionism is that both perceptions and social activity are based not on our direct apprehension of 'objective reality' ... but rather on systems of meaning that are provided by culture, developed through social interaction, and produced through claims-making activities that advance particular views of the world. The 'reality' of social life thus consists of myriad social constructions that are taken for granted by members of particular cultures and subcultures. (p. 26)

(See also Chapter 5 on terminological control theory, which focuses on the rhetorical aspects of social constructivism.)

A more complex understanding of crisis management. The understanding of management behind the staged approaches is based on a prescriptive perspective, positing that it is possible to define rules and norms – including best practices – for the crisis management process as such, and thereby to reach a higher degree of control and predictability. There is no doubt that organizations with a formal crisis preparedness are, by default, in an better position than those organizations that are unprepared. However, not everything can be planned.

Some researchers, therefore, recommend that crisis managers take a more emergent perspective, claiming that a planned process will always contain 'something more' and/or 'something less' than initially decided. Other researchers recommend a contingency approach, arguing that there is no 'one best way' to manage a crisis. Organizations are not independent closed entities but interdependent open systems that constantly have to adapt to changes. The appropriate way to manage a crisis depends on the kind of crisis and environment with which one is dealing (see also Cameron's contingency theory of crisis communication in Chapter 6).

The contingency approach can be seen as an alternative to the widespread idea of *best practice*. Best practices are 'ways of doing things' that are considered superior to other 'ways of doing things' and they are used as a benchmark for multiple if not all organizations (Champ, 1989; for best practices in crisis communication, see Chapter 6). The idea of best practice has been criticized for not taking the differences between organizations and their dynamic context into consideration. Best practice in one organization is not necessarily best practice in another. In most cases, it is not possible to transfer a normative idea about how to manage in crisis situations from one organizational context to another, despite how generic the idea may be. The idea always has to be recontextualized or 'translated'.

Other researchers go a step further, recommending an approach inspired by complexity theory. Complexity theory is the study of interaction processes within complex systems. In *Crisis Management in a Complex World* (2008), Dawn Gilpin and Priscilla Murphy, two proponents of this approach, argue that complexity theory is particularly relevant to organizational crises 'because of its focus on uncertainty and unpredictability' (p. 7). Complexity theory is introduced by the two scholars as no less than a paradigm shift. From a complexity perspective, crises are defined as complex adaptive systems that show the following features:

1. Complex systems are composed of interacting agents.
2. The agents' interactions alter the system over time.
3. Complex systems are self-organizing.
4. Complex systems are unstable.
5. Complex systems are dynamic and have their own history.
6. Complex systems have permeable and ill-defined boundaries.
7. Complex systems are irreducible.

The focus in this approach is on organizational learning, and not on prevention and preparation. We will never be able to control and predict complex systems. However, these systems are not completely random. They just follow another logic.

A formal crisis preparedness for 'routine crises' in stable and well-known contexts will still be relevant. However, it is also important to create a strong organizational *crisis culture*, that is either a culture based on a high degree of crisis awareness or reliability, or a culture that is resilient and able to bounce back. A formal crisis preparedness will never be better than the organization (the crisis culture) in which this preparedness is embedded. This catapults us directly into the last section of this chapter.

BOX 3.3

MINDFUL CRISIS MANAGEMENT

In *Managing the Unexpected* (2001; 2007), Karl E. Weick and Kathleen M. Sutcliffe established five principles on how to practise mindful crisis management. This approach is inspired by so-called high-reliability organizations (HROs) and how they deal with the unexpected. The concept of HROs was originally coined by Karlene Roberts and refers to organizations that have succeeded in avoiding catastrophes in an environment where the risk of accidents is high: aircraft carriers, air traffic control systems, nuclear power plants, wildland firefighters, and emergency medical treatment. Weick and Sutcliffe (2001) explain that the 'unexpected' does not necessarily have to be a major crisis. The unexpected is triggered by a simple sequence in organizational life: 'A person or unit has an intention, takes action, misunderstands the world; actual events fail to coincide with the intended sequence; and there is an unexpected outcome' (2001, p. 2; see also Turner & Pidgeon, 1997, p. 117).

The first three principles of mindful crisis management are principles of anticipation while the last two are principles of containment.

Principle 1: Preoccupation with failure

HROs encourage reporting of errors and near misses. They accept that failure is an option and learn more.

Principle 2: Reluctance to simplify

HROs do not accept simplifications. They simplify less and see more.

Principle 3: Sensitivity to operations

HROs are attentive to where the work gets done, because this is also where the latent failures are to be found. This is not so much an aspect of crisis management as it is an aspect of the unexpected.

Principle 4: Commitment to resilience

HROs combine anticipation and resilience. They keep errors small and improvise when it is necessary to keep the system functioning.

Principle 5: Deference to expertise

HROs cultivate diversity and avoid rigid hierarchies in high-tempo situations.

Weick and Sutcliffe claim that every other type of organization can learn from and imitate HROs and their mindful approach to crisis management. HRO proponents have been in heated debate with the proponents of NAT (i.e., Natural Accident Theory) (Perrow, 1984).

Source: Weick and Sutcliffe (2001; 2007).

THE DEBATE ON ANTICIPATION VS. RESILIENCE

As we touched upon in the general introduction, it is hard to imagine a better time to publish a textbook on organizational crises, crisis management, and crisis communication than today. This is, among other things, due to the fact that an important shift in our understanding of crisis management and crisis communication is currently taking place. Central to this shift is the debate on *anticipation* vs. *resilience*.

Resilience is a concept that emerged within different scientific disciplines in the 1970s. It began within biology, more precisely within the study of ecological systems (for an overview of the field, see Simonsen, 2014). In his article 'Resilience and stability of ecological systems' (1973), Canadian Professor of Ecological Sciences Crawford S. Holling defined two types of behavior regarding how the continuity of an ecological system can be maintained: (1) stability, that is the ability of a system to return to an equilibrium state after a temporary disturbance; and (2) resilience, that is the ability of a system to absorb change and disturbance and maintain the same relationships between populations or state variables. If the continuity of the ecological system is to be maintained by stability, it must be possible to predict or anticipate the disturbances that will affect the system in the future. This is best achieved in simple ecological systems that are characterized by few predictable changes. If we are talking about complex ecological systems characterized by many unpredictable changes, the continuity of an ecological system is best maintained by resilience. Resilience does not presuppose that a system is able to predict the future, only that it can design systems that can absorb future events in whatever unexpected form they may come.

American risk management researcher Aaron Wildavsky introduced the concept to the social sciences and initiated the debate on anticipation vs. resilience with his book *Searching for Safety* (1988). He defined the two concepts as follows: 'Anticipation is a mode of control by a central mind; efforts are made to predict and prevent potential dangers before damage is done … Resilience is the capacity to cope with unanticipated dangers after they have become manifest, learning to bounce back' (p. 77). What are the consequences of this debate to the practice of crisis management?

If you decide to have anticipation as your strategy, you must focus on prevention and preparation 'sinking resources into specific defenses against particular anticipated risks' (p. 220). This is the rationale behind the strategic, proactive, and process-oriented perspective on crisis management presented in the previous section. The ultimate goal of this approach must be to eliminate the unexpectedness of the world.

If you decide to have resilience as your strategy, you must focus on a different type of crisis management 'retaining resources in a form sufficiently flexible – storable, convertible, malleable – to cope with whatever unanticipated harms might emerge' (ibid.). The crises you have to manage will always be unanticipated; that is, either they were not taken into consideration in the existing crisis management plan, or the plan failed. Instead you have to follow 'plan B'.

A small example from everyday life may illustrate the difference between anticipation and resilience as 'crisis management strategies'. In cities of a certain size, the city council will usually make attempts to regulate traffic and prevent accidents through the use of traffic-light systems. This common policy, including the way traffic lights are placed at important intersections, can be defined as anticipation. In other words, the traffic lights form part of a plan. But let us now imagine that one day there is a major power cut which lasts several hours. Suddenly, the traffic lights no longer work. In this situation, the conditions of uncertainty, ambiguity, and time pressure are aggravated. Neither drivers nor pedestrians know when and how it is safe to cross the intersection. It is also difficult for them to interpret the behavior of other drivers or pedestrians as they hesitatingly make a move forward. Will they hold back if you continue driving or walking? And how long will they accept staying behind you while you are monitoring the intersection? Here you can no longer rely on anticipation. Instead, you need to be resilient. One way to be resilient is to *improvise*.

Organizational improvisation

How does improvisation work in an organizational context? Is organizational improvisation like jazz or theater improvisation? Can you always improvise, or are there certain conditions that must be fulfilled before it is possible? French crisis management researcher Christophe Roux-Dufort is one of the very few scholars who have conducted empirical studies of organizational improvisation in crisis situations. Based on existing literature, Roux-Dufort and Vidaillet (2003) reviewed the definitions and conditions for improvisation. The following four characteristics were recurrent in most definitions of improvisation:

- Improvisation is characterized by the temporal convergence of planning and executing action. There is little or no time between the sequences of the management process (situational analysis, decision making or planning, and execution).
- Improvisation is action guided by intuition in a spontaneous way. The improvisors must rely on their ability to use previous experience.
- Improvisation is based on an underlying minimal structure that on the one hand guides action, but on the other hand is also transformed by the very same action. Improvisation is not just pure 'invention'.
- Improvisation is based on a combination or reconfiguration of existing resources (cf. the concept of *bricolage*, to create something from a variety of available things).

Certain conditions are necessary before improvisation can be applied as a strategy:

- Contextual conditions (e.g., urgency and surprise).
- Organizational and behavioral conditions (e.g., flexibility of the role system and interactions among people).

Based on a follow-up case study of a crisis involving several groups of actors, Roux-Dufort and Vidaillet (2003) concluded: (1) that if there is no shared sense of urgency and surprise among the actors involved in the crisis, it will be difficult to improvise; (2) that the greater the level of urgency and surprise, the lower the level of improvisation – that is, beyond certain critical thresholds, conditions favoring improvisation become conditions hindering improvisation (e.g., when a sense of urgency develops into high stress); (3) that the involvement of actors with strong professional identities in the management of the crisis leads the actors to rely on their identities and to repeat the roles they have learned; and (4) that if there are no interactions among the different groups of actors, this will hinder the process of collective sensemaking, which is necessary to improvise.

These conclusions are very important. First of all, Roux-Dufort and Vidaillet emphasize that pure improvisation only exists in the world of artistic performances. In organizations, improvisation will always be framed by certain contextual and organizational conditions. Second, the two scholars demonstrate – without using the term – that communication (called 'interactions' in the article) plays a key role for improvisation. Without interactions among people, across professional identities and fixed roles, nobody will be able to improvise.

CASE STUDY 3.1

DEMA'S COMPREHENSIVE PREPAREDNESS PLANNING

The Danish Emergency Management Agency (DEMA) has developed a guide for all types of organizations as a voluntary tool to improve the quality of existing preparedness planning or to begin new planning activities. The guide follows the principles of what DEMA calls *comprehensive preparedness planning*: 'The purpose of the planning for each organization is to strengthen its ability to prevent incidents, where it is possible, and to manage them when it is necessary. In other words, preparedness planning is about creating resilient organizations' (p. 5). The planning concept is divided into seven general areas: (1) programme management, (2) planning assumptions, (3) prevention, (4) training, (5) exercises, (6) evaluations, and (7) crisis management plans. Below you will find the section on 'Core task 4: Crisis communication' (pp. 36–37) which is part of area 7. Read the description and then answer the questions.

Crisis communication

During a crisis, a massive and sudden pressure for information typically rises from the media, citizens, partner organizations and other stakeholders. A crisis therefore puts demands on the organization's communication which by far exceeds what it is used to in day-to-day operations. It can be necessary to set up a dedicated crisis communication team, that can ensure a timely, reliable, and open crisis communication through the organization's own and external channels. Such a team can also help lay the foundations for constructive relations with the news media. The following conditions regarding the crisis communication team should be described in the organization's general crisis management plan and related documents:

Tasks – An instruction or action card outlining the team's various tasks, such as:

- Updating the organization's webpage with information on the crisis management.
- Responding to inquiries from journalists, concerned citizens, etc.
- Press releases and interviews for radio, TV and Internet news media.
- Direct warning of affected/threatened citizens via available media and technology.
- Information in foreign languages for tourists, ethnic minorities, and foreign media.
- Coordination of information to the public with external partners that are also involved in responding to the crisis in question.

Management – The head of the crisis communication team (often the head of the normal communication unit) must be a member of the crisis management unit. Competences vis-à-vis the person leading the crisis management unit must be described clearly.

Organization – It should be clear if the individual members of the crisis communication team are expected to stay at their normal work stations, or if they should work directly from the crisis management room or an adjacent room.

Staff – The crisis communication team will typically be a strengthened version of the normal communication unit, but the group of people and the allocation of roles will not necessarily be the same. In addition to the 'usual' communication employees there can for example be a need for leaders and experts tasked with making live media statements.

Resources – A resilient webpage that can manage many simultaneous visitors is one of the most important resources for updated crisis communication. More specialised means can be the setting up of a press centre or a call-centre with dedicated telephone lines and an advertised email address for questions and answers. In this case the organization needs instructions for activating and manning rooms and technical facilities, standard reply guides for operators that can be adapted to the particular crisis, etc.

Procedures – Additional action cards, templates, etc. can lay down procedures for:

- Activation of the crisis communication team (preferably before but otherwise immediately after the first meeting of crisis management unit).
- Establishment of systematic media monitoring and media analysis – partly to contribute to the combined situation picture, partly as basis for press strategies and to ensure that any errors in the media's coverage of the organization are corrected.
- Agendas for internal meetings in the crisis communication team.
- Involvement of the crisis communication team in the crisis management unit meetings. Press strategy and media coverage should be a fixed item on the agenda.
- Permanent contact person for journalists with a fixed telephone number during the crisis (press duty officer).
- Contact details for persons in charge of communication at partner organizations.
- Prepared drafts for press releases, fact sheets with background information, etc.
- Distribution lists for press releases and communication briefings (email).
- Instructions regarding who can speak to the media on behalf of the organization (spokesman hierarchy), specifying who in the organization journalists may quote directly, and who are only allowed to provide background information to the media.
- Procedure that, if necessary, dictates a centralisation of all crisis communication to ensure that the organization speaks with one voice only.

Discussion questions

- How would you classify this document? As a representative of the tactical, reactive, and event-oriented perspective on crisis management, or as a representative of the strategic, proactive, and process-oriented perspective? Why?
- How does DEMA understand *communication*?
- Who are the primary stakeholders in a crisis situation?

Source: Comprehensive Preparedness Planning (DEMA, 2009).

CHAPTER SUMMARY

In this chapter, we have explored old and new perspectives on crisis management. We have taken a helicopter view of the development from the tactical, reactive, and event-oriented perspective to the strategic, proactive, and process-oriented perspective, which has become the dominant paradigm, and then again from the simple broad perspective to the complex broad perspective, including new understandings of crises and crisis management. The chapter concluded with a brief introduction to the debate on anticipation vs. resilience and how resilience can take the form of organizational improvisation.

 Further reading

DuBrin, A.J. (Ed.) (2013). *Handbook of Research on Crisis Leadership in Organizations*. Northampton, MA: Edward Elgar.

Roux-Dufort, C. (2009). The devil lies in details! How crises build up within organizations. *Journal of Contingencies and Crisis Management*, 17(1), 4–11.

Smith, D. (2006). Modelling the crisis management process: Approaches and limitations. In D. Smith & D. Elliott (Eds.), *Key Readings in Crisis Management: Systems and Structures for Prevention and Recovery* (pp. 99–114). London. Routledge.

CRISIS MANAGEMENT (II): STAGED APPROACHES – BEFORE, DURING, AND AFTER CRISIS

4

CHAPTER OVERVIEW

This chapter introduces the reader to the staged approaches that constitute the core of the strategic, proactive, and process-oriented perspective on crisis management. These staged approaches are based on the conceptualization of crises as a life cycle encompassing three stages: a pre-crisis, a crisis, and a post-crisis stage. The chapter also includes a brief presentation of the most important disciplines and tools, such as signal detection, risk management, issues management, crisis management plans and teams, and organizational learning, applied in one or more of the three stages.

INTRODUCTION

Within the broad strategic perspective on crisis management, researchers as well as practitioners apply a *staged* approach: that is, they view a crisis as having a life cycle and divide the crisis management process into a number of stages or phases. Each of these has a range of disciplines and tools. The more disciplines and tools, the more finely meshed the individual stages or phases of the models, and this makes it necessary to introduce a certain number of substages.

Fink (1986) made an early distinction between four stages in what he called the 'anatomy of the crisis', namely (1) *the prodromal stage*, (2) *the acute stage*, (3) *the chronic stage*, and (4) *the crisis resolution stage*. As it appears, Fink's distinction is very much based on the metaphor of a disease. First there are only a few symptoms, then the disease breaks out and develops, and finally it reaches a climax, in which the patient either dies or recovers. Following this metaphor's logic, Fink defined a crisis as 'a turning point for better or for worse' (p. 15).[1]

Almost 10 years later, Mitroff (1994) expanded the model to include five stages: (1) *signal detection*, (2) *probing and prevention*, (3) *damage containment*, (4) *recovery*, and (5) *learning*. In this model, the stages no longer represent stages in the life cycle of a crisis, but are different types of crisis management interventions. In his efforts to provide an integrative framework for the study and practice of crisis management and crisis communication, Coombs (1999) established a three-staged approach where each macro-stage is divided into three micro-stages: (1) the pre-crisis stage (*signal detection*, *prevention*, and *preparation*), (2) the crisis stage (*recognition*, *containment*, and *restitution*), and (3) the post-crisis stage (*evaluation*, *institutional memory*, and *post-crisis actions*).

In the following three sections, we will provide a detailed introduction to the three macro-stages, as we understand them, including some of the most important disciplines and tools in the crisis management process. Along the way, we will also discuss the theoretical and practical value of crisis management plans, life cycle models, and anticipation.

THE PRE-CRISIS STAGE

With a perspective on crisis management that is both proactive and process oriented, the focus will naturally be on the pre-crisis stage. If an organization has decided to establish crisis preparedness for the first time, the conceptualization and implementation of this practice or function will take place during this stage. Which type of crisis preparedness will be the best? How comprehensive must it be? How must it be organized and implemented to be as effective and efficient as possible? If the organization already has it, then it is also during this stage that the existing preparedness is maintained – for example, by means of crisis simulations held at regular, fixed intervals. Unfortunately, crisis management researchers have rarely taken a holistic perspective on the pre-crisis stage. Instead, they have devoted most of their time to the study of specific components, such as the crisis management team or the crisis management plan. Olaniran, Williams and Coombs (2012) and Portal and Roux-Dufort (2013) are the first books to provide a systematic introduction to the management of the pre-crisis stage.

'The best way to manage a crisis is to prevent one' goes an old saying that cannot be repeated too often. 'The second best way to manage a crisis is to prepare for one' is another saying that cannot be repeated too often either. In the pre-crisis

---

[1] In their 2012 article 'Tracking the evolution of the disaster management cycle: A general system approach', Christo Coetzee and Dewald van Niekerk demonstrate that the idea of disaster phases – what we in this chapter call a staged approach – is not a new conceptual invention. These concepts have been around since the early 1920s, first within sociology (e.g., Prince, 1920, who distinguished three phases: the emergency period, the transition period, and the rehabilitation period), then within psychology (e.g., Stoddard, 1968, who also distinguished three phases: the pre-emergency, emergency, and post-emergency phases). However, it was not until the 1970s that the disaster management cycle became a general framework in disaster and emergency management.

Table 4.1 Overview of the pre-crisis stage

The pre-crisis stage

Focus	To prevent crises from breaking out
	To prepare the organization for handling the crises that have become manifest anyway
Challenge	To identify as *early* as possible weak signals revealing that a crisis is building up
	To activate the crisis preparedness of the organization at the *right* time
Disciplines	Risk management, issues management, stakeholder management
Tools	Signal detection including media/social media monitoring, reporting on near misses, early warning systems, whistleblower arrangements, etc., crisis management team, crisis management plan, media training, simulations

stage (see Table 4.1), the focus is on preventing crises from breaking out, but also on preparing for handling crises that have become manifest.

Regarding prevention, the biggest challenge is to identify signals as early as possible that reveal a crisis is building up. This is called signal detection. At first, it sounds like an easy task. Is it not just a question of keeping an eye on the organization and its environment? That is correct. But it is not as easy as it sounds. First, *when* and *where* do you have to be vigilant? Both the organization and its environment are complex and dynamic phenomena over which neither the CEO nor the crisis management team can have a complete overview. Second, on *what* do you have to keep an eye? In the literature on the subject, it is often stated that it is a question of identifying 'weak signals'. The earlier you discover these signals, the greater the chance that you will prevent the crisis from entering the crisis stage. But the earlier you are looking out for weak signals, the weaker the signals are and the easier they are to miss. Finally, *how* can you keep an eye on the organization and its environment?

SIGNAL DETECTION

Most crisis management researchers recommend that organizations practise signal detection, or have early warning systems. 'If anything is at the heart of Crisis Leadership, it is Signal Detection', Mitroff (2004) claims. Signal detection is about anticipating the future from a vantage point in the present and is inspired and/or applied by disciplines such as strategic management, scenario planning, futurology, information science, and semiotics.

Within signal detection, there is a distinction between two types of signals: strong and weak signals. It is easy to identify strong signals, because they are located within what futurologists define as a trend (e.g., a decrease in turnover over a number of years, as reflected in sales figures, annual reports, etc.). It is less easy to identify weak signals because they either are not located within a trend or constitute by themselves the starting point of a new trend.

Signal detection in crisis management is about identifying weak signals, revealing that something is not as it should be, that something is developing in the wrong way. But perhaps we should replace the concept of signal with the concept of sign (or cue)? Signals are characterized by a tight conventional relationship between their expression and content level. It makes them easy to interpret, or decode. Signs, on the contrary, are characterized by a much looser relationship between the two levels. In other words, they are less easy to interpret and there is more space for 'reading something' into the situation that is not there (cf. Weick's criticism of crisis management plans later in this section).

BOX 4.1

TEN PRINCIPLES OF SIGNAL DETECTION

Ian Mitroff and the USC Center for Crisis Management have established ten principles for signal detection:

Principle (1): All crises are preceded by early warning signals.

Principle (2): Signals are not self-amplifying or self-blocking.

Principle (3): Signals do not exist by themselves. They are part of, and a reflection of, the overall structure of an organization.

Principle (4): Signal detection is a direct reflection of our priorities.

Principle (5): Signal detection necessitates signal detectors.

Principle (6): Different crises require different detectors.

Principle (7): Not all signals are alike.

Principle (8): Every signal detector needs a signal monitor.

Principle (9): Signals have to be transmitted to the right people.

Principle (10): Individual signal detection is not enough.

Source: Mitroff (2004).

Signal detection can be practised in different ways. Most of the tools are information collection and analysis systems. Some examples of these include: early warning systems (EWSs) developed within disaster or emergency management, or the near-miss and near-accident reporting systems that aim for organizational self-improvement and which have become popular in for example the transportation and health-care industries. Media monitoring can also be defined as a kind of signal detection. Despite the fact that everybody studying and/or working within this field seems to agree on how important signal detection is, very little research has actually concentrated on this component of the pre-crisis stage.

Risk management

Risk management is a popular tool in private as well as public organizations when it comes to crisis prevention. As formulated by Beck (1992), a risk is a 'not yet event' that may transform into a real crisis event. Or as Heath (2006) defines it: 'A risk is an occurrence that can have positive or negative consequences of varying magnitudes, the occurrence of which and the effects of which can be variously predicted, controlled, and harmful or beneficial. In this context, *a crisis is a risk manifested*' (p. 245).

The purpose of risk management is to describe one or more key activities performed by an organization, to identify the risks associated with these activities, to assess how serious these risks are, and, finally, to decide what must be done about them. Are the risks acceptable when considering the costs to alleviate them? Must they be reduced? Must they be transmitted to or shared with other actors (e.g., an insurance company)? Or must the activities be stopped because they are too dangerous? Risk management is divided into a series of iterative processes, including the following:

- *Definition* of the object or context of risk management (cf. the key activities mentioned above).
- *Risk analysis* consisting of (1) *risk identification* and (2) *risk assessment*. Risk identification consists of the identification of all credible events or failure scenarios related to the activities that may harm people and the environment or lead to loss of material or immaterial values. Techniques such as bottom-up analysis (e.g., failure modes and effects analysis) or top-down analysis (e.g., fault tree analysis) can be used to solve this task. Risk assessment consists of the quantification of all the risks associated with the activities (estimation of probabilities and magnitude of consequences applying probabilistic models).
- *Risk treatment* is the process of selecting and implementing measures to modify risk. Risk treatment can include avoiding, reducing, sharing (transfer of risk), or retaining risk (accept of risk).
- *Risk management planning* consisting of (1) *risk decision making* and (2) *risk implementation*. These last two processes consist of formulating a strategy or action plan, including making cost–benefit calculations of the consequences of the decisions made by the organization.

The risk understanding represented by this approach to risk management is based on the natural scientific or technical idea of the *objective risk*, which can be calculated by using probability theory. The risk of an unwanted scenario is calculated by multiplying the expected frequency by the expected consequences. However, it must be emphasized that there are alternative risk understandings, such as the psychological theory of the *experienced risk*, the anthropological theory of the *selected risk*, and the sociological theory of the *constructed risk* (cf. Chapter 1).

Issues management

Another widespread way to prevent crises from breaking out is issues management. Just as a risk may develop into a crisis, an issue may also develop into a crisis.

However, this takes place in a different context. While risk management traditionally has a strong focus on managing *internal* organizational phenomena, issues management has a strong focus on *external* organizational phenomena, that is phenomena related to the legal, political, economic, and social environment of the organization. Further, risks are often considered objective while issues are viewed as subjective or linked to certain social actors and their interpretations.

An issue has been defined as 'an unsettled matter which is ready for decision' (Chase, 1984, p. 38) and as 'a contestable point, a difference of opinion regarding fact, value, or policy, the resolution of which has consequences for the organization's strategic plan' (Heath, 1997, p. 44). The most important difference between these two definitions is that while Chase emphasizes that an issue is ready for decision, Heath is more interested in the content of the issue.

Behind the definitions is a common set of ideas that are rooted in the concept of *legitimacy gap* (Sethi, 1977). Private and public organizations are social institutions dependent upon society's acceptance of their role and activities in order to survive and grow. Businesspeople call it their 'license to operate'. If an organization, let's say a private company, starts manufacturing its products in a way that is seen as problematic, a gap between business performance and societal expectations will open up and the company risks losing its legitimacy. In such a case, the whole situation would have turned into an issue.

The most popular approach to issues management is the Jones-Chase issues management process model (1979; see also Chase, 1984). It consists of five steps: (1) issue identification, (2) issue analysis, (3) issue change strategy options (a reactive, adaptive, or dynamic change strategy?), (4) issue action programming, and (5) evaluation of results. This model was originally created for the management of public policy issues. It considers communication a tactical resource and is inspired by the 'Lasswell formula' (Lasswell, 1948) in its approach to issues communication.

Robert L. Heath and Tony Jaques have developed two alternative approaches to the Jones–Chase model. The former author introduced a strategic issues management (SIM) approach based on rhetoric (meaning), resource dependence theory, and corporate social responsibility (Heath, 1997; Heath & Palenchar, 2009). The latter has contributed an integrated model of issues management and crisis management (Jaques, 2014). The four issues management experts mentioned here have different viewpoints when it comes to the relationship between issues (management) and crisis (management). Jones and Chase do not address this relationship at all. Heath defines crisis as a 'risk manifested', but also reminds us about preventing a 'crisis from becoming an issue' (Heath & Palenchar, 2009, p. 285).

Stakeholder management

Issues do not just circulate by themselves in the 'issues arena' (Luoma-aho & Vos, 2010; Vos et al., 2013; see also Chapter 8). They are 'carried' around by individuals, groups of individuals, or organizations that provide them with names and speak in favor of or against them. We call these 'carriers' *stakeholders*. Put a little differently, issues management first becomes an effective discipline when the organization is able to 'put a name and face' to those issues that are of strategic importance; this is the intersection of issues management and stakeholder management.

One element that crises have in common is that they can harm the external and/ or internal stakeholders of an organization (e.g., customers, the local community, employees, suppliers, competitors, investors, politicians, governmental stakeholders, the media). It is therefore no surprise to find stakeholders included in many of the most popular crisis definitions (see, for example, Pearson & Clair, 1998, and Chapter 2).

The most widespread definition of stakeholders, including the field of crisis management, is Freeman's (1984) definition: 'Organizations have stakeholders. That is, there are groups and individuals, who can affect, or are affected by, the achievement of an organization's mission' (p. 52). However, there is another definition which seems to fit better within a crisis context, namely that by Gray et al. (1996). According to their definition, a stakeholder is any human agency that can be influenced by, or can itself influence, 'the activities of the organization in question' (p. 45). The difference between the two definitions amounts to the difference between the *mission* of an organization and its *activities*. A mission is based on an explicit intention. Such an intention can trigger a crisis directly or indirectly, for example if the product or the production processes of the company is viewed as problematic, but activities is a broader category, including *unintended consequences of purposive action* (Merton, 1936).

A simple way to practise stakeholder management in the pre-crisis stage is to draw a generic, organization-centric, stakeholder map where the organization is placed in the middle surrounded by all its stakeholders (the so-called hub and spokes model). In this approach, the key questions are: Who are the stakeholders of the organization? What stakes do they have? And how will they affect the organization in a crisis situation?

A more sophisticated way to practise stakeholder management is to draw a specific stakeholder map where both the organization and its stakeholders are placed in a larger network together with other actors (e.g., *intermediaries*) (Frandsen & Johansen, 2015b). This approach adds a range of new questions: Which actors enact which stakeholder roles in which situations? One and the same person can be an employee, a customer, and an investor in relation to their organization. What relations are there between the individual stakeholder groups? Are there alliances or conflicts that can develop into a crisis (or during a crisis)?

Whether we choose one approach to stakeholder management or the other, we must expect that a crisis will change the stakeholders' stakes – including the network of relationships of which they are part. This is a challenge for every type of graphical representation that will always appear as static.

Most stakeholders have a direct stake in the organization, and that does not stop when the organization is facing a crisis. However, as we will see in Part 2 of this book, there are stakeholders who have a stake in the crisis *as such*, and not in the organization or in the other stakeholders involved in the crisis. They can be categorized as *third parties*.

Considering how crucial the role of stakeholders is in a crisis situation, it is surprising how under-investigated this topic is. However, there are a few exceptions. Alpaslan et al. (2009) have developed a stakeholder theory of crisis management.

Their research has produced two insights. First, that the stakeholder model of corporate governance will lead a more proactive and accommodative type of crisis management. According to the authors, this means, for example, that a broader set of stakeholders than mandated by law will be involved in crisis preparations, and that stakeholder relations based on mutual trust and cooperation will be developed. Second, that the salience of stakeholders may change in crisis – that is, stakeholders are dynamic. The first of these insights is clearly based on normative stakeholder theory claiming that all stakeholders' interests have intrinsic value (Donaldson & Preston, 1995).

Acquier et al. (2008) have investigated the operational value of stakeholder theory for crisis management. These French researchers apply an analytical approach to stakeholder management. They agree with their American colleagues that stakeholders can behave dynamically in crisis situations, but disagree when it comes to the value of normative stakeholder theory. They conducted a case study of how a large public transportation company in France managed a complicated crisis involving many different sub-crises, issues, and stakeholders, in which a part of the building site of a new metro line belonging to the transportation company collapsed under a school in a dense urban environment. Their research also produced some important insights, including the concept of 'stakesholder': that is, actors that are concerned with multiple issues of a crisis. Instead of managing stakeholders individually, it is better to manage 'stakesholders' and the flow of issues coherently.

The practical value of the research presented above can be summed up as follows: we tend to have an oversimplified view of the relationship between an organization and its stakeholders, and we take the stakeholders' existence, identity, and interests for granted; in reality, however, stakeholders are dynamic actors that may change, especially in ambiguous and complex crisis situations.

From prevention to preparation

In this section, we take a look at two of the most important tools of organizational crisis preparedness: the *crisis management team* (CMT) and the *crisis management plan* (CMP). They are the very incarnation of crisis preparedness. We have put the CMT and CMP in the pre-crisis stage – as part of the preparation for handling different types of crises – but they are not activated until a crisis occurs (or during a crisis simulation). As we shall see, the CMT and CMP even cover part of the post-crisis stage.

What does an effective CMT and an effective CMP look like? There is no definitive answer to this question. Especially not if the answer has to be applicable to all types of crises and all types of organizations. On the one hand, CMTs and CMPs have not yet been researched to a very great extent. On the other hand, the normative templates recommended by the 'how-to' literature are often based on personal experience, which may be fragile ground. However, a *heuristic* approach to problem solving – consisting of asking questions and applied to situations where there is no optimal, but only a satisfactory solution – may serve as a starting point.

What made the organization decide to implement a (new) CMT or CMP? Is the organization a private company? If so, does it operate in foreign markets?

Is the organization a public organization? If so, does it have a political dimension? How many members will the CMT have? What tasks will it have? Will it be permanent or will it be flexible and change from crisis to crisis? Which organizational functions must be represented in the CMT? How long will the CMP be? Will it be divided into subplans? Who is in charge of the CMT or CMP? How will the CMT or CMP be implemented? And so forth.

By answering these preliminary questions, you will get a platform for continuing with the establishment of a CMT and CMP that are specific to your organization.

Crisis management team (CMT)

A CMT can be defined as a group of people, designated by the CEO or another top manager, who are responsible for the crisis management practice or function of an organization. Thus, in a crisis situation, it will typically be the members of the CMT who make the important decisions, such as when to activate the crisis preparedness and how to coordinate the response activities. Before and after the crisis situation, it is also the members of the CMT who will be in charge of evaluating and updating the crisis preparedness on the basis of what the organization may have learned from a crisis.

The size, structure, and modus operandi of a CMT varies from organization to organization. Some CMTs are small (less than five members) while others are big (more than five members). Some CMTs are permanent while others are organized in a more flexible way. According to Jaques (2014), it is common practice today to designate a core team which assembles during a crisis regardless of its severity. Specialists are then added depending on the skills and knowledge needed to handle the crisis. In terms of organizational design, the CMT can be described as a horizontal project structure.

In most cases, the CMT is a cross-functional group consisting mainly of middle managers representing the key functions of the organization: corporate communication, security, finance, production, marketing, and human resource management. The CMT often also includes the CEO, a lawyer or legal advisor, a representative of the board, and in some cases an external communication consultant (cf. the lists in Pauchant & Mitroff, 1992, and Frandsen & Johansen, 2004). However, the CMT must never be the executive team under another label. The CMT is responsible for:

1. Conceptualizing and implementing the CMP(s) as part of the organizational crisis preparedness.
2. Activating and enacting the CMP in crisis situations (including selecting an appropriate spokesperson).
3. Evaluating and updating the CMP after a crisis (simulation).
4. Taking care of problems not covered by the CMP (e.g., providing counsel).

The members of the CMT risk running into problems in the following two extreme situations: if they *agree* too much, and if they *disagree* too much. If they agree too much about what will happen in a crisis situation, they end up with the psychological phenomenon described by Janis (1972) as *groupthink*. Groupthink occurs within a group of people in which the desire for consensus is so strong that it leads to dysfunctional decision making. If the opposite happens, that is if the members of the CMT disagree too much about what will happen in crisis situations, they end up with an internal conflict. Bergeron and Cooren (2012) conducted a study of how the participants in three crisis management teams interacted and had difficulties in creating a collective framing of the crisis situation, mainly due to differences in professional and organizational background.

Crisis management plan (CMP)

A CMP can be defined as a *document* representing the text genre that we call *plans*. It consists of a selection of *components* depending on the type of organization, its history, and its culture.

The CMP is a document or text. This has two important implications. First, as every other document or text, the CMP will be part of a communicative process involving senders, receivers, points in time and space, etc. This process begins when the CMP is introduced for the first time (implementation), and the process is repeated every time it is necessary to activate the CMP (in real crisis situations, during drills, and simulations). Second, in order to facilitate this communicative process, the CMP must have a cover page and an introduction informing the receiver about the aim and purpose of the CMP. It must also be written in an accessible style so that the receivers can read and understand the content. The CMP is not 'just another' document. It is what Lammers (2011) calls an *institutional message*, that is a message that carries institutional logics and that is characterized by endurance, reach, incumbency, and intentionality.

The CMP is a plan. By plan we understand a set of instructions telling members of the organization how they should think, behave, and communicate in future crisis situations of a certain type. The CMP consists of *components*. These components can be combined in different ways according to the approach to crisis management. The structure of the components often follows the life cycle of crises. Some of the most important components are listed in Table 4.2.

How useful are CMPs? They are the hallmark of the strategic, proactive, and process-oriented approach to crisis management. The adoption of a CMP by an organization is often considered a sign of institutionalization of the idea of crisis preparedness (cf. the general introduction). Ideally, nobody questions the functional value of a CMP: that it can be used to prevent and handle crises, the individual stages, and the transition from one stage to another.

CMPs also seem to have a symbolic value. A group of Norwegian researchers has examined how crisis preparation among leaders is carried out and communicated to the rest of the organization and what impact this has on the risk perception and psychological well-being of the employees. The results of their survey conducted in five different organizations revealed that crisis preparedness, including CMPs, was associated both with lower perceived risk as well as with increased well-being among employees (Selart et al., 2013). To put it differently, a CMP seems to be 'effective' even before it is activated in a crisis situation.

Nevertheless, there are scholars who warn organizations against relying too much on CMPs. Karl E. Weick and Kathleen M. Sutcliffe are two of these scholars. They claim

Table 4.2 Components of crisis management plans

Components of CMP	Including
Introduction	Specification of relationship with other (sub)CMPs
Activated the last time	Date and place of most recent crisis simulation and/or crisis
Crisis management team (CMT)	Activation process List of members (functions) Location (room) Contact sheet Roles and responsibilities
Information input from pre-crisis stage	Crisis portfolio Risk identification and assessment Issues identification and analysis Stakeholder map
Crisis communication plan (CCP)	Integrated with the communication strategy and policy of the organization Prescribed messages (i.e., press releases) Crisis dark sites Q&As External/internal spokesperson(s) Offline/online spokesperson(s)
Scenarios for crisis stage	Integrated with the value statement and CSR policy of the organization
Business continuity management	BCM plan
Information input from post-crisis stage	Logbook Learning outcome Updating of CMP

that plans can do the opposite of what was intended. Instead of guiding and facilitating the crisis management process, plans can make things worse (Weick & Sutcliffe, 2001; 2007). Their arguments are as follows.

Plans create expectations that influence what people see, their perceptions, and reduce the number of things people notice. Plans are based on expectations, and expectations can be so strong that they influence what we see. The argument is that we impose our expectations on the signs we interpret, especially signs that are ambiguous, and if the interpretations do not correspond to our expectations, we will 'fill in the gaps' and 'read between the lines' (Weick & Sutcliffe, 2001, p. 79).

Plans preclude improvisation. The sequences of actions described in the plans and designed to manage a future crisis restrict attention to what is expected and limit our view of our capabilities to what we have now. Weick and Sutcliffe refer to

Henry Mintzberg's criticism of strategic planning and what he calls the 'fallacy of predetermination'. Planners plan in stable and predictable contexts and therefore they are lulled into thinking that the world will unfold in a predetermined manner.

Plans presume that consistent high-quality outcomes will be produced time after time if people repeat patterns of activity that have worked in the past, that is routines. The problem with this way of thinking, which is often reinforced by crisis simulations, is that routines cannot handle the unexpected. Weick and Sutcliffe suggest that we learn from 'High Reliability Organizations' which have understood that 'reliable outcomes require the capabilities to *sense* the unexpected in a *stable* manner and yet *deal* with the unexpected in a *variable* manner' (2007, p. 67; cf. Chapter 3).

Another scholar who is sceptical about the usefulness of CMPs, at least a certain category of plan, is Clarke (1999). He makes a distinction between two different perspectives on CMPs. The first perspective is functional or rational common-sense planning. From this perspective, the purpose of plans is to tell the members of the organization how to solve a problem – in our case how to prevent and/or handle a crisis. According to Clarke, functional planning is possible under conditions of relatively low uncertainty where information can be gathered and trusted. The second perspective is symbolic planning. Under conditions of high uncertainty rational planning becomes more difficult, and the instrumental utility of plans decreases. In these cases, the plan and the planning process *themselves* become the function. From this perspective, the purpose of plans is not to tell the organization how to solve a problem, but to claim expertise. Clarke calls these plans *fantasy documents*. They are first of all rhetorical instruments used by organizations and experts to convince citizens and employees that they have the necessary expertise, and that they are in control.

Behind the discussion on the usefulness of CMPs lies a more general discussion about human rationality, context, information, uncertainty, and expectations.

THE CRISIS STAGE

The crisis stage represents what the narrow tactical, reactive, and event-oriented perspective on crisis management would define as the crisis *as such* (cf. Chapter 3). This is the moment when the organization becomes aware of the crisis, when the damage control starts, when the organization runs out of resources, and when the overview vanishes into the air. In the 'how-to' literature this is the moment when the situation gets 'hot', the 'shit hits the fan', the 'perfect storm' materializes. The focus is on coordination and damage containment. The biggest challenge is to activate the organizational crisis preparedness at the right time and in the right place. The risk of ending up with a double crisis is high (cf. Chapter 2). In this section, we will briefly look at two important aspects of the crisis stage: *crisis decision making* and the *crisis communication plan* (Table 4.3).

Decision making in crisis situations

There are people who claim that the crisis stage begins with a decision ('We are in crisis!') and that it also ends with a decision ('Now the crisis is over!'). However, none

Table 4.3 Overview of the crisis stage

The crisis stage

Focus	To coordinate the crisis preparedness systems
	To mitigate the negative consequences of the crisis
Challenge	To activate crisis preparedness in the most appropriate way, at the most appropriate place and time, to manage the crisis
Disciplines	Crisis communication, crisis decision making, reputation management, business continuity management
Tools	Crisis communication plan, crisis dark site, holding statements, hotline, logbook, spokesperson

of these decisions are necessarily one-off, clear-cut, final decisions made at the right time and in the right place. The first decision is typically made after the crisis has become manifest – that is, too late to be of any help. The second decision is typically made before the crisis is over – that is, too early to be of any help. Put simply, timing is a challenge. When, for example, did the top management of Volkswagen decide that the 'Dieselgate' scandal was manifest, and that the German automobile manufacturer was in crisis? On September 18, 2015, when the US Environmental Protection Agency announced that Volkswagen had cheated on emissions tests by means of an illegal software? Or on September 23, 2015, when the CEO of Volkswagen, Dr. Martin Winterkorn, resigned? Or later?

A crisis is a time when important decisions must be made by the CMT in order to respond as quickly and effectively as possible. It is also a time when the conditions for decision making are unusual. The decisions have to be made by a team of people who may agree or disagree about the crisis (cf. the previous section on groupthink and collective framing). The members of the CMP are only partly informed about the situation, and it is difficult to collect more information. They only have limited time to make the decisions, and they feel stressed.

Most crisis decision-making theories are based on a rational–analytical approach to decision making and belong to the same tradition as the prescriptive perspective on crisis management that we referred to in the previous chapter. According to these theories, decision making is a purely cognitive activity where a rational human being first identifies all the alternative solutions to a problem, then calculates all the consequences of each of these solutions, and finally makes his or her decision by selecting what seems to be the most appropriate solution. A primary interest within this approach is how to prevent 'irrational' factors such as stress and emotions from having an impact on the decision-making process.

However, since the late 1980s, crisis management researchers have become increasingly interested in the tradition of naturalistic decision-making theory (Lipshitz et al., 2001). Instead of beginning with formal models of decision making, the researchers began by conducting field research to try to discover the strategies people used in natural settings. Gary Klein is one of the pioneers in the field of naturalistic decision making. His recognition primed decision (RPD) model is a model of how people make quick, effective decisions when faced with complex situations. In this model, the decision maker is assumed to generate a possible course of action, compare it to the constraints imposed by the situation, and then select the first course of action that is not rejected. RPD has been described in diverse groups including ICU nurses, fire commanders, chess players, and stock market traders. It functions well when there is time pressure and when information is incomplete and goals poorly defined.

Crisis communication plan

The crisis communication plan is sometimes used as a synonym for the CMP as such, but in our case the term refers to a specific 'plan in the plan' activated at the very beginning of the crisis stage. Like the CMP it consists of a series of components linked to each other by what you may call a simple 'communication model': (1) What is the overall communication strategy? (2) Who is the sender? (3) Who is the receiver? (4) What is the key message? (5) Which channels will be used? The answers to these questions will normally be formulated in terms of:

- Crisis communication strategy (integrated with CMP)
    - o For example, to 'over-communicate' (a strategy applied by Scandinavian Airlines during the Dash 8-Q400 crisis, cf. case study 6.1).
- Spokesperson(s)
    - o External/internal
    - o Online/offline
    - o Source credibility
    - o Spokespersons hierarchy.
- Stakeholder list
    - o Primary/secondary stakeholders
    - o External/internal stakeholders
    - o Intermediaries.
- Prescribed messages
    - o Press releases
    - o Blogs
    - o Fact sheets
    - o Q&As.
- Media list
    - o Legacy media
    - o Internet and social media.

It is important for an organization to have a crisis communication plan and to be able to activate it when the crisis breaks out. However, it is also important to keep in mind that such a plan will often be based on a simplified understanding of communication as transmission of messages or distribution of information.

In this book, we follow the principle: *no crisis management without crisis communication, and no crisis communication without crisis management* (cf. the general introduction). Communication cannot be reduced to an activity that takes place after the management issues have been sorted out. The members of the CMT do not first make their decisions and then communicate these decisions to the other members of the organization. Decision making is a communication activity from the beginning. We shall return to this principle in Chapter 5 (cf. terminological control theory).

THE POST-CRISIS STAGE

Unfortunately, the post-crisis stage has not yet been subjected to the same amount of research as the pre-crisis stage. It seems as if both researchers and practitioners find this part of the crisis life cycle less attractive. However, this does not mean that this stage is without importance. If the disciplines and tools applied in the pre-crisis stage will help you manage the individual organizational crises, those applied in the post-crisis stage, especially organizational learning, will perhaps help you get rid of organizational crises as such. In this section, we will concentrate on three important aspects of the post-crisis stage: (1) evaluation, (2) learning, and (3) implementing change after crisis (Table 4.4).

Evaluation of the crisis management process

It is difficult to evaluate anything until you know what happened during the crisis. Therefore, any kind of evaluation must start with the collection of relevant information. This is not a problem if the CMT has used a logbook, registering all important events that took place during the crisis, including contacts from the news media.

Two types of evaluations are relevant before the information collected can be transformed into knowledge that the organization and its members can learn from: (1) evaluation of the consequences of the crisis, and (2) evaluation of the crisis management process. The first type includes the economic, human, material, and symbolic consequences of the crisis. These consequences can be measured in different ways, from the measurement of investors' reaction to the crisis, or decrease in stock price, and reputational damage, to media monitoring. The second type of

Table 4.4 Overview of the post-crisis stage

The post-crisis stage

Focus	To learn, to change, to start again
Challenge	To learn from and remember the experience that the organization and its members have gained
Disciplines	Organizational learning, opportunity management, change management
Tools	Incident report, logbook, evaluation (media coverage, crisis management process)

evaluation concerns the performance of the organization. Did the CMT succeed in coordinating efforts and resources? Did the CMP work as expected? How was the reaction among external and internal stakeholders?

Organizational learning

Organizational learning is, without doubt, the most important aspect of the post-crisis stage. Larsson (2010) defines organizational learning as follows: 'Organizational learning applies to efforts where individuals and collectives in organizations … gain knowledge from the past to deal with the present, or use knowledge from an earlier crisis when managing a new crisis, especially to correct previous shortcomings and mistakes' (p. 714).

There are several sources for learning from a crisis: (1) the most recent crisis that your organization has experienced; (2) past crises involving organizations from the same industry; (3) past crises involving organizations from different industries; (4) near misses; and (5) crisis simulations. The more you go down this list, the less the learning potential. The first source has the biggest learning potential: a recent crisis that involves yourself as a member of the organization. Sources (1) to (3) all represent real, full-blown crises; (4) represents real, but not full-blown crises; and (5) represents full-blown, but not real (only realistic) crises.

Argyris and Schön's (1978) theory of organizational learning is often brought into play to understand how, and to what extent, organizations can learn from crises. Argyris and Schön take a psychological perspective on learning, introducing a distinction between two basic types of learning:

- *Simple-loop learning* is defined as the simple process in which a mistake is detected and corrected by using a different approach, but without changing the initial goal. This is the most superficial type of learning process. The organization has learned something, but the process has not changed its self-understanding or the reference frame inside which it is reflecting, acting, and communicating.
  As an example (inspired by case study 11.1), a Danish children's clothing manufacturer is accused by the media of badly handling a product recall. The company has forgotten to inform the public authorities about the discovery of traces of cancer-causing chemicals in T-shirts produced in Asia – which is required by Danish law. Information given to customers who have purchased the T-shirts is also limited. The company detects the error, corrects it, and continues to sell children's clothes produced in Asia.
- *Double-loop learning* is defined as the more complicated process in which a mistake is detected and corrected but where the process leads to a rethinking of the initial goal.
  Continuing the example (inspired by case study 11.1), the Danish children's clothing manufacturer understands that the problem is not to improve the company's product recall procedures in accordance with Danish law, but to avoid product recalls as such, that is to improve the supply chain system.

French crisis management researcher Christophe Roux-Dufort is a pioneer when it comes to crisis and learning. He has criticized the widespread idea that organizational crises offer an opportunity for change, an idea that has also become popular among crisis communication researchers (see, for example, the brief introduction to renewal discourse theory in Chapter 6, and the epilogue). However, the fact that the same types of crises keep repeating themselves over and over again reveals that crises instead offer an opportunity for the consolidation of existing management beliefs and practices (Roux-Dufort, 1999).

One vital aspect of learning from crises centers on the barriers to learning. Two other pioneers within this sub-field, Denis Smith and Dominic Elliott, have listed the following barriers: rigidity of core beliefs, values, and assumptions; ineffective communication and information difficulties; focus on single-loop learning; centrality of expertise; and disregard of outsiders (Smith & Elliott, 2007; see also Pergel & Psychogios, 2013).

CRISIS SIMULATIONS

Many private and public organizations make use of crisis simulations or exercises in order to test the quality of their crisis preparedness. In addition to organizing training excercises under conditions resembling the conditions of a real crisis, crisis simulations also make it possible to discover structural, procedural, and/or resource-related weaknesses of crisis preparedness – and help to develop it further.

However, there are experienced consultants such as the Argillos consultants who warn against believing too firmly in the benefits of crisis simulations. Robert and Lajtha (2007) have identified three drawbacks to the traditional approach to crisis management training, including the periodic 'day out' to participate in a crisis simulation. First, these kind of excercises may provoke adverse psychological reactions – feelings of dissatisfaction, doubt, and distrust – *on the part of the participants.* They do not benefit very much from spending a day away from a tight work schedule in order to participate in a scenario that does not unfold realistically. Second, there may be doubts about the learning value of such excercises. Most of them follow a predictable annual cycle and are emergency evacuation drills. In short, they quickly become 'routine exercises' without any real learning potential. Finally, such exercises are often based on flawed assumptions about the nature of crisis and the practical implications for effective response. An example of flawed thinking is the impression, generated by the concentration of training into single 'D-Day' exercises, that crisis management skills are devoted only to sudden and immediate responses.

CRITICISMS OF STAGED APPROACHES

As already mentioned, the strategic, proactive, and process-oriented perspective in general, and the staged approaches in particular, are based on the understanding of crises as a life cycle, which is linear and sequential. This understanding is manifest in

Herbane (2010a) when he defines business continuity management as an approach covering 'the entire chronology and timeline of a crisis, which comprises of three key stages – pre-crisis, trans-crisis and post-crisis' (p. 46).

The definition of crises as a life cycle has recently been subject to criticism. First, it is not always possible to determine the time and place for each of the three stages, and they may well be dislocated. Drennan and McConnell (2007) conclude their criticism by emphasizing that what might be a crisis stage for some at this moment does not become a crisis stage for others until later. They point to the September 11, 2001, terror attacks on the United States as an example. For citizens, first responders, and the fire and police departments who responded, the crisis began immediately. But for organizations like the CIA, which had difficulties explaining intelligence failures and defending its own legitimacy in the months following, the crisis evolved more slowly. The same thing happened during the financial crisis of 2008–2009, when many companies held warehoused goods that could sit on the shelves for two years and therefore did not feel the consequences of the crisis until other companies were already on the way out of it. This created different kinds of challenges for the crisis planners. After all, how do you explain that your organization has just entered a crisis stage because of a financial crisis that many consider to be already over?

Second, several crises can easily occur at the same time and must be handled in parallel. This creates a situation in which a company can find itself in both a pre-crisis stage and a crisis stage at the same time. Scandinavian Airlines, for example, was hit by a number of crises in 2001 – from a price-fixing case to an accident at Linate Airport in Italy to the 9/11 attacks – all of which had to be handled at the same time.

Third, it is not only stages but also disciplines and tools that may overlap. Tony Jaques, consultant and former issues manager at Dow Chemicals in Australia, is one of the practitioners who have criticized crisis life cycle models. Inspired by disaster management where the elements of the management process form tightly related processes rather than isolated disciplines and tools, he has developed an *issue and crisis management relational model*. This model is characterized by having a non-linear structure: 'the relationship between different activities is not a stepwise, linear process … It comprises clusters of related and integrated disciplines that may be undertaken in sequential fashion but equally may operate simultaneously' (Jaques, 2014, pp. 13–14; see also Jaques, 2007). He emphasizes that two of the most important substages of the pre-crisis stage – prevention and preparation – *should* in fact most often happen at the same time. Like Gilpin and Murphy (2008), he also reminds us of the fact that organizational learning is not a process which takes place exclusively during the post-crisis stage. There are learning loops related to every activity within the entire crisis management process.

CHAPTER SUMMARY

This chapter has introduced the reader to the staged approaches to crisis management, which is based on the idea of a crisis life cycle encompassing three stages: a pre-crisis stage, a crisis stage, and a post-crisis stage. To be more specific, we have looked at some of the most important disciplines and tools applied by crisis managers in private and public organizations, from signal detection to organizational learning. Finally, we have also taken a critical stance on some of these elements (i.e., the crisis management plan or CMP). Thus, together with the previous chapter, this more practically oriented chapter provides the reader with an advanced, up-to-date introduction to crisis management.

 Further reading

Robert, B., & Lajtha, C. (2002). A new approach to crisis management. *Journal of Contingencies and Crisis Management*, 10(4), 181–191.

Wicks, D. (2001). Institutionalized mindsets of invulnerability: Differentiated institutional fields and the antecedents of organizational crisis. *Organization Studies*, 22(4), 659–692.

CRISIS COMMUNICATION (I): RHETORICAL AND TEXT-ORIENTED APPROACHES

5

▌ CHAPTER OVERVIEW ▌

This chapter and the next introduce the reader to four of the most important theories of organizational crisis communication: (1) image repair theory, (2) terminological control theory, (3) situational crisis communication theory, and (4) contingency theory. The chapter first provides an overview of the field, then a detailed introduction to two theories follows, representing the rhetorical and text-oriented tradition, their sources of inspiration and basic assumptions, their preferred research design and methods, together with a short summary of their further developments and the criticisms they have generated.

INTRODUCTION

In the two previous chapters we looked at organizational crisis management and how this discipline has developed from a narrow perspective to a broad perspective: from a tactical, reactive, and event-oriented approach to a strategic, proactive and process-oriented approach (and beyond). We also looked at how there has recently been a shift from the traditional focus on anticipation to a new focus on resilience: from a focus on crisis preparedness in the pre-crisis stage to a focus on the ability of the organization to bounce back and maintain its structure and functions after the crisis has become a reality.

Crisis management is a complex discipline consisting of many components. In this chapter and the next we shall look at perhaps the most important of these components: *crisis communication*. Many of the most spectacular organizational crises in the last few years have accelerated and developed into so-called *double crises* due to bad crisis communication (for a definition of double crises, see Chapter 2). A good example is 'verbals' from the CEO of a private company. The crisis known today as the Deepwater Horizon oil spill began on April 20, 2010, when the BP-owned Deepwater Horizon oil rig exploded and sank in the Gulf of Mexico. The oil spill turned into a double crisis only a few weeks later due to some unfortunate statements made by BP CEO Tony Hayward (Bergin, 2012). First, he tried to downplay the incident, describing the oil spill as 'relatively tiny' in comparison to the 'very big ocean' (May 13, 2010). Later he declared: '[W]e're sorry for the massive disruption it's caused to their lives [Gulf Coast residents]. There's no one who wants this thing over more than I do, I'd like my life back' (May 30, 2010). Both statements contributed to create an image of BP as a selfish company. However, good crisis communication may also contribute to preventing a crisis from developing with serious consequences, not only for the organization itself, but also for its stakeholders.

We shall look at four of the most important theories of organizational crisis communication which each in their way describe, explain, and recommend how and why organizations communicate or should communicate when facing different types of crisis situations. Some of these theories are descriptive, while others are (also) normative. In particular two of the theories - William L. Benoit's image repair theory (IRT) and W. Timothy Coombs' situational crisis communication theory (SCCT) – have dominated the field until recently. Avery et al. (2010) conducted a bibliometric study of trends in the use of crisis communication theory in public relations research and its applications between 1991 and 2009. The study resulted in the identification of 66 articles published in 16 different academic journals. Benoit (co-)authored 19 of the 66 articles, while Coombs (co)authored 14 of them. Thus, the two American researchers were responsible for half of all the articles identified.

The four crisis communication theories selected for this chapter and Chapter 6 share an interest in examining how a crisis can damage the image, reputation, and/or legitimacy of an organization, and how the organization can protect or repair its symbolic capital (for definitions of these key concepts, see Chapter 3). However, before we compare and evaluate the four theories, we must first provide an answer to a definitional question which seems difficult to avoid: What is crisis communication?

WHAT IS CRISIS COMMUNICATION?

Surprisingly enough, only a minority of scholars have found it necessary to take up the challenge of trying to define what they understand by crisis communication. Either they take for granted that we already know what we are talking about, or they introduce definitions that are insufficient (see, for example, Fearn-Banks, 1996, who defines crisis communication as the 'dialogue' between the organization and its publics).

Sturges (1994) is one of the few scholars who has tried to define what he understands by crisis communication, and his definition has so far been adopted by many crisis communication researchers (cf. Sellnow & Seeger, 2013; Coombs, 2015). Inspired by the study of the dynamics of the public opinion process, and the conceptualization of a crisis as a process or life cycle with a series of stages – in this case Fink's (1986) model in four stages – Sturges makes a distinction between three different types of external crisis information:

(1) Instructing information, that is '[i]nformation that tells people affected by the crisis how they should physically react to the crisis' (p. 308).

(2) Adjusting information, that is '[i]nformation that helps people psychologically cope with the magnitude of the crisis situation' (p. 308).

(3) Internalizing information, that is '[i]nformation that people will use to formulate an image about the organization' (p. 308).

These three types of crisis information are presented here as mutually independent communication strategies, but, in reality, they combine in different ways depending on where the crisis is in the life cycle. In order to be as effective as possible, crisis communication must adapt to each stage in the process. The combination of communication strategy and crisis stage is illustrated in Figure 5.1.

According to Sturges, the organization must focus on internalizing information in the pre-crisis stage in order to create certain expectations among its stakeholders about how it will manage a crisis situation. A private company, for example, can create a reputation for itself as a socially responsible organization. Likewise, a public emergency organization can organize a large emergency drill in order to show the local community that the organization is well prepared.

In the crisis stage, on the contrary, the organization must concentrate first on the instructing information and then on the adjusting information. It is more important for a private company that its customers and investors are informed about how they must behave in a crisis situation (such as providing information about where and when to return a defective product that may cause harm), or about the potential

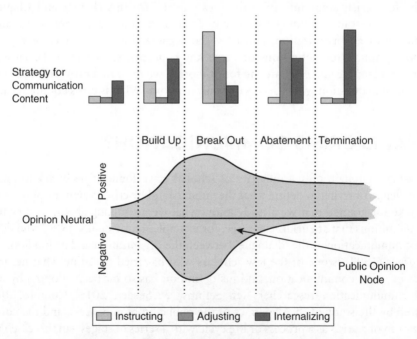

Figure 5.1 Communication content strategies by crisis phase

Source: Sturges (1994, p. 310).

consequences of the crisis (such as a fall in share prices), than being told 'what a great company we are'. Similarly, it is more important for a public emergency organization to take care of citizens' safety, and offer crisis intervention such as emergency psychological care to the victims.

As already mentioned, Sturges' (1994) definition has been adopted by many crisis communication scholars. However, no one has pointed out that his distinction between the three types of crisis information and their distribution according to a staged approach to crisis management is questionable, not least because of how he understands the concept of image or reputation. By presenting these three types of crisis information as *sequential categories*, with each contributing a specific communicative effect, Sturges overlooks an important thing: that is, both the instructing and the adjusting information reveal how competent a particular organization is at managing a crisis. In a crisis situation, the reputation of an organization is at play all along the course of events, and also when it is communicating instructions and helping victims cope with the crisis. Stakeholders or people get impressions of an organization from every aspect of its behavior – not only before or after the crisis, but during the whole process.

Recently, Coombs (2015) has emphasized that crisis communication is not one phenomenon, but many closely related phenomena. His definition of crisis communication is made up of two parts: (1) managing information (collecting and analyzing crisis-related information) and (2) managing meaning (influencing how people perceive the crisis and the organization in crisis). Each of these two parts exists in two variations: (1) public crisis communication (directed toward external stakeholders) and (2) private crisis communication (directed toward employees or exchanged among members of CMTs). As in Sturges (1994), these four types of crisis communication are distributed according to a staged approach to crisis management. However, Coombs' definition is also problematic because of the implicit understanding that it is possible to separate information from meaning.

BOX 5.1

ANTI-HANDBOOK OF MEDIA FAILURE

French crisis management scholar Patrick Lagadec has written a small, ironic anti-handbook that explains what an organization in crisis must do to be sure to experience a media failure (Lagadec, 2000):

- Be silent, absent-minded and evasive.
- Say, 'No comment!'
- Use denials systematically.
- Use 'reassuring' statements.
- Demonstrate a complete lack of humbleness.
- Shift the blame to others.
- Do not inform anyone about anything.
- Problematize those who inform.

CRISIS COMMUNICATION RESEARCH: AN OVERVIEW

As mentioned in the general introduction, crisis communication is a dynamic discipline that has developed with great speed. This is reflected, among other things, in the multiple crisis communication theories that have been developed in recent years. Some of these theories lie at the heart of conversations between researchers and have high potential for development. Coombs' situational crisis communication theory is a good representative of this group of theories. Other theories are more peripheral and do not seem to possess the same potential for development. This applies to the theory of excellent crisis public relations, presented by Fearn-Banks (1996) and Marra (1999, 2004), which is based on the excellence theory developed by James E. Grunig and a group of public relations researchers between 1985 and 2002.

Crisis communication theories can be divided into schools or traditions depending on the criteria in use. Some researchers apply a *chronological* approach (using time as the criterion) in their accounts of how the field is structured and/or how it has developed. If a chronological approach is applied, expressions such as *young, mature, progress,* or *growth* will often dominate. In his introduction to the first volume of *Crisis Communication* (2014a), Coombs includes a section entitled 'The short history of crisis communication by decade', which is clearly based on such a chronological approach:

- 1980s:
  - Crisis communication appeared in the late 1980s. The first publications were written by practitioners offering advice based on their own experience.

- 1990s:
  - Crisis communication research in the proper sense of the word emerged from the fields of rhetoric and marketing. Three important theories are developed: image restoration theory (Benoit, 1995), corporate apologia (Hearit, 1994), and situational crisis communication theory (Coombs, 1995).

- 2000s:
  - The crisis communication field explodes. New theories appeared: contingency theory (Cancel et al., 1997, 1999), renewal discourse theory (Ulmer et al., 2007), and rhetorical arena theory (Frandsen & Johansen, 2007).

- 2010s:
  - Globalization and digital crisis communication.

Other researchers apply a *systematic* approach (using research themes as the criterion) in their accounts of how the field is structured and/or how development has occurred. If a systematic approach is used, expressions such as *position*, *dominance*, *alternative*, *paradigm*, or *turn* will often dominate. A good example of such a systematic approach is Timothy L. Sellnow and Matthew W. Seeger's *Theorizing Crisis Communication* (2013) where crisis communication theories are categorized by themes such as crisis development, warning, crisis outcome, emergency response, mediated crises, influence, risk management, and ethics.

In this book, we have chosen to divide the most important crisis communication theories into two large research traditions, each with its own lines of development, sources of inspiration, basic assumptions, and preferred research designs and methods.

The first tradition is the *rhetorical* and *text-oriented* tradition. Researchers who represent this tradition are inspired by classical rhetoric, the new rhetoric, and the study of apologia. They are interested in describing *what* an organization in crisis says – and *how* it says it – when that organization has to defend itself verbally against accusations of wrongdoing.

The second tradition is the *strategic* and *context-oriented* tradition. Whereas the first tradition is rooted in the old rhetorical tradition, researchers who represent this second tradition are inspired by far more recent disciplines such as marketing, public relations, social psychology, management, and organizational studies. They are primarily interested in explaining not only *where*, *when* and *to whom* an organization in crisis communicates, but also *why*. They find the answer to this question in the situation or the context of a crisis.

These two traditions share some similarities. When we claim that the first of the two is text oriented and the second context oriented, it is a qualified truth because the rhetorical tradition in crisis communication research is also interested in context. Consider, for example, Bitzer's (1968) concept of the rhetorical situation, defined as: '[a] complex of persons, events, objects, and relations presenting an actual or potential exigence which can be completely or partially removed if discourse, introduced into the situation, can so constrain human decision or action as to bring about the significant modification of the exigence' (p. 3). Likewise, the context-oriented tradition is also interested in text, in particular crisis-responding strategies. Another similarity is the significance ascribed by both traditions to the reputation of an organization. Reputation is seen as something valuable, a symbolic resource or capital, which can be damaged in a crisis and which must be protected or repaired.

Despite these similarities, there are also important differences. The rhetorical tradition is rooted in the apologia tradition, which is based in turn on the idea of *attack* and *defense*. The result is a strong focus on the crisis stage and the use of crisis response strategies. The strategic tradition is inspired by studies in management and organization, which means that the stages *before* and *after* a crisis are also included. It also means that many other types of crisis communication, besides response strategies, are subject to analysis.

BOX 5.2

WHAT IS (A) THEORY?

This chapter focuses on crisis communication theories, but what is a theory? Sellnow and Seeger (2013) define a theory in the following way: '[I]n its most basic form, a theory is simply an explanation created for something that needs further understanding. Theory is an abstraction of reality, a way of framing, modeling and understanding what is observed to be happening' (p. 15). It may be useful to distinguish between various types of theory, as follows.

Theory can be defined broadly as what gives structure to our knowledge about a specific field of study. In its simple version, such a structure is purely descriptive. In ancient Greek, *theoria* meant 'to look at the world'. In most cases, however, we do not call these structures theories, but use terms such as typology, classification, and taxonomy. Image repair theory and its typology of strategies represent this understanding of theory.

Theory can also be defined more narrowly as a set of abstract statements from which empirically testable hypotheses can be derived (the principle of falsifiability). According to this definition, the function of theory is to explain causal relations and patterns in the field of study. Situational crisis communication theory and its evidence-based approach represent this understanding of theory.

In interpretive and critical approaches, researchers emphasize the value of working with multiple theories that can illuminate different aspects of a situation – or they deconstruct or reconstruct theories.

Normative theories are hypotheses or statements about what is right and wrong, desirable or undesirable, just or unjust, in organizations or in society. Evaluation is separated from description and explanation. The crisis consulting offered by agencies often represents this understanding of theory.

Further reading: Sellnow and Seeger (2013).

THE RHETORICAL AND TEXT-ORIENTED RESEARCH TRADITION

The rhetorical and text-oriented research tradition has roots that go back more than 2000 years to Greek and Roman antiquity. At that time, a demand for theoretical and practical knowledge about how to speak eloquently and, especially, how to defend oneself persuasively and convincingly in political and legal contexts arose within the Greek *polis* and the Roman *forum*. The answer to this demand was the invention of rhetoric. Apologia, or self-defense, remains one of the most important rhetorical genres.

Among the representatives of the rhetorical and text-oriented research tradition we have selected two American rhetoricians who have both contributed, directly or indirectly, to the field of crisis communication: namely, William L. Benoit and his *image repair theory*, and Keith Michael Hearit and his *terminological control theory*.

Benoit's research has been described as 'the definitive work on the strategies used by apologists' (Hearit, 2006, p. 83). He has established a general theory that covers all categories of verbal defense strategies (with the exception of silence) applied by all categories of social actors (individuals, organizations). Hearit, on the contrary, has established a more specific theory, analyzing in depth one single strategy, the apology, which, as we shall see, has recently become a very popular crisis response strategy.

The two introductions to image repair theory and terminological control theory follow the same structure: (1) a short presentation of the researcher and his research, (2) sources of inspiration, (3) basic assumptions, (4) the theory/theories, and (5) further developments and criticisms.

Image repair theory (IRT)

Benoit developed a rhetorical theory about how and why individuals and organizations defend their reputation by applying a set of image repair strategies when accused or suspected of wrongdoing. The theory is based on numerous case studies examining how, for example, American presidents (Richard Nixon, Ronald Reagan, Bill Clinton, George W. Bush), royalty (Queen Elizabeth), actors (Hugh Grant), athletes (Tonya Harding, Tiger Woods), and private companies (AT&T, USAir, Sears, Texaco, Walmart) have used verbal defense strategies with greater or lesser success. Image repair theory can be applied as a theoretical approach for understanding the communicative behavior of individuals or organizations in crisis situations, and – to a lesser extent – as a practical tool for managing a crisis.

The most comprehensive exposé of Benoit's theory can be found in *Accounts, Excuses, and Apologies* (Benoit, 1995). The theory has remained almost the same for the past 20 years, including in the revised second edition of *Accounts, Excuses, and Apologies* (Benoit, 2015).

Before we take a closer look at the theory, we must emphasize that Benoit makes a distinction between image repair discourse and crisis communication. He defines crisis communication as a broader category, including image repair discourse, but also messages about other types of crises such as natural disasters and terrorism where the focus on image and reputation is less strong (Benoit, 2015). However, since the late 1990s, he has described his theory as an applicable approach to the study of 'messages that respond to corporate image crises' (Benoit, 1997, p. 177; see also Benoit, 2004). In any case, during the past 20 years, image repair theory has been disseminated within the field of crisis communication and has become a very popular approach.

Moreover, we are not just talking about one single theory, but about two theories that are both highly relevant to the study of crisis communication. In parallel to image repair theory, Benoit has also developed a theory of persuasive attacks, which seems interesting from a multivocal arena perspective and which will also be introduced in this section.

Sources of inspiration

Image repair theory is inspired by two disciplines that have both contributed substantially to the study of verbal self-defense: rhetoric and the sociology of accounts.

Within rhetoric, Benoit is inspired by Ware and Linkugel's (1973) theory of *apologia* (for an overview of apologetic rhetoric, see Towner, 2009). Ware and Linkugel represent what rhetoricians define as generic criticism, a tradition that originated in Edwin Black's criticism of neo-Aristotelian rhetoric in *Rhetorical Criticism* (1965) and in Lloyd Bitzer's (1968) article on the rhetorical situation. This article is based on the assumption that genres emerge through the repeated response to recurrent and comparable rhetorical situations. Thereby, genres become part of the exigence that constitutes the rhetorical situation. Benoit is also inspired by Burke's (1970) theory of purification. The feeling of guilt is the pivot of this theory. A feeling of guilt represents an undesirable state of affairs, which occurs when expectations concerning a specific behavior are violated. An attack on the reputation of an individual or an organization – alleging that their behavior is less than perfect – may provoke a feeling of guilt. The individual or the organization can reduce or remove this feeling by applying two types of purification strategies (victimage and mortification).

Within the sociology of accounts, Benoit is inspired by Scott and Lyman's (1968) theory of accounts. Scott and Lyman define an account as 'a statement made by a social actor to explain unanticipated or untoward behavior' (p. 46), introducing a distinction between two basic types: (1) *excuses* (defined as an explanation in which the social actor admits that the act in question is bad, wrong, or inappropriate but denies full responsibility) and (2) *justifications* (defined as an explanation in which the social actor accepts responsibility for the act in question, but denies the pejorative quality associated with it).

In the second edition of *Accounts, Excuses, and Apologies*, Benoit is also inspired by social psychology and Fishbein and Ajzen's (2010) theory of reasoned action. According to this theory, persuasive communication will always try to create, strengthen, or change attitudes. Attitudes have two components: (1) beliefs (descriptions of the world, or knowledge) and (2) values (positive or negative evaluations). Each attitude consists of several pairs of beliefs/values. A threat to image also has two components, blame and offensiveness, which correspond to Fischbein and Ajzen's concepts of belief and values. Based on the theory of reasoned action, Benoit can reformulate his image repair strategies as attempts to change or create new beliefs (or values) about an offensive act and the accused's blame for this act.

Basic assumptions

Image repair theory is based on two axiomatic assumptions, and the second presupposes the first. Benoit claims, as the first assumption, that communication is a goal-oriented activity. On this point he does not seem to differ from many other rhetorical theorists, from Aristotle to Kenneth Burke, who see communication as always having a purpose. Second, Benoit claims that a key goal of communication is to maintain a favorable reputation. Reputation is valued as important because it contributes to a healthy self-image and because it provides us with influence. Benoit often uses terms indiscriminately that seem similar to the concept of reputation, but which, in fact, belong to different disciplines: ethos (rhetoric), face (micro-sociology), image and reputation (branding).

Theory (1): Image repair theory

The basic image repair situation, which serves as the platform for the verbal defense strategies, is rather simple. It can be presented as a process with two phases (see Table 5.1).

As mentioned, the basic image repair situation is simple. However, it can become more complex in several ways. This happens, for example: (1) when the accuser is not the same as the victim of the crisis, but, say, the news media; (2) when multiple actors are under accusations of wrongdoing (e.g., the car industry); (3) when one actor acts in defense of another actor (Benoit describes this as third-party image repair); and (4) when image repair strategies are used preemptively. No matter how simple or complex the image repair situation may be, it is the same image repair strategies that are applied. These strategies represent the cornerstone of image repair theory.

Benoit has established a typology of verbal defense strategies applied by individuals or organizations to repair a reputation that has been damaged when facing a crisis. He distinguishes between five general strategies, three of which are divided into two or more subcategories (for an overview, see Table 5.2).

The first general strategy is *denial*. This strategy has two subcategories: *simple denial*, in which the accused simply denies having performed the undesirable event and/or being responsible for it; and *shifting the blame*, where the accused blames another individual or organization for being guilty of the undesirable event.

The second general strategy is *evading responsibility*. Here, the accused tries to evade or reduce responsibility for the undesirable event or action. This strategy has four subcategories: *provocation*, where the accused claims that he or she was provoked to act, or, put another way, that the accused was a scapegoat, and that others share the blame; *defeasibility*, where the accused claims that the event or action was

Table 5.1 The basic image repair situation

Process	Example
Phase (1): from attack to crisis An undesirable event takes place An actor accuses or suspects another actor for being responsible for the undesirable event The image of this actor is threatened	The Tesla Model S, an electric car sold on the Norwegian market, does not live up to customer expectations regarding acceleration and horsepower. A group of dissatisfied Tesla owners accuses Tesla Motors on Facebook for not keeping its promises to customers
Phase (2): from crisis to image repair The accused or suspected actor defends itself against the attack by means of one or more image repair strategies If the defense is successful, the image of this actor will be repaired	In a press release, Tesla Motors defends itself against the attack. The car producer promises to investigate the problem

Table 5.2   Benoit's typology of image repair strategies

General strategies	Subcategories
Denial	Simple denial Shifting the blame
Evading of responsibility	Provocation Defeasibility Accident Good intentions
Reducing offensiveness of event	Bolstering Minimization Differentiation Transcendence Attack accuser Compensation
Corrective action	
Mortification	

Source: Benoit (2015).

due to a lack of information or ability, and hence not entirely his or her own fault; *accident*, where the accused claims that the event or action occurred accidentally; and finally *good intentions*.

The third general strategy is *reducing offensiveness*, in which the accused tries to mitigate the negative effect of the undesirable event or action. This strategy has six subcategories: *bolstering*, where the accused attempts to strengthen the audience's positive perception of him or her, for example by referring to actions performed in the past or to his or her ethos; *minimization*, where the accused attempts to minimize the number of negative effects associated with the offensive event or action; *differentiation*, in which the accused attempts to distinguish the act performed from other similar, but less desirable events or actions; *transcendence*, where the act is placed in a different – positive – context or frame of reference that reduces the perceived offensiveness; *attack the accuser*, for example by questioning the credibility of the accuser; and, finally, *compensation*, where the accused attempts to reduce offensiveness by remunerating the offended part.

The fourth general strategy is *corrective action*. Here, the accused responds to an attack by making an attempt to correct the problem. This strategy has no subcategories. The fifth and last general strategy is *mortification*, where the accused accepts responsibility, apologizes, and asks for forgiveness. This strategy has no subcategories either.

Theory (2): persuasive attacks

Inspired by Ryan (1982) and his idea of treating *kategoria* (accusation) and *apologia* (apology) as a 'speech set' (p. 254), Benoit and Dorries (1996) established a typology of

Table 5.3 Benoit and Dorries' typology of persuasive attacks

Constitutive elements	Rhetorical strategies
Perceived offensiveness: An offensive act has occurred and the target of complaint is alleged to be responsible for the act	*Increased offensiveness:* • Extent of the damage • Persistence of negative effects • Effects on the audience • Inconsistency • Victims innocent or helpless • Obligations to protect victim
Perceived responsibility: The act must be perceived as offensive by an audience for the accused's image to be at risk	*Increased responsibility:* • Accused committed the act before • Accused planned the act • Accused knew likely consequences of the act • Accused benefited from the act

Source: based on Benoit and Dorries (1996).

persuasive attacks. A persuasive attack comprises two constitutive elements: offensiveness of an act and responsibility for this act. The goal of each type of persuasive attack is to *increase* either offensiveness or responsibility – or both (Table 5.3).

Benoit's theory of persuasive attacks has attracted far less attention than his image repair theory, and it has not been developed to the same extent as its counterpart. However, it clearly anticipates a multivocal approach where there are multiple senders and receivers.

The *blame game*, to which we shall return in Chapter 8, resembles the combination of a persuasive attack and an image repair strategy. Hood (2011) defines a blame game as follows: 'As a social process, blaming must involve at least two sets of actors, namely blame makers (those who do the blaming) and blame takers (those who are on the receiving end). Those two roles come together in "blame game" – a term that came to be heavily used in the 2000s' (p. 7).

Further developments and criticisms

Image repair theory (IRT) has developed in many different directions since the publication of *Accounts, Excuses, and Apologies* (Benoit, 1995). One direction taken by many researchers is to conduct IRT-based case studies within areas of society where this has not been done before or where only a few studies have been conducted. One of these areas is the world of sports, where athletes and their related organizations are often involved in crises. We only need to mention Lance Armstrong, Tiger Woods, Joseph Blatter (FIFA), and Michel Platini (UEFA). *Repairing the Athlete's Image: Studies in Sports Image Restoration* (Blaney et al., 2012) is a good illustration of how IRT can be applied within this area. Other researchers have developed IRT by shifting from a qualitative to a quantitative research design, conducting surveys or doing experiments to see which image repair strategy is the most effective regarding a specific crisis type according to the respondents (see, e.g., Dardis & Haigh, 2009).

Other researchers again have contributed theoretically to the further development of IRT by combining this theory with other theoretical frameworks such as contingency theory (see, for example, Pang, 2006, and Chapter 6).

IRT has been the object of some criticism. Burns and Bruner (2000) claim that the meta-language in which Benoit's theory is formulated may lead to certain misinterpretations. This applies in particular to the concepts of image, restoration, strategy, the identity of the target (the accused), text, and context. The use of the concept of image and image restoration, for example, may lead to the misunderstanding that the image of an organization is unitary and homogeneous, and that it can be restored back to its previous state. According to Burns and Bruner, this will reduce a rather complex process to a simple 'two-step sequence' (p. 50). They also recommend that IRT should adopt a more audience-oriented approach. Benoit (2000) has replied to this criticism.

Terminological control theory (TCT)

Like his fellow countryman, Keith Michael Hearit has developed a rhetorical theory about how and why individuals and organizations engage in verbal self-defense, when they are accused of wrongdoing and face a crisis. But the similarities between the two theories end there. First, what people are defending according to Hearit is not so much their image or reputation as their social legitimacy. Second, Hearit is more interested in corporate apologia, namely crisis communication in the business world.

Hearit has not yet provided us with a comprehensive presentation of his theory in the shape of a book. However, the various theoretical components, which when put together form what we call terminological control theory, have been presented in a series of articles published in the 1990s. These articles contain detailed case studies of how private companies representing the automobile and computer industries handle what Hearit calls 'public relations crises'. He is, however, the author of a book entitled *Crisis Management by Apology* (2006), but it is devoted to the study of one particular crisis response strategy: the apology.

Sources of inspiration

Hearit is inspired by the new rhetoric, in particular the stream of research known under the name of *corporate* or *organizational rhetorics* that goes back to the 1980s and is represented by scholars such as J. Michael Sproule, G. N. Dionisopoulos, and S. L. Vibbert (for an overview of this tradition, see, for example, Cheney et al., 2004).

Hearit is, in particular, inspired by Kenneth Burke's theory of *terministic screens*: 'Even if any given terminology is a reflection of reality, by its very nature as a terminology it must be a selection of reality; and to this extent it must function also as a deflection of reality' (Burke, 1966, p. 45). A terminology – in our case, crisis communication – is placed as a screen between us as human beings and the outside world, leading our attention in a specific direction. Therefore, even the apparently innocent act of *naming* a crisis is an important strategic act. To name a crisis is not just a simple nominalistic operation: to name something is in fact to *define*, and to *argue* that something exists (is real) or does not exist (is not real) (cf. Hearit, 1994; see also case example 1.2 in Chapter 1 about the 'naming wars' that took place during the 2009 flu pandemic). This is the core of terminological control theory: in any crisis situation, it is important for the organization in crisis to be able to control the terminology and thus to influence the interpretations and counter-interpretations used and produced by the actors involved.

Another important source of inspiration is the theory of *social legitimacy*. According to this theory, companies exist in a state of dependency upon their environment: they can only survive if they are able to convince their stakeholders that they live up to established norms and values. Legitimacy functions as an organizational resource enabling organizations to attract the resources necessary for survival (cf. Suchman, 1995).

Basic assumptions

Hearit takes up a social constructivist stance on organizational crises, claiming that crisis communication has a constitutive role (Hearit & Courtright, 2003, 2004). Hearit does not refute that there is an objective reality and that all crises, therefore, must be human made. He refutes that it should be possible for us human beings to give a pure and complete description of an objective reality. A crisis does not become a crisis until it has been ascribed a specific meaning by people (because of their symbolic intervention in the course of events).

The foundation of Hearit's social constructivist stance is a criticism of what he calls the 'positivist temptation' – or the generic approach to crises. This approach is based on the assumption that (types of) crises are objective phenomena sharing the same – stable – characteristics with other (types of) crises. Crises can therefore also be handled using the same crisis management tools, as far as the crisis type sets up the limits for which choices the organization can make regarding crisis management and crisis communication. In the positivist or generic approach 'things speak for themselves', and the crisis management process must follow suit. Crisis communication is, therefore, understood as information about an objective reality.

According to Hearit, the positivist (or generic) approach has its limitations. Certain crises display stable characteristics while other crises – which we still call and consider *crises* – do not display such characteristics. Four types of factors contribute to make these crises 'unclear': (1) cultural variability, (2) extended length, (3) multiple numbers of participants, and (4) the inability to identify a cause or a guilty party.

Hearit claims that crisis communication is the core of the crisis management process: 'We assert that communication, rather than being one variable in the crisis management mix, actually constitutes the nature and being of the crisis itself' (Hearit & Courtright, 2004, p. 202). At the same time, he warns us against reducing crisis communication to 'a unitary rhetorical event, focused only on one organization' (Hearit & Courtright, 2003, p. 92). Crisis communication also includes the communicative activities of the other actors involved in the crisis.

Theory (1): Terminological control theory

The social constructivist or symbolic approach serves as the basis for Hearit's most important contribution to crisis communication research, namely his theory of *terminological control* or *definitional hegemony*: 'Crises are terminological creations conceived by human agents and, consequently, are managed and resolved terminologically' (Hearit & Courtright, 2003, p. 87).

Just like Benoit's basic image repair situation, terminological control can be presented as a process including a certain number of phases (Hearit, 1994). In the first phase, an action is committed that is considered wrongful by (certain parts of) society. This wrongdoing can be traced back to a specific organization. In the second phase, an accusation – what the rhetoricians call a *kategoria* – is made against the organization, which is made responsible for the wrongdoing. The third phase represents the organizational crisis as such. As a consequence of the accusation for wrongdoing the organization ends up in a legitimacy crisis: (part of) society views the organization either as incompetent, unprofessional, and unable to 'get the job done' (lack of *pragmatic legitimacy*) or as indifferent to the laws, rules, values, and norms of society (lack of *ethical legitimacy*) (Hearit, 1995b). In the fourth phase, the organization in crisis defends itself against the accusation. The fifth phase marks a potential ending of the crisis to the extent that the apologia performed by the organization allows it to restore its legitimacy and to continue its business (Table 5.4).

The reason Hearit can be considered a representative, even a good one, of the rhetorical or text-oriented approach to crisis communication is his primary research interest in the communication strategies applied by organizations in crisis. Based on his studies of public relations crises in the automobile industry (e.g., Audi, Chrysler,

Table 5.4 Hearit's terminological control theory

The process of terminological control

Wrongdoing	
Kategoria	
Legitimacy crisis	Types of legitimacy: • Pragmatic legitimacy • Ethical legitimacy

Apologia	Corporate apologia strategies:
	(1) Persuasive accounts
	(2) Expressing sorrow
	(3) Using dissociation strategies
	   • Opinion/knowledge dissociation
	   • Individual/group dissociation
	   • Act/essence dissociation

Ending of crisis	

General Motors, and Volvo), Hearit has identified three main strategies for *corporate apologia* (Hearit, 1994, 1995a, 1995b).

The first strategy is *persuasive accounts*: that is, the organizations' attempts to provide convincing and plausible accounts of a crisis situation that will serve as counter-interpretations of, for example, the interpretations found in the news media. The utilization of this strategy allows the organizations to reassert terminological control or to exercise definitional hegemony over the interpretation of the course of events. The second strategy is to *express sorrow* for what has happened. It is, however, also often an attempt to minimize responsibility for wrongdoing.

The third and last strategy is the strategy to which Hearit devotes most of his work on crisis response strategies. He introduces Polish rhetorician Chaïm Perelman's concept of strategy of *dissociation*: that is, the strategies in which an organization accused of wrongdoing attempts to distance itself from the wrongdoing. According to Perelman, the primary dissociation consists in separating appearance from reality; that is, separating what *looks* like reality from what actually *is* reality. Hearit distinguishes between three basic types of dissociation representing three prototypical stances of denial, differentiation, and explanation.

Denial uses an opinion/knowledge dissociation corresponding to ancient Greek philosophy's distinction between *doxa* or the people's opinion (the sophists' position) and *episteme* or the philosophers' truth (Plato's position). In this strategy, the accusations raised against an organization are described as mere 'opinions' that do not represent 'actual knowledge' of the event that created the crisis. When applying this strategy, an organization claims for example that 'the journalists believe they know what is going on in our company in this critical situation', but 'the truth is that only our CEO has this knowledge'.

Differentiation uses an individual/group dissociation. When applying this strategy, an organization claims for example that a 'few employees', and not the 'company as such', are responsible for the wrongdoing.

Finally, explanation uses an act/essence dissociation. In this strategy, an organization accused of wrongdoing admits that some wrongdoing has occurred, but claims that the act is not representative of the essence or 'true nature' of the organization: 'Many employees think that because we refuse to negotiate with these people, we are against trade unions in general. However, nothing could be more wrong.'

Theory (2): Apologetic ethics

Although the terminology is a little different, Hearit's study of the apology as a crisis response strategy in *Crisis Management by Apology* (2006) is unfolded within the same process model as his terminological control theory. Focusing on the apology as a speech act and as a public ritual (Rothenbuhler, 1998), he examines how the process begins with the transgression of a social order followed by *kategoria* leading to a legitimacy crisis, and how it ends with an apology followed by forgiveness (if the apology is successful). However, the aim of the book is not only to describe or explain, but also to introduce the reader to an apologetic ethics, that is a set of normative guidelines for how to produce the best apology, ethically speaking (Hearit, 2006, Chapter 4).

The philosophical foundation of this new communicative ethics is casuistry. Contrary to the traditional understanding, casuistry does not define ethics as a kind of science or codex of general rules and principles covering all cases without any exceptions. Instead, ethics is viewed as a kind of practical wisdom based on the fact that ethical rules and principles are never exhaustive and that we need to include the circumstances of each case. Viewed from this perspective, we will never be able to make an absolute ethical judgment, but have to look at the circumstances from case to case. Hence the name casuistry.

Hearit applies this way of thinking to apologies as a crisis response strategy. First, he defines a paradigm case, or situation in which the ethical considerations are so clear cut that everybody can agree on whether it is ethically acceptable or not. This paradigm case then serves as a standard against which more complex ethical situations can be measured. The paradigm case comprises two dimensions: (1) the manner of the communication (an ethical apology must be truthful, sincere, timely, voluntary; it must address all stakeholders and be performed in an appropriate context) and (2) the content of the communication (an ethical apology must explicitly acknowledge wrong-doing, fully accept responsibility, express regret, identify with injured stakeholders, ask for forgiveness, seek reconciliation, fully disclose relevant information, provide an explanation, and offer appropriate corrective action and compensation).

Second, he sets up a list of complicating circumstances that could justify departures from the paradigm case or standard: catastrophic financial losses, grave liability concerns, a moral learning curve, the problem of full disclosure, and discretion. In this way, the apologetic ethics becomes 'a method by which to ethically judge the apologetic decision making offered by individuals and organizations (Hearit, 2006, p. 77).

Further developments and criticisms

Surprisingly few crisis communication researchers have followed in Keith Michael Hearit's footsteps. His terminological control theory and his social constructivist approach are mentioned again and again, but have not yet had the breakthrough they deserve. His apologetic ethics, in particular his understanding of *social order*, has been criticized for being too monolithic and for not taking into account multicultural contexts and situations in which one party feels offended and demands an apology, but where the other party does not understand why he or she should have offended someone and therefore does not find it necessary to offer an apology.

In a previous study (Frandsen & Johansen, 2010a), we have suggested use of the concept of *meta-apology* to solve this problem. By meta-apology we understand 'an apology where the apologist is no longer apologizing for what he or she may have done – because he or she actually does not have to, according to their own sociocultural order – but for the negative effects that the act committed by the apologist may possibly have caused' (p. 362). Both the Danish prime minister in the Cartoon Affair in 2005–2006, and Pope Benedikt XVI, Head of the Roman Catholic Church, when in 2006 his speech in Regensburg was misunderstood, used this strategy (cf. Chapter 7).

We are convinced that we will see more meta-apologies in the future. In today's interconnected world, a crisis can easily become global, and consequently organizations risk facing multiple socio-cultural orders more often at one and the same time.

CHAPTER SUMMARY

This chapter has introduced the reader to two representatives of the rhetorical and text-oriented research tradition: William L. Benoit's image repair theory and Keith M. Hearit's terminological control theory. The strength of this first group of crisis communication theories is their attempt to describe and classify the crisis response strategies applied more or less successfully by organizations in crisis.

 Further reading

Benoit, W. L. (2004). Image restoration discourse and crisis communication. In D. P. Millar & R. L. Heath (Eds.), *Responding to Crisis: A Rhetorical Approach to Crisis Communication* (pp. 263–280). Mahwah, NJ: Lawrence Erlbaum.

Hearit, K. M., & Courtright, J. L. (2003). A social constructionist approach to crisis management: Allegations of sudden acceleration in the Audi 5000. *Communication Studies*, 54(1), 79–95.

CRISIS COMMUNICATION (II): STRATEGIC AND CONTEXT-ORIENTED APPROACHES

6

CHAPTER OVERVIEW

In this chapter, we continue our introduction to four of the most important theories of organizational crisis communication. It focuses on two theories representing the strategic and context-oriented research tradition, on their sources of inspiration and basic assumptions, their preferred research design and methods, together with a short summary of their further developments and the criticisms they have generated. The chapter concludes with a short presentation of the most recent research themes in crisis communication.

INTRODUCTION

In the previous chapter, two theories representing the rhetorical and text-oriented research tradition in organizational crisis communication – Benoit's image repair theory and Hearit's terminological control theory – were presented. These two theories were first and foremost interested in describing what an organization in crisis says, and how it says it, when it has to defend itself against accusations of wrongdoing. The most prominent result of this stream of research is the identification of crisis response strategies. These strategies have already been described in great detail. In this chapter, we shift to the strategic and context-oriented research tradition in organizational crisis communication. We have selected two representatives that share a common interest in using situational variables or contingency factors as analytical and practical guidelines.

THE STRATEGIC AND CONTEXT-ORIENTED RESEARCH TRADITION

The roots of the strategic and context-oriented research tradition are much more recent than those of the rhetorical and text-oriented tradition. Both public relations and management and organization studies are children of the twentieth century. Within the same decade, two of the most influential books in these disciplines were published: *Effective Public Relations* (Cutlip, Center & Broom, 1952) and *Organizations* (March & Simon, 1958).

The aim of the strategic and context-oriented research tradition is to provide us with an answer to the question: What will be the most effective crisis response strategy in a crisis situation? Among the representatives of the strategic and context-oriented research tradition we have selected two American public relations scholars who have both made important contributions to the field of crisis communication: W. Timothy Coombs and his *situational crisis communication theory* (SCCT) and Glen T. Cameron and his *contingency theory*. However, their contributions are fairly different. Whereas SCCT is a middle-range theory, focusing exclusively on crisis communication, contingency theory is of more general nature (a public relations theory) taking its starting point in a critique of James E. Grunig and the excellence theory. Its contribution to the field of crisis communication was developed first of all by researchers such as Augustine Pang and Yan Jin.

The two introductions to SCCT and contingency theory follow the same structure as the two introductions in Chapter 5: (1) a short presentation of the researcher and his research, (2) sources of inspiration, (3) basic assumptions, (4) the theory/theories, and (5) further development and criticisms.

BOX 6.1

METHODOLOGICAL CONTROVERSIES

Which research designs and methods are the most appropriate for the study of organizational crisis communication? Over the past two decades there have been some methodological controversies, in particular between scholars who are in favor of using experimental designs and those who prefer to conduct case studies.

The first group of scholars often criticizes the representatives of the rhetorical and text-oriented approach, such as Benoit and Hearit, for being dependent on 'simple lists of crisis response strategies and the use of case studies to develop recommended courses of action. While useful to generate ideas, case studies are not a method for building causal relationships and, therefore, not very precise when used to create recommendations for the utilization of crisis response strategies' (Coombs, 2006b, pp. 242–243). 'While case studies can be insightful, their results are more speculation than evidence. The crisis case studies utilize qualitative research methods, resulting in the speculative nature of their findings' (Coombs, 2015, p. 184).

The second group of scholars seldom reply to this criticism, but find support in Flyvbjerg (2006) where five misunderstandings or oversimplifications of case study research are identified and rejected:

(Continued)

(Continued)

- Misunderstanding (1): General, theoretical (context-independent) knowledge is more valuable than concrete, practical (context-dependent) knowledge.
- Misunderstanding (2): One cannot generalize on the basis of an individual case; therefore, the case study cannot contribute to scientific development.
- Misunderstanding (3): The case study is most useful for generating hypotheses, that is in the first stage of a total research process, whereas other methods are more suitable for hypotheses testing and theory building.
- Misunderstanding (4): The case study contains a bias toward verification, that is a tendency, to confirm the researcher's preconceived notions.
- Misunderstanding (5): It is often difficult to summarize and develop general propositions and theories on the basis of specific case studies.

Flyvbjerg rejects all five, claiming that we need to reconsider the value of case studies. Combining research design with human learning theory, he introduces the Dreyfus model of skill acquisition, which consists of the following five stages: (1) novice, (2) advanced beginner, (3) competent, (4) proficient, and (5) expert (Dreyfus & Dreyfus, 1980, 1986). The progression from stage (1) to stage (5) involves the following variables or components: role and status of rules and plans, type of knowledge, situational perception, context, and intuition. According to Flyvbjerg, only case studies allow us to become true experts.

Further reading: An and Cheng (2010).

Situational crisis communication theory (SCCT)

Coombs has developed a theory about how situational variables (to be more precise: stakeholders' attribution of crisis responsibility to an organization in crisis) can serve as the basis for choosing the most appropriate crisis response strategy. The theory has been given different names over the years. First it was called the symbolic approach because it emphasized how communication can be used as a symbolic resource in attempts to protect the organization's image or reputation (Coombs, 1998). However, since 2000, the name of the theory has remained the same: situational crisis communication theory (SCCT).

Coombs has contributed to our body of knowledge about organizational crises, crisis management, and crisis communication in important ways. He is the (co-) author of several books, including *Ongoing Crisis Communication* (1999) and *Applied Crisis Communication and Crisis Management* (2014b). He is the (co-) editor of *The Handbook of Crisis Communication* (2010) and the impressive four-volume collection of master works in *Crisis Communication I–IV* (2014c). Regarding research methodology, he has been one of the strongest promoters of an experimental approach to the study of crisis communication. Regarding practice, he has been able to transform his research findings into normative guidelines (Coombs, 2015).

However, his most important contribution remains his SCCT, which is based on the social psychological theory of causal attributions and which has generated an array of new concepts such as relational history, relational damage, crisis or performance history, Velcro and halo effect, paracrisis, etc.

Sources of inspiration

SCCT is inspired by theories of social psychology and public relations, which, permanently or for a shorter period, have left their mark on its development.

The most permanent source of inspiration is attribution theory, a stream of research within social psychology, from Fritz Heider's studies of 'naive psychology' to Harold Kelley and Bernard Wiener (for an overview, see Försterling, 2001). Attribution theory is based on the assumption that to make sense of the world, people develop explanations about what is happening and why people are acting certain ways. People will always try to gain cognitive control, explaining to themselves spontaneously 'why something happened', in particular if it is something negative. Attribution theory is the theory of these *causal attributions* made by social actors in an attempt to assign the responsibility for an event or an action to someone or something.

Attribution researchers such as Wiener have introduced a series of causal dimensions that they claim influence how people produce causal attributions. Coombs has adopted Wiener's distinction between:

- *Stability* (Is it ongoing?): How often has an organization been involved in a crisis situation? If an organization often has been involved in crises before, even if it may not be the fault of the organization this time, there is a tendency that people will attribute more responsibility to the organization.
- *Controllability* (Can I change it?): Is the organization able to control the situation? If the crisis is controlled by external factors, there is a tendency that people will attribute less responsibility to the organization. However, if it is within the control of the organization, people will attribute more responsibility to the organization.
- *Locus of control* (Whose fault is it?): If a crisis is triggered internally or related to internal factors in the organization, there is a tendency that people will attribute more responsibility to the organization.

According to this distinction, the worst imaginable organizational crisis is a crisis (type) in which the organization is involved frequently, a crisis where the organization is expected to be in control, and a crisis that originates from within the organization. In such a situation, the stakeholders will ascribe responsibility for the crisis to the organization and not to some external factor.

A less permanent, but still important, source of inspiration is relationship management. Ledingham and Bruning's (2000) theory of *relationship management* defines the relationship between an organization and its stakeholders as the core of public relations. It is assumed that an organization builds up a relationship with its stakeholders over time and that this relationship has an impact on the reputation of the organization. From this perspective, a crisis can be defined as *relational damage* to the *relational history* of the organization and its stakeholders (Coombs, 2000).

Basic assumptions

Whereas Hearit's basic assumptions are ontological by nature (cf. his social constructivist approach to the study of crisis communication), Coombs' assumptions are primarily epistemological: that is, he argues that crisis communication would benefit from an *evidence-based management* approach. Like its counterparts in medicine and pedagogy, evidence-based management is rooted in empiricism. Rousseau (2006) defines evidence-based management as the translation of principles based on best evidence into organizational practice (see also Pfeffer & Sutton, 2006).

Theory: situational crisis communication theory

In 1995, Coombs published a journal article entitled 'Choosing the right words'. In it he presented a set of guidelines for the selection of the appropriate crisis response strategy.

Coombs' theory of crisis communication is based on the assumption that the best way to protect the reputation of an organization in crisis is by selecting the crisis response strategies that best fit the reputational threat presented by the crisis. The theory consists of three components: (1) a list of crisis response strategies, (2) a framework for the categorization of crisis situations, and (3) a procedure for matching a given crisis situation with the right response strategy.

How can the reputational threat of a crisis be assessed? Coombs defines it as a two-step process. The first step is to identify the *crisis type*. As mentioned in Chapter 2, Coombs' crisis typology comprises three clusters: a victim cluster (e.g., natural disasters), an accidental cluster (e.g., technical breakdown accidents), and a preventable cluster (e.g., organizational misdeeds).

The second step is to determine whether there are modifiers or intensifying factors that may influence the attribution process among stakeholders. Coombs is particularly interested in three factors. The first is the *crisis history*: that is, whether or not the organization has experienced similar crises (or crises at all). The second factor is *prior reputation* (Coombs, 2007) or *good work* (Coombs, 2006a). How favorable was the relationship between the organization and its stakeholders before the crisis? Coombs and Holladay (2001, 2006) demonstrated that a favorable prior reputation does not seem to have any larger effect (the so-called *halo* effect), whereas a negative prior reputation reinforces the attribution of crisis responsibility. If, for example, an organization is known for treating its stakeholders badly, this will stick to the organization and reinforce the attribution of crisis responsibility, a phenomenon that Coombs and Holladay call the *Velcro* effect. The first two factors have today been collapsed into what Coombs calls the *performance history*.

The third factor is the crisis itself. How severe is it? If it is a severe one, crisis responsibility will increase.

Causal attributions (Table 6.1) represent a key factor in the selection of an appropriate crisis response strategy. Coombs (2007) and Coombs and Holladay (2006) have identified three important consequences of the attribution of crisis responsibility to an organization: (1) negative impact on the organization's reputation, (2) altered purchase behavior, and (3) increase in negative *word of mouth*.

Table 6.1   The causal attribution process

The attribution process: from crisis type to crisis response strategy

Which crisis type?	Victim, accident, or preventable crisis?
Which intensifying factors?	• Crisis history • Prior reputation • Severity of crisis
Attribution of crisis responsibility	Degree of reputational threat
Selection of appropriate crisis response strategy	Defensive or accommodative strategy?

Attribution theory is the link between situational variables such as crisis type and crisis history (performance history) and the selection of crisis response strategies. Depending on whether an organization has been assigned a low, moderate or high responsibility, it will benefit from applying either a defensive or an accommodative response strategy. In his list of crisis response strategies, Coombs makes a distinction between four postures: (1) the denial posture where the organization in crisis claims there is no crisis; (2) the diminishing posture where the organization in crisis attempts to minimize the organization's responsibility; (3) the rebuilding posture where the organization in crisis provides compensation and/or apologizes for the crisis; and (4) the bolstering posture where the organization in crisis tells its stakeholders about past good works. Bolstering strategies, the purpose of which is to create a positive picture of the organization, can be combined with any of the other crisis response strategies (Table 6.2).

Table 6.2   Coombs' typology of crisis response strategies

Crisis response strategies

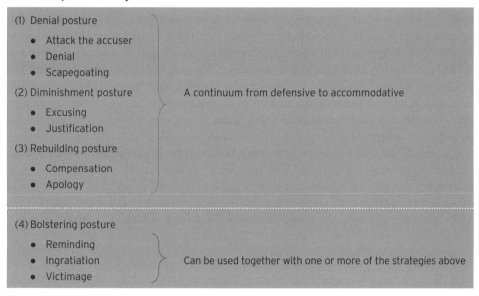

Source: Coombs (2015).

Further developments and criticisms

SCCT has been developed further by a large number of researchers. Almost every important aspect of this framework has been investigated, based on research questions such as: Does the attribution of crisis responsibility among key stakeholders change over time (during the post-crisis stage)? Do the stakeholders' emotions and stakes affect the attribution process? Do pictures enhance the effect of crisis response strategies? And so forth.

Recently, Benoit (2015) has criticized SCCT for assuming that the crisis type can be determined a priori. According to Benoit, this is only possible in some situations. In other situations, our 'perception of reality, such as whether blame should be internal to an organization or assigned to an external target, is socially constructed through messages' (pp. 36–37).

The experimental research design applied in SCCT-related research has many advantages, but also a few disadvantages. As emphasized by Rousseau (2006), 'Evidence-based management … derives principles from research evidence and translates them into practices that solve organizational problems. This isn't always easy. Principles are credible only where the evidence is clear, and research findings can be tough for both researchers and practitioners to interpret' (p. 256).

Contingency theory (CT)

Another representative of the strategic or context-oriented research tradition is the American public relations scholar Glen T. Cameron. Just like Coombs, he is interested in examining how situational variables, or what he calls *contingency factors*, have an influence on where, when, and how an organization communicates to its external stakeholders in a crisis situation. However, as we shall see, Cameron operates with a much larger battery of variables, or factors, than Coombs.

Cameron has contributed important insights to public relations research in general and to the study of strategic conflict management and crisis communication in particular. First, he problematized James E. Grunig's normative theory of public relations as symmetrical two-way communication, suggesting that we replace it with a contingency theory of accommodation. Second, with Augustine Pang and Yan Jin, he has applied this general framework within the field of crisis communication, demonstrating how the communication of an organization in crisis is dependent on crisis contingency factors and how the organization *positions* itself vis-à-vis different stakeholder groups.

Cameron has not published a comprehensive presentation of his contingency theory in the shape of a book. The two foundational articles are: 'It depends: A contingency theory of accommodation in public relations' (Cancel et al., 1997) and 'Testing the contingency theory of accommodation in public relations' (Cancel et al., 1999). For an overview of contingency theory, see Pang, Jin and Cameron (2010).

Sources of inspiration

The all-important source of inspiration in Cameron's research is contingency theory. This theory emerged within management and organization studies at the beginning of the 1960s as a reaction to the universalistic approach that was dominant at the time. According to this approach, it is always possible to identify a solution to an organizational problem that is the best solution for *all* organizations. Contingency theory rejects this approach, claiming that the solution to an organizational problem will always be dependent on a series of situational variables that make it more obvious to search for the best solution for each *individual* organization. Among the situational variables scrutinized by management and organization scholars in the 1960s and the 1970s were (1) uncertainty and dependency regarding the external and internal environment of the organization, (2) technology (not only production machines, but the entire production process), and (3) size of the organization. Two of the questions typically raised by contingency theory were: 'Are there general principles of organization structure to which all organizations should adhere? Or does the context of the organization – its size, ownership, geographical location, technology of manufacture – determine what structure is appropriate?' (Pugh, 1973, p. 19).

BOX 6.2

BEST PRACTICES IN CRISIS COMMUNICATION

Seeger (2006) defines best practices in crisis communication as a grounded theoretical approach for improving the effectiveness of crisis communication in the context of large crises managed by public agencies. The following ten best practices were identified by means of an expert panel process, including members of the National Center for Food Safety and Defense, who were asked to review and critique a number of practices generated from the research literature:

(1) Crisis communication is most effective when it is part of an ongoing and integrated process (cf. the staged approaches in Chapter 4) and when it is part of the decision-making process right from the beginning.
(2) Pre-crisis planning is important.
(3) The organization managing crises must accept the public as a legitimate and equal partner who has the right to be informed about what is happening.
(4) The organization managing crises must listen to the concerns of the public, take these concerns into account, and respond accordingly.
(5) Crisis communication is most effective when it is driven by honesty, candor, and openness.
(6) The establishment of strategic partnerships before a crisis occurs is important.
(7) Effective communication with the news media is important. Media training for spokespersons is part of pre-crisis planning.
(8) Spokespersons must demonstrate appropriate levels of compassion, concern, and empathy.

(Continued)

(Continued)

(9) The organization managing crises must accept the uncertainty and ambiguity inherent in crisis situations.

(10) Crisis communication must include messages of self-efficacy, helping people to restore some sense of control over the crisis situation.

Seeger (2006) emphasizes that these best practices for crisis communication are 'general standards rather than specific prescriptions' (p. 242) and that crises are unique events that can be expected to evolve in unexpected ways.

Further reading: Covello (2003).

Basic assumptions

Contingency theory is based on the assumption that public relations models, and in particular the normative theory of public relations as two-way symmetrical communication, are too limited and rigid in their descriptions of the public relations activities of organizations, including crisis communication. Thus, Cameron criticizes the excellence theory for being unrealistic. The practice of public relations is too complex to be contained within a single model. If you ask the communication director of a private company why he or she handled a specific issue, including the stakeholders related to this issue, in this or that way, that director will in most cases *not* answer 'We always use symmetrical two-way communication', but will instead respond: 'It depended on so many factors!' Cameron also criticizes the excellence theory for being neither the most effective nor the most ethical way to practise public relations.

It goes without saying that Cameron's criticism of James E. Grunig also is a criticism of the excellent crisis public relations theory within the field of crisis communication.

Theory (1): Contingency theory

The key concepts in Cameron's contingency theory of accommodation in public relation are *advocacy, accommodation, continuum, stance* (or *position*), and *contingency factor* (see Table 6.3).

Advocacy and *accommodation* represent the two extremes of a continuum indicating which stance or position an organization takes in its public relations work. That is to say, the way the organization positions itself toward a particular external public at a particular point in time in a particular situation. Advocacy is when the organization argues for its own case. Accommodation is when the organization gives in. Between the two extremes there is a wide array of stances where advocacy and accommodation are combined. It is important to emphasize that a stance or position is not the same as a specific strategy or a specific tactic (a specific way to communicate, for example, or a particular crisis response strategy) or the result of the interaction with the external public. The focus is on the decision-making process taking place prior to the interaction and which is crucial for the strategies

Table 6.3 Key concepts of contingency theory

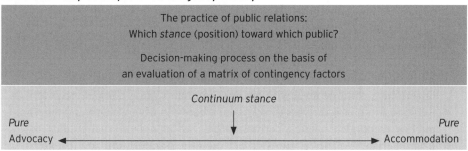

Source: Frandsen and Johansen (2009c).

and tactics the organization utilizes. The organization can take different stances toward different external publics. It can also change its stance toward the same public in a dynamic situation.

The situational variables, or contingency factors, listed by Cameron play a key role to the extent that it is here that the contingency principle is located. Originally, Cameron distinguished between external and internal factors (see below). However, after having conducted a series of empirical studies, he started distinguishing between predisposing variables and situational variables (Cancel et al., 1999). The predisposing variables exist before an organization enters into a situation or interaction with a particular external public. The situational variables influence how an organization shifts its stance toward an external public as the situation plays out.

Cameron operates with no less than 87 different contingency factors either identified in previous studies and the public relations literature or established by Cameron himself on the basis of interviews with public relations professionals. The contingency factors of the external environment of the organization include the following categories:

- Threats (litigation, government regulation, potentially damaging publicity, scarring of company's reputation, and legitimizing activists' claims)
- Industry environment (dynamic or static number of competitors/level of competition, richness or leanness of resources)
- General political and social environment/external culture (degree of political and social support of business)
- The external public (size and/or number of members, degree of source credibility, level of media coverage, relative power of organization and public, etc.).

The contingency factors of the internal environment of the organization include the following categories:

- Threats (economic loss, marring of the personal reputation of the company's decision makers, etc.)
- Company characteristics (open or closed culture, economic stability or the organization, formalization, hierarchy, etc.)

- Communication department characteristics (number of practitioners, type of past training of employees, representation in top management, location of communication department, degree of autonomy, etc.)
- Top management characteristics (political values, management style, support and understanding of public relations, etc.)
- Individual characteristics (training, tolerance or ability to deal with uncertainty, comfort level with change, communication competency, etc.)
- Relationship characteristics (level of trust between organization and external publics, ideological barriers between organization and external public, etc.)
- Characteristics of the relationship between the organization and its external publics.

For the complete lists of external/internal or predisposing/situational contingency factors or variables, see Cancel et al. (1997, 1999).

Theory (2): The factor–position–strategy model

It was not until the mid-2000s that Cameron's contingency theory of accommodation became a genuine theory of crisis communication. It was in particular Augustine Pang and Yan Jin who contributed to this development. Pang (2006) combined Cameron's concept of conflict positioning and Benoit's image repair theory, transforming this combination into a so-called *factor–position–strategy* model of crisis communication (see Table 6.4).

Table 6.4 The factor-position-strategy model of crisis communication

External/internal factors (conditions) ↓	Five important crisis contingency factors: <ul><li>Threat perception and assessment of the organization (type, duration, level)</li><li>The involvement of top management in the crisis</li><li>Influence and autonomy of the communication department during the crisis</li><li>Influence and role of legal advisors</li><li>Significance of stakeholders</li></ul>
Crisis position (reaction in decision-making process) ↓	Continuum (*stance*)
Strategy (communicative action)	Verbal defense strategies: <ul><li>Denial</li><li>Evading responsibility</li><li>Reducing offensiveness</li><li>Corrective action</li><li>Mortification</li></ul>

Source: Pang (2006).

Further developments and criticisms

Apart from the research conducted by Pang and Jin, the contingency theory framework has not been developed further during these past years. Contingency theory distinguishes itself by its very elaborated understanding of the context of crisis management and crisis communication, including a large number of contingency factors. However, we need to learn more about how all these factors can be operationalized. Will it be a kind of crisis communicative SWOT analysis or a similar type of situational analysis?

CASE STUDY 6.1

SCANDINAVIAN AIRLINES AND THE DASH 8 Q400 CRISIS (2007)

Scandinavian Airlines, or SAS, is the flag carrier of Sweden, Norway, and Denmark and the largest airline in Scandinavia.

On September 9, 2007, the pilots on flight SK1209 bound for Aalborg in the western part of Denmark alerted the control tower at Aalborg Airport that they had difficulties with the landing gear of the Dash 8 Q400 aircraft, produced by Canadian aircraft manufacturing company Bombardier, with 4 crew members and 69 passengers aboard. After circling above the airport for almost an hour, and after moving the passengers away from the mid-section of the turboprop airliner, the pilots landed the plane at 4.10 p.m. A few seconds later, the landing wheel under the right wing broke, the propellor went through the cabin, and the plane tipped over onto the grass. Miraculously, no one was seriously injured. Later the same day, SAS described the incident as a 'controlled emergency landing'.

In its first press release, SAS Group Corporate Communications announced:

Scandinavian Airlines regrets to confirm that one of its aircrafts, a Dash 8-400 (Q400) with flight number SK1209 from Copenhagen to Aalborg was involved in an accident at Aalborg Airport at 16:10 hrs local time today. Although no further details are available at the moment we can confirm that there were 69 passengers and 4 crew onboard. We can confirm that 5 passengers have been lightly injured during evacuation. SAS is doing everything possible to help all passengers. (SAS, September 9, 2007)

At the first press conference held on September 9, Danish Deputy CEO of SAS John Dueholm announced that SAS had been in contact with Bombardier and had decided to view the accident in Aalborg as an 'isolated incident'. SAS also announced that it considered the Dash 8 Q400 aircraft a 'safe and secure aircraft', although the new aircraft type had been plagued by 'child illnesses' and 'low technical irregularity', as mentioned in a report from the Swedish Accident Investigation Board (*Jyllands-Posten*, September 10, 2007).

In the days following the accident in Aalborg, the Danish news media were packed with critical headlines: 'Crash-landed aircraft had problems before' (*Jyllands-Posten*, September 10, 2007) and 'Same aircraft type was criticized for

(Continued)

(Continued)

lack of safety' (*Politiken*, September 10, 2007). The media accused SAS for not having maintained its aircraft properly and for operating with aircraft that were not airworthy.

Three days later, on September 12, another of SAS's Dash 8 Q400 aircraft was in dire straits. Flight SK2748, en route from Copenhagen to Palanga in Lithuania, had to make an emergency landing at Vilnius Airport at 1.36 a.m. Once again, the pilots had difficulties with the landing gear, and, again, nobody was injured. SAS sent a crisis team to Vilnius and all passengers were offered help. As expected, the news media were again packed with negative headlines: 'SAS faces a severe trust crisis' (*Jyllands-Posten*, September 13, 2007) and 'The coffers are empty and the credibility has been damaged' (*Politiken*, September 13, 2007).

In SAS's communication department in Denmark, the employees worked on finding the right name for the crisis. SAS does not at any time use the word *crisis* in its press releases, letters, and statements distributed to the media and its customers. Instead, expressions like *incident* and *accident* are used. However, during the entire crisis, as stated by former press officer Jens Langergaard (personal communication), the communication department was conscious about delimiting the crisis to the Dash 8 Q400 aircraft, and not to the SAS fleet of aircraft or activities in general. The department succeeded in making the newspapers refer to the 'Dash 8 crisis', and not the 'SAS crisis'.

On October 3, SAS Group Corporate Communications announced:

> Following an extensive inspection program and parts replacement, SAS is now returning Dash8/Q400 aircraft to traffic. SAS chose to ground the entire Q400 fleet following two accidents, in Aalborg on September 9 and Vilnius on September 12, to replace parts identified as the cause of the accidents. This involved an actuator in the main landing gear that was affected by corrosion. At an early stage, SAS decided to replace all actuators, whether they showed signs of corrosion or not. Accordingly, SAS took actions that went a step further than those required by the civil aviation authorities and the aircraft manufacturer. SAS has conducted extensive inspections of the main landing gear and the nose gear, and undertook much more comprehensive inspections than those required by the civil aviation authorities and the aircraft manufacturer. SAS will initiate discussions with Bombardier regarding compensation for the costs and lost income incurred due to the aircraft being grounded for about three weeks.

Slowly, the news media started to focus on the role and responsibility of Bombardier, the Canadian aircraft manufacturing company.

The CEO of SAS Denmark, Susanne Larsen, was on board the first Dash 8 that took off after having gone through a meticulous extensive inspection.

A little more than a month later, on October 27, for the third time a Dash 8 Q400 got into difficulties. Flight SK2867 from Bergen to Copenhagen had to make a controlled emergency landing in a blanket of foam on the runway at Copenhagen Airport (Kastrup) at 4.00 p.m. The explanation was a defective landing wheel. The very same day, SAS announced that 'The SAS Group has decided to ground the entire fleet of Dash 8-400 aircraft until further notice' (SAS, October 27, 2007). The following day, an unscheduled meeting of the board of directors was held and it was decided to 'discontinue the use of this type of aircraft'. Deputy CEO John Dueholm declared:

The Dash 8 Q400 has given rise to repeated quality-related problems and we can now conclude that the aircraft does not match our passengers' requirements concerning punctuality and regularity. SAS's flight operations have always enjoyed an excellent reputation and there is a risk that use of the Dash 8 Q400 could eventually damage the SAS brand. (SAS, October 28, 2007).

On March 10, 2008, Scandinavian Airlines made public that it had agreed a settlement with Bombardier and Goodrich regarding the accidents involving the Dash 8 aircraft in the autumn of 2007:

The details of the agreement are confidential but SAS Group confirms the total financial compensation is slightly more than SEK 1 billion in the form of a cash payment and credits for future firm and optional aircraft orders. As part of the agreement, the Board of Directors of SAS AB has approved an order for 27 aircrafts, with an option for a further 24 aircrafts. (SAS, March 10, 2008)

Discussion questions

- How and to what extent can the four theories of organizational crisis communication introduced in Chapter 5 and this chapter (image repair theory, terminological control theory, situational crisis communication theory, contingency theory) be applied in an analysis of SAS's crisis communication during the Dash 8 Q400 crisis in 2007? Try to be as specific as possible when applying the key concepts and models of each approach.
- How and to what extent can insights from the four theories be applied in practice to help SAS manage the crisis?
- What are the strengths and weaknesses of each approach?

Sources: Media coverage in national daily newspapers, letters to customers from SAS, and press releases on www.sas.dk (collected between September 9, 2007 and March 10, 2008).

ALTERNATIVE THEORIES AND EMERGING RESEARCH THEMES

In Chapter 5 and this chapter, we introduced the reader to four of the most important theories of organizational crisis communication. However, this does not mean that there are no alternatives left. Far from it. Among the existing alternative theories, we could for example have selected renewal discourse theory: that is, a theory about an 'optimistic discourse that emphasizes moving beyond the crisis, focusing on strong value positions, responsibility to stakeholders,, and growth as a result of the crisis' (Ulmer & Sellnow, 2002, p. 362; see also Ulmer et al., 2007).

One of these alternative theories deserves to be presented in more detail, namely Karl E. Weick's theory of retrospective sensemaking. The aim of this theory is to study situations where organizational sensemaking breaks down, typically in a crisis situation where demands on sensemaking can be severe. Weick's (1988) study of the Bhopal disaster and his study of the Mann Gulch fire (Weick, 1993) are often regarded as paradigmatic exemplars of how to conduct a sensemaking study, and also the starting gun for a stream of research labelled *crisis sensemaking*. The studies conducted within crisis sensemaking are first and foremost characterized by qualitative case studies with the purpose of examining how organizational members create meaning at an organizational micro-level as a crisis unfolds in various contexts, or how sensemaking takes place at a societal macro-level at the end of a crisis through the study of reports and other documents from public inquiries (for an overview, see Maitlis & Sonenshein, 2010).

We must also expect to see new alternative theories emerging from ongoing research. Among the most important emerging research themes are: crisis communication and social media, internal crisis communication, and emotional crisis communication, including (1) the emotions expressed by stakeholders as a response to crises and the crisis response strategies applied by organizations in crisis, and (2) the emotions expressed by an organization and its members when facing a crisis (cf. Chapters 9 and 12).

CHAPTER SUMMARY

This chapter has introduced the reader to situational crisis communication theory and contingency theory, focusing on their sources of inspiration, basic assumptions, theories (in a more precise sense of the word), further developments, and criticisms. The strength of this second group of theories is their attempt to explain and predict the use of crisis communication based on specific contextual variables and factors.

—— 📖 —— Further reading ——————————————————

Cancel, A. E., Cameron, G. T., Sallot, L. M., & Mitrook, M. A. (1997). It depends: A contingency theory of accommodation in public relations. *Journal of Public Relations Research*, 9(1), 31–63.
Coombs, W. T. (1995). Choosing the right words: The development of guidelines for the selection of the 'appropriate' crisis-response strategies. *Management Communication Quarterly*, 8(4), 447–476.

CRISIS COMMUNICATION ACROSS CULTURES

7

CHAPTER OVERVIEW

This chapter explores the intercultural and/or multicultural dimensions of organizational crises, crisis management, and crisis communication and their influence on the interaction with stakeholders across cultures. After an introduction to the concept of culture, including the two most important approaches to the study of culture, this chapter examines how culture affects the practice of crisis management and crisis communication at national, organizational, and community levels.

INTRODUCTION

We have now reached the fifth and last dimension of our multidimensional approach to organizational crises, crisis management, and crisis communication. In Chapter 1, we started out looking at the societal dimension, focusing on risk sociology in general and on Ulrik Beck's theory of the risk society in particular. Then we examined the definitional and typological dimension (Chapter 2), the managerial dimension (Chapters 3 and 4), and the communicative dimension (Chapters 5 and 6). The intercultural and/or multicultural dimension completes the circle.

Why is it important to include this dimension? Are intercultural differences still important? Do we not live in a globalizing world? The situation is in fact a little paradoxical. On the one hand, we claim that the process of globalization, including the rise of new information and communications technology (ICT), inevitably will lead to a reduction of cultural differences. On the other hand, cultural differences still seem to play a key role when organizations are involved in a global or international crisis.

In 2004, Marion Pinsdorf wrote a book entitled *All Crises are Global* in which she claimed that no crises are local. Even if they start as local crises in a specific geographic area, they do not stay local, or they have global consequences.

A globalizing world is first of all a *connected* world. We are, for example, currently experiencing a global ethical turning point, in which new standards and expectations among consumers and citizens are emerging regarding the behavior of companies not only in their home country, but also when they operate in host countries. On April 24, 2013, the eight-story commercial building of Rana Plaza in the Savar Upazila of Dkaha in Bangladesh collapsed. More than 1,100 people died and 2,500 people were rescued. The building hosted a bank, shops, and clothing factories. The factories inside the building employed around 5,000 people and manufactured apparel for brands such as Benetton, Bonmarché, Childrens Place, El Corte Inglés, Mango, and Walmart. The Rana Plaza disaster illustrates the new global ethical turn and how a local crisis had global repercussions. It caused international outrage and lead to newspaper headlines such as 'Enough fashion victims'. How could these companies allow workers to work in a building where three extra floors had been built over the original authorized level (and which was built on a pond in the first place)? And why did management order the workers to carry on work when cracks had appeared the day before, and the shops and bank on the lower floor of the commercial building had closed immediately on discovery of the cracks? Was it related to short production deadlines due to 'fast fashion' (designs that quickly change) and the need to meet orders on time?

BOX 7.1

HOST CRISIS VERSUS GLOBAL CRISIS

Coombs (2012, 2014a) introduced a distinction between *host crises* (where a crisis breaks out in one or more host countries, in which an organization has assets, but not in the home country of the organization), and *global crises* (where the same crisis breaks out in both the home country and one or more host countries). By making such a distinction, Coombs draws attention to the fact that organizations that operate internationally risk being involved in crises in host countries.

Due to the ICT revolution, a crisis, conflict, or issue in one country, such as a supply chain issue or an ethical dilemma (see case study 7.1), quickly spreads to other countries, becoming well known all over the world. Consequently, organizations may have to manage crises in different cultural contexts where different cultural values and norms are a reality. See for instance the attacks on the French supermarket chain Carrefour in China following the Olympic Torch Protests in France in 2008 (Coombs, 2012).

Further, global crises are much more complex, for instance when the crisis management in the home country is in conflict with the crisis management in the host country. The Cartoon Affair in 2006 is an excellent example of such a conflict. The Danish dairy, Arla Foods, had to handle a consumer boycott of its products in the Middle East caused by reactions to the publication of 12 cartoons depicting the prophet Muhammad in the Danish newspaper *Jyllands-Posten* in 2005. However, the way the company handled the boycott (insertion of ads in Saudi Arabian newspapers dissociating the company from the cartoons) was met with criticism from some stakeholder groups (cf. Frandsen & Johansen, 2010b). Thus, cultural diversity can lead to controversy in host countries and to global crises.

Further reading: Coombs (2012).

Today, consumers focus more on what is going on elsewhere. Therefore, we can expect to see more global crises. According to Boin (2009), 'the crises of the future will be increasingly transboundary in nature' (p. 367). However, global crises have to be managed locally. This calls for insights into local socio-cultural norms and local stakeholder expectations, which can be very different. To strengthen cultural awareness, this chapter starts with an introduction to the concept of culture and the two most important approaches to the study of culture. Then we look closer at how culture can have an influence on crisis management and crisis communication at three different levels: (1) the national or regional level, (2) the organizational level, and (3) the community level.

DEFINING CULTURE

Culture is a small word, but it covers many things. As stated by management scholar Mats Alvesson (2013), 'Culture is a tricky concept as it is easily used to cover everything and consequently nothing' (p. 3). In other words, it is also important to know what culture is *not*. For example, how do we distinguish between culture and social structure? Culture and social structure can be said to represent the same phenomenon but in different ways. According to Alvesson (2013), culture describes social action as depending on the meaning it has for those involved, while social structure describes social action from the point of view of its consequences on the functioning of the social system. This distinction is appropriate because cultural meanings may change without changing social structure, just as a change in social structure, such as the change of specific formal rules or regulations, may not necessarily lead to changes of cultural meaning.

Within the business world, culture started attracting attention in the 1970s and especially in the 1980s. It was mostly about intercultural differences and barriers to communication among businesspeople from different national cultures who were going to sell, buy, and negotiate. However, differences in organizational cultures combined with national cultural aspects started to gain attention too. This stemmed largely from the question of why some organizations, such as Japanese companies at the beginning of the 1980s, were better at resisting crises than others. What was the role of the organizational culture?

APPROACHES TO THE STUDY OF CULTURE

Two approaches are dominant within the study of culture: the functionalist approach and the interpretive or symbolic approach. As will become evident, these two approaches determine the choice of methodology for the study of crises and culture. Common to both approaches is the idea that culture, be it national cultures or organizational cultures, never will form a homogeneous entity. Culture can always be broken down into various *subcultures*, and it can always be studied at various *levels*. In nation-states, there are regional and local cultures. In organizations, there are functional and professional cultures.

The functionalist approach

The first approach is the functionalist approach, also called the *values* approach. This approach focuses on the norms and values that differentiate people in one culture from people in another culture. Dutch management scholar Geert Hofstede and American organizational culture scholar Edgar Schein are two of the most prominent representatives of this approach. The functionalist approach is aligned with Schein's view that organizational culture has a double function: to overcome problems of external adaptation to the environment and of internal integration of processes in order to ensure growth and survival of the organization.

Hofstede considers culture to be 'the software of the mind' (1991). Using a computing metaphor, he defines culture as 'the collective programming of the mind that distinguishes the members of one group or category of people from another' (2001, p. 9). However, he also states that part of the programming of human nature is inherited. Thus, culture is a mixture of something inherited and something learned.

Hofstede is renowned for his study in the 1970s of IBM and its worldwide subsidiaries, in which he revealed important cross-national cultural differences. He identified four, and later five, cultural dimensions that can explain differences when comparing national cultures: (1) *power distance*, (2) *uncertainty avoidance* (the extent to which individuals within a culture are made nervous by situations that are unstructured, unclear, or unpredictable and the extent to which these individuals attempt to avoid situations by adapting strict codes of behavior), (3) *individualism vs. collectivism*, (4) *masculinity vs. femininity*, and finally (5) *long-term vs. short-term orientation* (Hofstede, 2001).

Hofstede's functionalist approach has been criticized from different quarters, especially his methodology and national cultural determinism (see Table 7.1). Nevertheless, many studies of intercultural differences have been based on Hofstede's findings. This is also the case within the field of crisis management and crisis communication.

Applying the functionalist approach: the Coca-Cola crisis of 1999

American public relations scholar Maureen Taylor was one of the first crisis communication researchers to apply Hofstede's approach in a study of intercultural differences and crisis communication. Taylor (2000) claimed that differences in

Table 7.1 Criticism of Hofstede's IBM study

Criticism	Hofstede's response
Surveys are not a suitable way of measuring cultural differences	Surveys should not be the only method used
Nations are not the best units for studying cultures	Agreed, but they are the only units available for comparison
A study of subsidiaries of one company cannot provide information about entire national cultures	The study was only used to measure differences between cultures, not entire national cultures
The IBM data are old and obsolete	The dimensions found have centuries-old roots. Only data stable across two subsequent surveys were maintained
Four or five dimensions are not enough	Additional dimensions should be independent from the ones already defined

Source: Hofstede (2002).

national culture, in particular regarding power distance and uncertainty avoidance, can explain why companies and consumers react differently to one and the same crisis. In a study of the Coca-Cola crisis in Belgium in 1999, Taylor tried to explain why national governments in six European countries reacted differently to this crisis, using the dimensions of power distance and uncertainty avoidance in these countries as observed in the Hofstede study. On June 14, 1999, more than 200 Belgian school children felt sick after drinking Coca-Cola. Following demands from the Belgian, French, and Spanish authorities, the Coca-Cola Company recalled 5 million bottles and cans of Coca-Cola. However, according to Taylor, the company reacted as an organization of low power distance and low uncertainty avoidance: it started by denying responsibility and expressing doubt about the claims of illness. Thus, it was viewed as an arrogant company. It was not until June 22 that the company finally took responsibility for what had happened, and the CEO went on Belgian television to explain and offer compensation.

According to Hofstede, countries that are high on the scale of power distance and uncertainty avoidance, such as Belgium, France, and Spain, have a high respect for power, and a high concern about security, written laws, and explicit rules; they are anxious about the unexpected, and find it risky to deviate from the expected norm. National cultures like these are less tolerant to risk and uncertainty and acutely attentive to isolated incidents that may lead to a crisis. This may explain their strong reactions to the Coca-Cola crisis: that is, obligatory product recall and boycott. Countries that are low on power distance and uncertainty avoidance and high on risk tolerance, such as Denmark, Norway, and Sweden, did not react in the same way. These countries did not see this kind of incident as a potential crisis and did not ask for a product recall. Thus, the Coca-Cola Company was able to meet the expectations of these Scandinavian countries but not the expectations of the more southerly European countries.

BOX 7.2

TRANSBOUNDARY CRISES

The concept of *transboundary crisis* (Boin, 2009; Falkheimer, 2013) is based on the idea that nation-states and organizations face threats or crises that risk crossing not only geographical boundaries but also functional and/or time boundaries. Nation-state borders do not constitute a barrier. A crisis more often threatens cities, regions, and countries. Furthermore, a crisis does not remain in its own functional category. It may start as a crisis in the public sector but then move to the private sector and vice versa, or it may move from one industrial sector to another. Finally, today's crises do not have time boundaries. The concept of transboundary crisis is well aligned with Beck's theory of the risk society (cf. Chapter 1) and with the complexity perspective of crisis management.

Further reading: Boin (2009).

The interpretive or symbolic approach

The second approach is the interpretive or symbolic approach. This approach is interested in how meaning is ascribed to phenomena of all kinds through social inter-action among people. The approach was inspired by two anthropologists: Clifford Geertz, who compares man to 'an animal that is suspended in webs of significance he himself has spun' (1973, p. 5), and Claude Levi-Strauss, who considers culture a system of symbols created through communication among people and common to a group of people and how they understand the world. Whereas the functionalistic approach sees culture as something primarily located in the mind of people, the interpretive or symbolic approach sees culture as something going on inside a group of people.

Swedish management scholar Mats Alvesson has developed this approach further in his research on organizational culture (see, e.g., Alvesson, 2013). He is also interested in the meaning aspect of what is being socially expressed. According to him (p. 4), people are meaning-seeking creatures, and meanings are negotiated and processed. This means that culture is something that people do, and that culture is dynamic, emergent, and dependent on the situational context. This approach is aligned with the approach that considers crises as social constructions that are negoti-ated among people (cf. Chapter 2).

Applying the interpretive or symbolic approach: the Coca-Cola crisis of 1999

What if we applied the interpretive or symbolic approach to the Coca-Cola crisis? How would we have to proceed? In this case, researchers would have to look for different interpretations of the crisis and different meanings ascribed to the actions and communication of the Coca-Cola Company. Johnson and Peppas (2003) also studied the Coca-Cola crisis. Interestingly, they found that contextual factors played an important role in the product recall and interpretation of the crisis in Belgium. According to them, the history of health crises in Belgium (mad cow disease and dioxin contamination, which led to a crisis of trust for government officials) called for a more 'calculated and sensitive approach to crisis management' (p. 22).

Most of the previous research on crisis and culture has applied a functionalist approach, considering national culture as a variable that affects crises in various ways. However, in recent years, the focus has started to shift from a functionalist to a social constructivist approach, and from an intercultural perspective to a multicultural one. Falkheimer and Heide (2006) were among the first scholars to point to the need for a new approach. According to these two Swedish scholars, most societies today include people with different linguistic, religious, political, and socio-cultural backgrounds. These people often understand and react to crises differently. This calls for more multicultural awareness and an interpretive approach.

CULTURE, CRISIS MANAGEMENT, AND CRISIS COMMUNICATION

Intercultural or multicultural dimensions represent an under-investigated area in the field of crisis management and crisis communication research. Communication scholar Betty Kamann Lee claimed that international crisis communication was 'underdeveloped, if not undeveloped' (2005b, p. 286), and that this was due to ethnocentrism or insensitivity towards cultural aspects. Ten years later, cultural aspects of importance to crisis management slowly started to attract more attention from researchers. Books including case studies of crisis communication from different parts of the world (George & Pratt, 2012, Coombs, 2014b), handbooks including sections on global crises (Coombs & Holladay, 2010) or devoted entirely to crisis communication research in different parts of the world (Schwarz et al., 2016a), as well as journal articles discussing new research approaches to culture and crisis, have started to emerge.

In an attempt to simplify and systematize the study of cultural aspects of crisis management and crisis communication, Frandsen and Johansen (2010c) established a model or framework for reviewing research on crisis across cultures. The model is presented in a revised version in Figure 7.1.

As it appears in Figure 7.1, the model combines two cultural levels that are mutually interdependent, namely national/regional culture and organizational culture, although more cultural levels could have been included. At the same time, the three columns indicate: (1) the interrelationships between the organization in crisis (before, during, and after the crisis), its internal crisis culture, and crisis management and crisis communication activities defined as a specific organizational practice taking place in a specific context; (2) the two cultural levels of national/regional culture and organizational culture; and (3) various types of stakeholders (across cultures) who perceive and react to organizational crises and how they are managed by the organizations. The remaining part of this chapter is structured in accordance with this model.

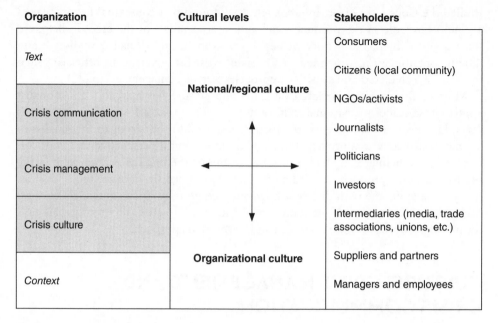

Figure 7.1   Cultural dimensions of crisis management and crisis communication

Source: Inspired by Frandsen and Johansen (2010c).

National culture, crisis management, and crisis communication

Most intercultural studies conducted so far within the field of crisis management and crisis communication have focused on the importance of national cultural differences. Some of the early studies investigated the airline industry. This industry is particularly interesting because, even though airline companies are headquartered in specific countries, they very often fly transnationally. Consequently, they handle passengers with many different cultural backgrounds, but they have to live up to the same kind of demands regarding safety procedures before, during, and after a flight, no matter where these passengers come from. Thus, it can be assumed that differences in the crisis management process are due in part to situational circumstances and/or to national or organizational cultural realities. Ray (1999) studied crises in American airline companies, focusing on organizational cultures, while Pinsdorf focused on national cultures in her article 'Flying different skies' (1991) and in her book *All Crises Are Global* (2004) (see also Haruta & Hallahan (2003) who apply an approach inspired by Geert Hofstede).

Pinsdorf's studies of airline crises demonstrated how language, communication problems, differences in media systems, variations in socio-cultural values and norms, and stakeholder expectations in different national cultures have an impact on the handling of airline crashes. In some cases, these factors even caused the crash. To illustrate: according to Pinsdorf, the handling of the serious crash of Japan Airlines' flight 123 in August 1985, where 524 people died, compared to the handling of the explosion over Lockerbie in Scotland of Pan Am flight 103 in December 1988, where 189 people perished, clearly made national cultural differences stand out.

In Japan, people had a strong focus on paternalistic and collectivistic values and expected the company to show a human face and take responsibility in cases like this. This meant that the company had to apologize personally and seek reconciliation. Following a detailed protocol, the CEO of JAL offered to resign immediately, families of the victims were offered help, and representatives from JAL participated in memorial ceremonies. In contrast to Japanese culture, American culture is more individualistic and capitalistic, and this may explain (at least to some extent) Pan Am's reaction to the crash. The company acted slowly, and although the company did show concern and care, the CEO did not apologize to the families of the victims, and they were not offered much help. This led to families and friends of the victims setting up a memorial homepage of the 'Victims of Pan Am 103' themselves, with the intention of 'seeking the truth about this tragedy and keeping the memory of our loved ones alive' (www.victimsofpanamflight103.org). The website is still active more than 27 years after the crash.

BOX 7.3

HOW DO COMMUNICATION PROFESSIONALS HANDLE THE CULTURAL ASPECTS OF CRISES?

It is difficult to navigate across cultures as a crisis manager, and organizations very often overlook the different reactions from customers, the press, and public authorities in different national cultures. If we look at how communication professionals handle the cultural aspects of crises, we know from the study of Oliveira (2013) that there is a gap between intention and practice, or what Argyris would have called espoused theory versus theory in use. Oliveira asked 25 communication professionals from the United States about their view on culture and crisis. The answers revealed that the majority of practitioners recognized that it was important to take cultural differences into account and to be able to adapt to the cultural characteristics of stakeholders, for instance in relation to language barriers, communication style, use of alternative communication channels, and tactics. However, this was seldom done in practice because they were not fully equipped to manage such crises. Therefore, according to Oliveira, it is vital that intercultural and multicultural situations are integrated in the course of crisis management/communication (cf. the epilogue).

Further reading: Oliveira (2013).

Another issue that has caught the attention of researchers is the issue of Western versus Eastern approaches to crisis communication. Lee (2004, 2005b) has pointed to the problem of ethnocentrism, an approach that either focuses exclusively on one's own culture or believes in the superiority of one's own culture. According to Lee, most of the studies of international public relations and crisis communication are based on a Western approach. Theories developed exclusively on the basis of Western culture, however, may lead to erroneous conclusions as to how to communicate in crisis situations in other parts of the world. Nevertheless, scholars such as Lee (2004, 2005a, 2005b) and Huang et al. (2005) have tested different crisis response strategies in a Chinese context. Lee has studied how consumers are influenced by the Western and Asian communities they belong to in their everyday life, and how underlying cultural factors have an impact on consumer reactions. For instance, differences in socio-cultural norms may explain variations in the use and interpretation of crisis response strategies, such as the 'no comment' strategy, compensation, and apologies. According to Lee (2004), the 'no comment' strategy was more easily accepted in China (cf. Confucius's maxim 'to think three times before you act') than in Western culture where it is often regarded as 'stonewalling'. Compensation gained more sympathy than apologies, perhaps because apologies in China are considered routine or a mere ritual. Thus, we need theories and models developed in a non-Western culture.

Apology across cultures is a field of special attention. In his book *Crisis Management by Apology* (2006), Hearit studied apologetic ethics or how to offer an ethically correct apology (cf. Chapter 5). Generally speaking, it is easier to offer an ethically correct apology when it takes place inside your own socio-cultural order. But it is less easy to offer such an apology when it takes place across two or more socio-cultural orders.

Hearit's (2006) study of the crisis that broke out in 2001 when the US Navy submarine *Greenville* collided with a Japanese fishing boat, the *Ehime Maru*, illustrates how difficult it can be to handle such a situation. The Japanese fishing boat carried Japanese students and teachers. Nine of them were reported missing after the collision. It turned out that a civilian on the *Greenville* had been steering the submarine at the time of the collision. The ritualistic components of the institutional apology to the Japanese families and society turned out to be very important, and it was difficult for the Americans to live up to this. Although officials including President Bush made an apology, the Japanese wanted an apology from the captain of the submarine himself. They wanted the captain to be personal, timely, to do it voluntarily, to take responsibility, and, importantly, to address the families of the victims as well as Japanese society. The captain did not live up to this in his first apology; he only did it once the Court of Inquiry had ended its investigations.

Globalization has created the need for a new type of apology. It is difficult to apologize in a globalizing world. How can you live up to conflicting expectations from people with so many different cultural backgrounds?

How should Danish Prime Minister Anders Fogh Rasmussen have communicated to a large group of Muslims who wanted him to apologize on behalf of the Danish newspaper *Jyllands-Posten*, after it had published the 12 cartoons that triggered the Cartoon Affair in 2005? In fact, he did not have to apologize. Freedom of expression is one of the fundamental values of Danish society. So he could either meet the expectations of his own socio-cultural order, or try to live up to expectations of the Muslims' socio-cultural order. It was impossible to do both. He ended up offering a serial apology but none of them was considered sincere by the Muslims. A solution to this dilemma could be to offer what we have named a *meta-apology*. By meta-apology we understand 'an apology where the apologist is no longer apologizing for what he or she may have done – because he or she actually does not have to, according to their own socio-cultural order – but for the negative effects that the act committed by the apologist may possibly have caused' (Frandsen & Johansen, 2010a, p. 362).

This was the solution chosen by Pope Benedict XVI, Head of the Roman Catholic Church, when he faced a misunderstanding of a lecture he gave on September 12, 2006, at the University of Regensburg in Germany. This lecture caused Muslims to ask him for an apology for having offended their prophet. But it was not until his third apology that Muslims were satisfied:

> I wish also to add that I am deeply sorry for the reactions in some countries to a few passages of my address at the University of Regensburg, which were considered offensive to the sensibility of Muslims. These in fact were a quotation from a medieval text, which do not in any way express my personal thought. I hope that this serves to appease hearts and to clarify the true meaning of my address, which, in its totality, was and is an invitation to frank and sincere dialogue with great mutual respect. (Frandsen & Johansen, 2010a, p. 360)

In this globalizing world, we must accept that we sometimes have to apologize for things that we are not used to apologizing for, because these things may be considered wrongful by people with differing socio-cultural orders.

BOX 7.4

CHALLENGES TO INTERCULTURAL CRISIS MANAGEMENT AND CRISIS COMMUNICATION

According to Jaques (2014), organizations have to keep an eye on cultural challenges when they are dealing with crises initiated in a foreign country, that is in situations where the crisis management process is removed from the culture and experience of head office executives. This means that the standard crisis response may not work in this context. Jaques identifies challenges related to the following:

- Long distance and multiple time zones (e.g., it can be difficult to get there quick enough; working across time zones is a constant limitation).
- Being a 'foreigner' outside the home country (e.g., extent of anti-foreign feeling about multinational corporations).
- Geographic diversity (e.g., possibility of isolating the problem while maintaining operations elsewhere).
- Portability of operations (e.g., relocating plants or facilities to avoid risks in a specific country).

(Continued)

(Continued)

- Technology–society mismatch (e.g., which standards to follow: 'our standard or local standard, whichever is the higher').
- Different national environments (e.g., language and culture, education systems, political, legal, economic systems, media systems, etc.).
- National employee differences (e.g., to manage the crisis locally while keeping head office in another country informed, and to work through local employees having a different language and other socio-cultural norms).

Further reading: Jaques (2014).

Organizational culture, crisis management, and crisis communication

Scholars are not just interested in how national cultural factors impact on the practice of crisis management and crisis communication. They are also focused on the impact of the organizational (sub)culture(s) of an organization and the crisis and communication culture. Pauchant and Mitroff were among the first to emphasize the importance of organizational culture. In their book *Transforming the Crisis-Prone Organization* (1992), they introduced a distinction between crisis-prepared and crisis-prone organizations. In order to find out whether an organization is crisis prone, they established a diagnostic model. It had the shape of an onion with four layers: (4) organizational strategies, (3) organizational structure, (2) organizational culture, and (1) the character of the individuals working for the organization. According to Pauchant and Mitroff, layers (1) and (2) represent the most invisible aspects. These aspects cover phenomena such as belief systems, codes of conduct, unwritten rules of what can be said and done, perceptions of crisis, etc. One way to study the crisis culture of an organization is to look at its faulty rationalizations, that is the way managers and employees talk about crises in order to protect themselves from them.

Organizational cultures are seldom homogeneous. They are fragmented and include conflicting subcultures. Furthermore, today's organizations are often multicultural workplaces where people from different ethnic groups work together. This becomes even more evident in multinational companies operating across borders. The organizational culture and the way an organization manages and communicates before a crisis breaks out will typically have an impact on how a crisis situation is managed. When an organization is under pressure, there is a tendency toward taking decisions based on routines. Which communication culture is predominant? How do the members of the organization talk about risk and crisis? Do employees speak up when something is wrong and are managers listening? Do the organizations have a corporate communication policy in times of crisis, and, if so, do they follow these guidelines?

It is also important that the members of an organization have developed a sensitivity to crisis – a crisis culture – recognizing that crises will happen at some point in time. One of the key characteristics of high-reliability organizations is their collective mindfulness. HROs (e.g., a trauma center in a hospital, a control tower in an airport, a nuclear plant, an aircraft carrier, etc.) have to operate in high-risk areas under difficult conditions. For this reason, they have developed specific ways of thinking, communicating, and managing the unexpected. Weick and Sutcliffe (2001, 2007) claim that other organizations can learn from HROs.

Marra (1999, 2004) examined the importance of the communication culture of an organization in relation to having a crisis management plan. He found that the communication culture is important in all three stages of a crisis: (1) before a crisis breaks out (i.e., risk communication and crisis preparations), (2) during the crisis (i.e., coordination and communication with stakeholders), but also (c) after the crisis (i.e., restoration of relationships with key stakeholders). According to Marra (1999), 'the communication culture is a far better predictor of successful crisis management than the presence or absence of a crisis communication plan' (p. 466). If the content or strategies listed in the plan are not supported by the communication culture of the organization, the plan risks failure. Marra illustrates his observations by referring to the proactive communication of AT&T, which had a culture of always communicating as much and as openly as possible. This helped it during the long-distance crisis of 1990. In contrast, NASA was supposed to communicate quickly (within 20 minutes) according to its own crisis plan, but the defensive and closed communication culture of the organization formed a barrier. It did not start communicating until six hours after the explosion of the Space Shuttle *Challenger* on January 26, 1986.

Wise's (2003) study of the successful crisis management response of a Connecticut hospital during the anthrax crisis of 2001 confirms Marra's observations that an organization's culture is more important than the plan in determining the success of its crisis management efforts. The hospital had established an open communication culture, and although it was advised not to announce publicly that it had a patient with anthrax until more test results were available, the management of the hospital followed the open communication culture policy. They did not have to consult the crisis communication plans – they knew what to do.

CASE STUDY 7.1

THE GIRAFFE MARIUS AND COPENHAGEN ZOO

On February 9, 2014, a young male giraffe named Marius was euthanized at Copenhagen Zoo. Giraffes are part of the European Breeding Programme, and the euthanization took place in accordance with this programme, which is meant to ensure a healthy and genetically diverse population of giraffes. As a member of the European Association of Zoos and Aquariums (EAZA), Copenhagen Zoo was not allowed to relocate animals to zoos outside of the organization, and it was not possible to find another zoo without creating inbreeding issues. Marius

(Continued)

(Continued)

could not stay with the herd at Copenhagen Zoo either, and sterilization was considered detrimental to the animal's quality of life. Therefore, euthanasia was the only realistic option.

The dissection of the giraffe that followed, conducted by a veterinarian, was opened to zoo visitors, including parents with children who could ask questions about the giraffe. According to Bengt Holst, Scientific Director of Copenhagen Zoo, this happened in accordance with the zoo's policy to educate people on nature and wildlife. This is normal practice in Denmark. Following the dissection, the zoo's carnivores were fed with the meat from the giraffe.

These events outraged people from all over the world, including citizens, animal rights campaigners, politicians, and the media. According to Copenhagen Zoo, it could follow how people woke up in the morning in different time zones. Once people had watched or heard the news, they started phoning the zoo or posting comments on Facebook accusing Copenhagen Zoo of behavingly wrongly in a very rude way:

- 'You murdered an innocent animal for NO GOOD REASON. To kill Marius in public, in front of CHILDREN, some of whom will be traumatised, is beyond belief! You deserve what you get now, Karma is coming.'
- 'You know that HITLER murdered millions of people for the exact same reason as you gave in the interview as to why your are killing this baby. Shame on you.'
- 'This is disgusting, there must be a wildlife park that could offer it a home … Not a Zoo will ever want to visit or support.'
- 'There is ALWAYS another way out than to euthanize a sound and healthy animal. You have acted directly wrong, and I hope it will have huge consequences.' and so on.

Some zoo employees received death threats. One man threatened to bring a machine gun to the zoo and kill employees the following day. However, these angry comments were also met with supportive reactions, especially from Denmark and visitors to the zoo, such as:

- 'It has ALWAYS been done like this. They are not evil people, and everything is probably thought through.'

And voices who were attacking the critics:

- 'I obviously don't understand what is happening in the real world. To go crazy because one giraffe is killed, and at the same time people don't mind eating pork chops. How hypocritical. New born calves are killed every day even though they are in perfect health – Get real.'

Copenhagen Zoo on international television

The Scientific Director of Copenhagen Zoo, Bengt Holst, had to answer questions from Hungarian, Dutch, German, and British television networks. In the United Kingdom, the reactions were much more intense and emotional. The British press was very aggressive. Bengt Holst (BH) was asked that if he allowed young school children to watch the dismemberment of the dead giraffe, why not just invite them in to see the killing? Bengt Holst's answer was that there was no education in seeing the killing, but a lot of education in seeing the dissection of the giraffe. The veterinarian could, for example, tell the children about the big heart.

When asked again whether the whole thing was cruel – that is, watching the dismemberment of the giraffe and seeing the lions feasting on it – and that it would make the children freak out, Holst emphasized that it was not cruel but natural. Carnivores live from meat and this meat comes from other animals. Every time an animal dies in a zoo, the animal is dissected. This is normal life in a zoo, whether in London or in Copenhagen.

The British journalist pointed out that the London Zoo would never show school children this process. To this, Holst responded that he could not understand why we should protect children from real life. According to him, school children could learn a lot from seeing what a fine animal the giraffe is: to see the big neck and all the vertebrates, and to learn that the big heart can pump the blood two metres up in the air to reach the brain.

At the end of the interview, the journalist agreed that nature could be cruel and that scientists were supposed to stand away from it. However, he found the language of Bengt Holst clinical and cold. Holst replied that he could not understand why talking about feeding the lions with meat from other animals was considered cruel or cold. It was all about natural animals and natural meat.

This interview created a lot of attention in Denmark because the British journalist was seen as aggressive, making accusations and giving lessons in his way of conducting the interview. In contrast to the journalist, Bengt Holst was perceived as answering in a very professional, authentic and eloquent way.

Together with the many critical Facebook comments from Danes as well as from people from all over the world, and not least from the UK, Copenhagen Zoo had to manage a cross-cultural crisis situation. However, there were more critical voices from abroad than from Denmark. Many Danes ended up defending Copenhagen Zoo.

Discussion questions

- What kind of crisis was Copenhagen Zoo facing? How would you manage the intercultural dimension of the crisis? How would you communicate?
- Why were people so angry? Why did the euthanasia of the giraffe trigger a 'shitstorm' on social media and attract attention from the news media all over the world? Does it matter that the giraffe was named Marius (cf. the killing of Cecil the lion by an American dentist in South West Africa on July 1, 2015)?
- How can we explain that there were more critical voices outside Denmark than inside? How do you interpret the interview?

Sources: Moberg (2015). Interview on Channel 4 News, February 9, 2014; articles from Danish newspapers; Copenhagen Zoo Facebook, February 2014.

CHAPTER SUMMARY

As we have seen in this chapter, researchers interested in global or international crisis communication have first of all focused on the importance of intercultural differences, applying a functionalist approach to the study of culture. However, recent studies seem to indicate that this approach is now being supplemented by new interpretive or social-constructivist approaches, and that focus has moved from national cultural aspects to multicultural aspects. Rhetorical arena theory and the multivocal approach to crisis communication, which is the topic of the next chapter, included this development when it predicted that:

> communication will be perceived as constitutive and interactive rather than as a simple tool, and the discipline and practice of crisis management and crisis communication will to a much higher extent take into account, not only the complexity and dynamics of organizational crises, but also important socio-cultural factors such as national culture, organizational (sub)cultures, communication cultures, and crisis cultures. (Frandsen & Johansen, 2010c, p. 564)

 Further reading

Falkheimer, J., & Heide, M. (2006). Multicultural crisis communication: Towards a social constructionist perspective. *Journal of Contingencies and Crisis Management*, 14(4), 180–189.

Taylor, M. (2000). Cultural variance as a challenge to global public relations: A case study of the Coca-Cola scare in Europe. *Public Relations Review*, 26(3), 277–293.

INSIDE THE RHETORICAL ARENA

In Part 2, we introduce the reader to a new approach to crisis communication based on rhetorical arena theory and the multivocal approach. According to this theory, we can gain a better understanding of organizational crises if we not only focus on the crisis communication produced by the organization in crisis, but also take into account the many other *voices* that start communicating when a crisis breaks out. A multivocal approach will also allow us to improve the crisis preparedness of the organization. After reading Part 2, the reader should be able to provide answers to the following questions:

- How do consumers, citizens, the news media, intermediaries (such as trade associations), managers, and employees communicate in a crisis situation?
- What are the practical implications of a multivocal approach?
- How will it change the organizational practice of crisis management and crisis communication?

THE RHETORICAL ARENA: A NEW THEORETICAL FRAMEWORK

8

CHAPTER OVERVIEW

Rhetorical arena theory (RAT) is neither a new stakeholder theory nor a new public sphere theory. The concept refers to the complex and dynamic social space that opens when a crisis occurs – a space inside which multiple voices, including the voices of customers, citizens, the news media, intermediaries such as trade associations, third parties, and the organization in crisis, start communicating. This chapter provides a detailed introduction to RAT and the multivocal approach, including the most important sources of inspiration, its basic assumptions and key concepts such as *arena* and *voice*, along with the macro and micro components of the model.

INTRODUCTION

In Chapters 5 and 6, we introduced the reader to four important theories of organizational crisis communication: image repair theory, terminological control theory, situational crisis communication theory, and contingency theory. Each of these theories has provided important insights regarding how private and public organizations communicate in a crisis situation. The rhetorical and text-oriented theories have taught us how organizations defend themselves by means of crisis response strategies. The strategic and context-oriented theories have shown how situational variables or contingency factors can help us select the appropriate response strategies. We have learned much, but this does not mean that all possibilities for new theory building are exhausted.

The purpose of this chapter is to introduce RAT and the multivocal approach, a theory and an approach that provide academics as well as practitioners with an alternative understanding of organizational crises, crisis management, and crisis communication. First, we evaluate previous crisis communication research. Second, to avoid misunderstanding, we define what RAT is – and what RAT is not. Third, we demonstrate how complexity theory, communication theory, and previous arena research inform our understanding of organizational crisis communication. Finally, we present the macro and micro components of the arena model.

EVALUATION OF PREVIOUS CRISIS COMMUNICATION RESEARCH

Our evaluation of previous crisis communication research can be summarized by five critical points:

> First, previous research has, to a large extent, focused on the type of crisis communication produced by the *organization in crisis*. The crisis communication produced by the other voices who are involved in the crises, directly or indirectly, as senders or as receivers, is seldom taken into account. In other words, crisis communication researchers have applied an organization-centric approach (cf. Chapters 5 and 6). There are, however, exceptions to this rule. Coombs and Holladay (2012b), for example, have developed a theory of sub-arenas.

> Second, previous research has largely focused on *crisis response strategies*: that is to say, the type of crisis communication produced during or immediately after the crisis event. Again, there are exceptions. One of them is renewal discourse theory where renewal is defined as 'a fresh sense of purpose and direction an organization discovers after it emerges from a crisis' (Ulmer et al., 2007, p. 177; see also Veil et al., 2011).

> Third, previous research has (again, to a large extent) conceptualized crisis communication as a process embracing *one* sender (the organization in crisis) and *one* receiver (all the stakeholders). Stakeholder theory was a theory of multiple stakeholders from the beginning (cf. Freeman, 1984; see also Frandsen & Johansen, 2015b), but this potential has not been exploited sufficiently (for an exception, see Marcus & Goodman, 1991).

> Fourth, previous research has mainly focused on *external* crisis communication – that is, communication to and with the organization's external key stakeholders, such as the media, customers, and investors, but not the employees.

> Fifth, previous research has so far not demonstrated great interest in the *relationship between crisis management and crisis communication*, including how both disciplines are embedded in the organization, its processes, structures, and cultures (cf. the epilogue).

RAT is an attempt to confront these points of criticism by applying a multivocal approach to crisis communication. It includes the multiple voices – the many senders and receivers – that start communicating when a crisis occurs. Before we take a look at the development of RAT, we would like to emphasize that the literature on crisis communication has sometimes come *very* close to describing an arena and the multiple voices, but without conceptualizing what the scholars have observed. Here are three examples:

(1) In her study of the *Exxon Valdez* oil spill in 1989, Murphy (1996) describes how this crisis attracts more and more actors: 'In the days following the spill, the crisis attracted ever more actors, each with their own version of the event and its solution: the Coast Guard, the Alyeska consortium, legislators, the media, animal rights activists, environmentalists, consumer groups and so forth. This multiplication of voices and solutions followed a dynamic similar to a chaotic system' (pp. 105–106).

(2) In his study of the crash of ValuJet Flight 592, Fishman (1999) first describes the dynamics of a crisis situation: '[A] crisis communication situation involves a dynamic or multi-dimensional set of relationships within a rapidly-changing environment' (p. 348). He then continues to describe how a type two focusing event (cf. Birkland's (1997) distinction) creates an arena: 'By contrast, a Type Two focusing event [a 'new' event] is neither routine nor pre-planned, and it opens a symbolic arena where various groups struggle about the interpretation and construction of social reality' (p. 354).

(3) However, the two scholars who come closest to grasping the complexity of crises and crisis communication are Hearit and Courtright (2003). They conclude their study of the Audi 5000 crisis in the 1980s by warning crisis communication researchers against reducing crisis communication to a 'unitary rhetorical event, focused only on one organization's response', and by reminding us of the fact that the 'discursive activities of multiple actors also must be taken into account' (p. 92). This is perhaps one of the most important statements ever made by a researcher within the field of crisis communication.

Whereas Murphy (1996) and Fishman (1999) focus on the multiplication of voices, and how these voices struggle over the interpretation of social reality, Hearit and Courtright (2003) criticize the organization-centrism that so far has characterized much crisis communication research.

RHETORICAL ARENA THEORY: DEVELOPING A MULTIVOCAL APPROACH

RAT takes as its starting point a very simple observation that anyone can make when a crisis occurs: that many actors (in our terminology, voices) start communicating in various ways. The list below contains some of the actors who most frequently are involved in an organizational crisis:

- The news media that cover and/or intervene in the crisis, making it accelerate with their revelations and breaking news.
- Consumers and citizens who express their attitudes or exchange opinions about the crisis on their social network, including social media such as Facebook and Twitter.
- PR experts who are asked by the news media to comment on the crisis, its causes, and consequences, including the crisis management efforts of the organization in crisis.
- Politicians who try to connect their political agenda to the crisis, for example by demanding more regulation within the policy area.
- Trade associations that protect the reputation of their industry.
- The employees working for the organization in crisis who are angry or frustrated and who are searching for information about what has happened.
- The management of the organization in crisis who tries to handle the crisis.

The aim of RAT is to study the *communicative complexity* that characterizes organizational crises, even the smallest of them, and to identify, describe, and explain patterns within the multiple communication processes taking place inside the arena. Who or what triggers these processes? Who or what keeps them going? Which constellations of actors and interactions are typical? What are the implications for practice?

What rhetorical arena theory is not

RAT is not a theory in the restricted sense of the word: 'a logically connected set of abstract statements from which empirically testable hypotheses and explanations can be derived' (Craig, 2013). It is more like a '"framework", a set of ideas from which a number of theories can be derived' (Parmar et al., 2010) – in our case, theories of specific aspects of multivocality. The remaining four chapters in this part are based on such theories.

RAT is not a new version of the public sphere theory as established by Jürgen Habermas (the deliberative model) or Niklas Luhmann (the mirror model). The multiple voices communicating in a crisis situation are not only located in the public sphere, but also appear in semi-public and private spaces. However, this does not mean that the public sphere does not play an important role in how a crisis develops over time.

RAT is neither a new version of the stakeholder theory as established by Freeman (1984) and many others (for an overview of stakeholder theories, see Friedman & Miles, 2006). We define stakeholder management as a specific organizational *gaze* cast by an organization on its external and internal environment (i.e., the stakeholders). It is very evident, for example, that Mitchell, Agle and Wood's (1997) model of stakeholder salience is a perception model. Some readers will probably ask: 'Do all the voices in the arena not automatically become stakeholders just because they are voices?' No, voices involved in third-party interventions – actors driven by other agendas, such as politicians or interest groups – only have a stake in the crisis *as such*, and not necessarily in the organization in crisis.

That RAT is not a new version of stakeholder theory does not mean, however, that stakeholders do not play an important role. But the stakeholder maps elaborated by private and public organizations as a management tool must from now on be viewed as part of a specific perspective on the arena allowing them to see some things – and to overlook others. One of the key insights of complexity theory is that none of the involved actors will be able to view the complex systems overall.

What rhetorical arena theory is

RAT is a set of ideas about the social space that opens up when a crisis breaks out – a social space located across our traditional distinctions between public and private, and between stakeholders and non-stakeholders. An arena is not a permanent space that will always be 'out there', including before and after a crisis. An arena, however, may open up or close down a long time before or after the so-called 'crisis event' (cf. Chapter 2).

The theory is based on two metaphors, *arena* and *voice*, which have been used for theory-building purposes (on metaphors and theory building, see Cornelissen and Kafouros, 2008).

The first metaphor highlights how the actors involved in a crisis struggle with each other regarding interpretation of not only the crisis itself, but also the handling of it. From such an agonistic perspective, dialogue and consensus are an exception, not the rule. According to Merriam-Webster's online dictionary, an arena is: (1) an area in a Roman amphitheater for gladiatorial combat; (2) an enclosed area used for public entertainment; a building containing an arena; (3) *a*: a sphere of interest, activity, or competition <the political *arena*>; *b*: a place or situation for controversy <in the public *arena*>. Thus, the word *arena* has a semantic structure including the following meanings: a physical or symbolic place or space; an exchange (struggle, competition, conflict, or debate) between two or more actors; and audiences that are watching the exchange.

The second metaphor highlights that there are many senders and receivers in the arena communicating to, with, around, or against each other. In our understanding of the concept of voice, there is a focus on the complexity of crisis situations, and not on power and suppression as is often the case in organizational communication (cf. Box 8.1).

BOX 8.1

AN APPROACH TO VOICES – POWER OR COMPLEXITY?

The research on voices is far more comprehensive than the research on arenas within the field of communication studies. In two chapters – 'Metaphors of communication and organization' (1996) and 'Revisiting metaphors of communication and organization' (2006) – published in two different editions of the *Handbook of Organization Studies*, Linda Putnam and her colleagues

(Continued)

(Continued)

examined seven metaphor clusters that represent alternative ways of looking at organization and communication and their relationship. Voice is one of these metaphor clusters, including subcategories.

According to these two chapters, voice researchers share an interest in 'the practices and structures that effect who can speak, when, and in what way' (Putnam et al., 1996, p. 389). They also understand communication as 'the expression or suppression of voice in organizational life' (Putnam & Boys, 2006, p. 556) and organization as a '*chorus* of member voices. But not all members have an equal voice and not all members of the chorus sing the same tune' (Putnam et al., 1996, p. 389). In the most recent chapter, the authors claim that voice has become a submetaphor within the broader category of discourse.

We define this approach to the study of voices as a *power approach*, focusing on the relationship between power and communication. We define our own approach as a *complexity approach*, focusing on the patterns produced by the interactions between multiple senders and receivers. However, this does not mean that the power issue is irrelevant to RAT.

Further reading: Putnam et al. (1996).

SOURCES OF INSPIRATION

RAT is inspired by three broad streams of research: (1) complexity theory, (2) arena theory, and (3) communication theory. In this section, we first briefly introduce our social science approach to complexity. Then we present how we understand arena and communication.

A social science approach to complexity

At the beginning of this chapter, we declared that one of our ambitions was to study the *communicative complexity* of organizational crises. Such a declaration makes it natural to bring up the following question: Can we apply already existing theories of complexity, or is it better to formulate a new approach? The thing is, we seem to face a paradox. On the one hand, we have never before used words such as *complex* and *complexity* so frequently. On the other hand, the existing theories of complexity have never really achieved a breakthrough within the field of organizational crisis management and crisis communication.

Complexity science is the study of *complex systems*, where we understand a complex system to be *a whole composed of a large number of parts*. These parts interact in ways that make them cause the system to display emergent patterns (Maguire et al., 2006). Complexity science has origins in many disciplines, including the natural sciences. Some scholars make a distinction between a European school of complexity (e.g., Prigogine and his theory of dissipative structures) and a North American school of complexity (e.g., Mandelbrot and his theory of fractals).

BOX 8.2

CHARACTERISTICS OF COMPLEX SYSTEMS

In his book *Complexity & Postmodernism: Understanding Complex Systems* (1998), South African philosopher Paul Cilliers provides us with a description of the characteristics of complex systems (pp. 3–5):

- Complex systems consists of a large number of elements.
- In order to constitute a complex system, the elements have to interact.
- Interactions are rich, that is, any element in the system influences, and is influenced by, any other.
- Interactions are non-linear.
- Interactions are typically short-range.
- There are positive and negative feedback loops of interactions.
- Complex systems are open systems.
- Complex systems operate under conditions far from equilibrium.
- Complex systems have histories.
- Individual elements are typically ignorant of the behavior of the whole system in which they are embedded.

Further reading: Cilliers (1998).

In the 1990s, complexity science entered the social sciences. The popularization of the so-called 'new science' paved the way for this development (cf. Prigogine & Stengers, 1984; Gleick, 1987; Waldrop, 1992). It began within management and organization studies (cf. the work of Ralph D. Stacey). The growing interest in studying complex systems also spread to the field of crisis management and crisis communication where two groups of researchers set an example.

The first group of researchers is represented by Priscilla J. Murphy and Dawn R. Gilpin (see Murphy, 2000; Gilpin & Murphy, 2006, 2008, 2010). These two researchers introduce a distinction between three different approaches to complexity science: (1) reductionist complexity science, representing a positivist, nomothetic approach; (2) soft complexity science, which is based on a sharp distinction between social ontology and natural ontology; and (3) complexity-based thinking, representing a 'radical epistemological shift that recognizes the contingent nature of all knowledge' (Gilpin & Murphy, 2008, p. 33). Gilpin and Murphy take their starting point in the last of these three approaches, claiming that there exists 'a middle ground between the use of complexity theory strictly as a metaphor and the insistence that it be quantitatively operationalized' (2008, p. 23).

The second group of researchers is represented by Matthew W. Seeger, Timothy L. Sellnow, and Robert R. Ulmer (see Seeger et al., 2003, 2010). This group of researchers combines three theories of organizational crises which are rooted in very different ontologies: (1) Weick's theory of sensemaking; (2) chaos theory (another term for complexity theory); and (3) organizational learning theory. They transfer the concepts of complexity from the natural sciences to the social sciences; that is, they apply these concepts in a metaphorical way: 'Chaos theory is applied as a metaphor for comprehending crisis communication's complexity' (Seeger et al., 2010, p. 493).

Although we sympathize with the agenda of the above-mentioned research groups, we have found it appropriate to define an alternative approach – a social science approach – to the study of the communicative complexity of organizational crises. Here are the basic principles of this alternative approach:

Ontology: the ontology of society (in our case, organizational crises) is different from the ontology of nature. Organizational crises are social constructions, not naturally occurring phenomena.

Epistemology: every type of quantitative and/or qualitative research design and research method can be applied.

Meta-language: the concepts imported from the study of complexity in the natural sciences can only be transferred as metaphors, that is as concepts that we will never be able to develop further as our 'own' concepts. Instead we will always feel obliged to reconfirm these metaphors because they represent what is left of the real thing, the 'new science'.

We find ourselves in a situation that reminds us of the situation in which British disaster sociologist Barry A. Turner found himself in the middle of the 1970s when he wrote *Man-made Disasters* (1978; see also Turner & Pidgeon, 1997). At a time when the literature on disaster management was sparse, he set out to conduct detailed studies of a large number of accident and disaster reports published by the British government between 1965 and 1975. Turner described his approach as 'the qualitative method of "grounded" theory, an approach which is very well suited both to the close, detailed examination of a little explored area and to the use of this examination to *build up a vocabulary, a set of concepts, and ultimately a theory of the novel topics under investigation*' (1997, p. xvii; our italics). Today, the results of this work are well known and have led to the conception of human-made disasters in terms of processes with long incubation periods, to the sequential model of incubation, and to new concepts such as perceptual rigidity, information ambiguity, and disregard of rules and instructions.

Arena theory

We are neither the first nor the only researchers to use the metaphors of arena and voice. We are, if not directly inspired, then at least informed by German PR researchers' redefinition of the public sphere as 'a forum for communication' inside which there exists certain arenas for actors to inform other actors and communicate with each other (cf. Bentele, 2005).

The pioneering publication is Jürgen Gerhard and Friedheim Neidhardt's working paper 'Strukturen und Funktionen der moderner Öffentlichkeit: Fragestellungen und Ansätze' (1990). The aim of this paper is to develop a conceptual framework for the sociological analysis of the public sphere.

Later in the 1990s, German risk sociologist Ortwin Renn developed a theory of political arenas that has some elements in common with RAT. Renn (1992) defined a political arena as the symbolic location of political actions that influence collective decisions or policies. Unlike Peters (1990), who distinguished between several arenas, Renn defined these arenas as *stages* within a single arena. At center stage, the main characters (i.e., the actors who seek influence) perform. Then comes a series of issues amplifiers or professional 'theater critics' and, finally, the audience. In contrast to traditional role theory or use of the theater metaphor, the audience will not watch a play where the actors have predetermined roles. According to Renn, an arena is more like a medieval court where the actors choose their own strategies. The outcome of an arena process will always be 'undetermined'. Actors applying different strategies may very well produce synergetic effects. A strategy may even lead to unwanted results. The interaction in the arena can also result in a change of the rules of the game being played in the arena.

More recently, Luoma-aho and Vos (2010) and Vos et al. (2013) have launched an agenda for research on *issues arenas*. Issues arenas refer to the interaction of stakeholders regarding an issue in the public debate in society. They are dynamic and require ongoing attention. They are like stages.

Communication theory

If we want to study organizational crises in a way that does justice to their complexity, we are forced to take what we have chosen to call the 'third step' in communication research. Over the last 60 years or more, communication has developed from a transmission paradigm where the focus is on the sender, the distribution of information, and the intended effect, to an interaction paradigm where the focus is on the receiver, the interpretation of messages, and the creation of meaning (Heath & Bryant, 1992). The same development can be seen within crisis communication research in the shift from a rhetorical or text-oriented approach to a strategic or context-oriented approach. Where image repair theory seems to have the sender as its hub (the verbal defense strategies of the organization), situational crisis communication theory is more aware of the receiver (attribution of crisis responsibility made by the stakeholders).

In our understanding of the shift from transmission to interaction, and from interaction to complexity, we are inspired by Luhmann's theory of social systems, including his understanding of communication (Luhmann, 1995). Luhmann defines communication as the 'processing of selection', a triple selection of information, utterance, and understanding:

This reflection also reveals why communication is never an event with two points of selection – neither as a giving and receiving (as in the metaphor of transmission), nor as the difference between information and utterance. Communication emerges only if this last difference is observed, expected, understood, and used as the basis for connecting with further behaviors. (1995, p. 141)

We define crisis communication as follows. Crisis communication is a complex and dynamic configuration of communicative processes which develop before, during, and after an event or a situation that is interpreted as a crisis by an organization and/or by other voices in the arena. Crisis communication also includes how various actors, contexts, and discourses (manifested in specific genres and specific texts) relate to each other.

THE ARENA MODEL

In continuation of our definition of crisis communication we have established an arena model that will serve as a set of analytical and practical guidelines. This model approaches crisis communication from two different but integrated perspectives: (1) from a *macro perspective*, that is the rhetorical arena as such, focusing on all the voices and all the communicative processes that take place in the arena during a specific organizational crisis; and (2) from a *micro perspective*, that is as part of the arena, focusing on the individual communicative processes. While the macro perspective provides us with an analytical and practical overview of the patterns of interaction between voices, the micro perspective shows us what characterizes each individual process in terms of context, media, genre, and text.

The macro component: patterns of interaction

When a crisis occurs, a rhetorical arena opens, in which multiple voices communicate. The communicative processes begin immediately or seriatim as the various voices enter or are forced into the arena. Each time a communicative process can be considered an intervention in or a contribution to the crisis, it becomes part of the arena (see Figure 8.1).

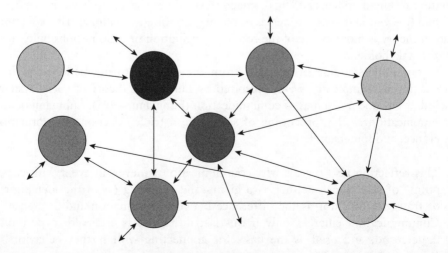

Figure 8.1   The arena model (1): macro component

The voices communicate in various ways. Some voices communicate *to* each other, other voices communicate *with* each other. Some voices communicate *against* each other or *past* each other, and, finally, there are voices that just communicate *about* each other. Dialogue or two-way symmetrical crisis communication – a key term in excellent crisis PR (cf. Fearn-Banks, 2001; Marra, 2004) – is just one possibility, and by no means the most frequent one, within this multitude of communication processes.

The relationships between the many voices in the arena are seldom based on equality. Often there are important differences in economic, political, and symbolic capital as well as in the distribution of power and access to the media. Likewise, there are important differences regarding how strategically well placed each individual actor is positioned both in regard to the public sphere (parliament, media, etc.) and in various semi-public networks (committees, think tanks, etc.).

Some examples

By patterns of interaction, we understand communicative processes that are combined with each other in ways that are so typical they even have their own name. Here are some examples:

- A verbal attack followed by a verbal defense (cf. Benoit's image repair theory and his theory of persuasive attacks) is considered one of the smallest patterns of interaction in the rhetorical arena.
- Third-party image repair is a complex version (in space) of the attack/defense scheme.
- A blame game is a dynamic version (in time) of the attack/defense scheme.
- This is also the case with the serial apology.
- The pattern of a multi-crisis is characterized by the involvement of many organizations in the same crisis.

The micro component: parameters of mediation

The micro component of the arena model consists of three elements (crisis communication, sender, and receiver) and four parameters (context, media, genre, and text) (see Figure 8.2).

The first and most important element is crisis communication. Since we have already defined what we mean by crisis communication (see above), we will confine ourselves to adding a few extra comments concerning communication as such. We understand communication as both a product (messages) and a process, in which and by which senders and receivers attempt to create meaning for themselves and for others in specific contexts. Thus, communication will always be contextualized. In addition, we apply a semiotic perspective: not only the spoken and written word, but also visuals, actions, and artifacts, may serve as resources when people communicate.

The next two elements of the model are senders and receivers. They do not just include the voice of the organization in crisis. Many other types of actors act as senders and receivers in the arena. All these voices are equipped with certain

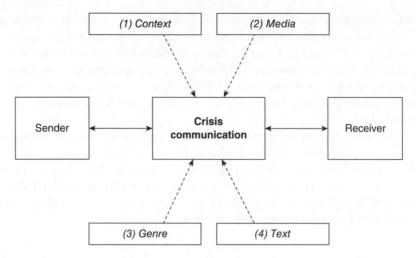

Figure 8.2   The arena model (2): micro component

'basic competencies'. They are, for example, able to make interpretations (including misinterpretations) of what is happening in the world in which they live, work, and experience crises. They are also able to act strategically, to follow a goal for a certain period of time.

Each communicative process is mediated by four parameters: *context, media, genre,* and *text.* The word *mediated* refers to the fact that the communicative processes in the arena are determined by specific choices made by the voices in relation to these four parameters. These choices influence the production and reception of crisis communication among the actors involved.

Context

The first and most complex parameter of mediation is the *context*. It consists of a specific set of internal or psychological and external or sociological contexts that 'filters' each individual communicative process.

By psychological contexts, we refer to the more or less fixed *cognitive schemes* that influence how people perceive and interpret various types of crises, including the causes and consequences of these crises. As Heath and Coombs (2006) state, 'A crisis type is the frame used to interpret the crisis' (pp. 203–204). The concept of psychological context is related to Weick's (1988) concept of enacted environment.

By sociological contexts, we refer to three types of contexts: (1) the *national–cultural* context, (2) the *organizational* context, and (3) the *situational* context. These three types are so closely embedded in each other that it can be difficult to distinguish between them.

The importance of the national–cultural context is evident when we are dealing with global crises and intercultural or multicultural publics. Social structures (political, legal, economic structures, the media system, etc.) and social norms (e.g., how to make the right apology, how to behave toward victims, etc.) may differ considerably. So how can expectations from voices with a different national–cultural background be met? (See Chapter 7.)

The organizational context also plays an important role in crisis communication. In the previous chapter we looked at differences between organizational cultures, for instance between having an open or a closed communication culture in a crisis situation. The formal status of the organization also has an impact on how crisis communication is or must be practised, as follows.

Private organization:

- If the company is publicly listed, it must observe certain rules regarding when to release negative or positive news.
- In a company it is possible to speak with 'one voice' by selecting one or two spokespersons who are allowed to speak on behalf of the company, and to tell employees to follow the CMP. If they do not do this, they risk not being part of the company in the future.

Public organization:

- If the organization is a hospital, it has to observe rules of privacy and discretion in relation to staff and patients.
- In a university or a municipality, it is more difficult to ask people to speak with 'one voice'. In the case of a university, professors are considered experts and are expected to inform citizens about their knowledge. The internal voices of a public organization often form a 'choir' where different tunes are sung – at the same time.

Finally, it can be important to take into consideration the organizational context of the *other* voices in the arena. Journalists have specific working norms and success criteria for their work. They are sometimes considered aggressive and rude. It is not uncommon to see a wrongdoer getting angry at journalists. However, if an organization understands the motives behind a certain behavior, it is easier to handle critical situations.

The third type of context is the situational context, including sender, receiver, time, place, and message. A crisis breaks out and develops at a certain point in time. The situation is fluid, but every time a communication process takes place inside the arena, it is important to know what the situation is at that specific point in time. Who is communicating to whom? What kind of alliances or conflicts do the different voices have? How is the crisis interpreted? Who are the negative voices and who are the positive ones? Will there be any third parties?

An important aspect of the situational context is timing. When will it be opportune to communicate? What kind of *crisis timing strategy* should be used? Will it be wise, in the case of a preventable crisis, to be proactive and to 'steal thunder', that is, to self-disclose a crisis before the crisis is discovered by the media or other voices, in order to reduce the risk of reputational damage? Claeys and Cauberghe (2012) demonstrated that organizations applying such a strategy are perceived to be more credible, and that 'stealing thunder' has the same impact on organizational credibility as the use of a crisis response strategy.

As we saw in Chapter 6, Cameron and his colleagues have established a framework with no less than 87 contingency factors. The context is indeed the most complex of the four parameters. In a crisis situation, it is important to identify the aspects of these three types of contexts that will most likely influence the crisis management and crisis communication activities of the actors involved.

Media

The second parameter is the *media*. By media we refer to a specific aspect of the communicative process: the 'carriers' of crisis messages. The spoken and written word, even the human body, are defined as media in this context. So are print media, electronic media, online media, social media, cell (mobile) phones, corporate media, etc. Thus, by media we do not refer to specific voices such as the voices of media organizations (cf. Chapter 10).

When communicating in a crisis situation, the choice of media type can have considerable influence on how, where, when, and why a crisis message is produced and/or received by the voices inside a rhetorical arena. Each media type displays certain communicative characteristics (e.g., its capability to create attention or its degree of interactivity), is linked to a specific set of attitude variables (e.g., credibility), and is used in specific situations in order to satisfy needs and demands (e.g., the willingness to share a message from specific media – named secondary crisis communication, cf. Schultz et al., 2011).

Austin et al. (2012) discovered that it is important to match information form (legacy media, social media, offline word-of-mouth communication) and source (organization, journalists, or user-generating content on social media). If the initial information about a crisis comes from voices on social media, people are likely to search for more information in other media (cf. Chapter 9).

Pang et al. (2014) examined the crossovers between social media and legacy media. The pervasiveness of social media has made the 'old' media change their ways of operating. It is no longer possible for them to ignore content originating from social media. A crisis may break out online, but when it gains traction it will typically shift to legacy media – though this is not always the case. This crossover depends on the newsworthiness of the crisis and the values of the journalists covering the story, such as the need to verify information from multiple sources. However, if the social media stories do hit the 'old' media, they gain credibility because they have been under the scrutiny of a journalist.

Schultz et al. (2011) studied the differences between the use of Twitter, blogs, and legacy media, and found, among other things, that people produce more secondary crisis communication when the story has crossed over into legacy media; that is, they talk more about newspaper articles than about blogs or Twitter news, despite the viral character normally attributed to social media. There is definitely a channel effect.

Finally, the media format also guides the crisis communication. It makes a difference if an organization only has two minutes during a TV news program to get its message through, or five sentences in a consumer program on TV, where the anchor makes use of special effects so that we know who are the good guys and who are the bad guys. It also makes a difference if an organization only have 140 characters on Twitter, an update on Facebook, or the possibility to make a full speech on a corporate website. The crisis communication message must adapt to the media format.

Genre

The third parameter is *genre*. Inspired by Swales (1990) we define genre as 'a recognizable communicative event characterized by a set of communicative purpose(s) identified and mutually understood by the members of the discourse community(s) in which it regularly occurs' (p. 58). A genre is a group or 'family' of texts that, besides sharing the same communicative purpose, also display common characteristics regarding message strategies. The existence of such a group or 'family' of texts is based on a process of institutionalization *in* communication.

Genre plays a defining role within the rhetorical or text-oriented tradition in crisis communication research (cf. the apologia tradition). However, surprisingly, the many text genres in use in a rhetorical arena are seldom subjected to study: namely, press releases or press conferences, published or organized by the organization in crisis, letters to customers or investors, news articles, editorials or cartoons, text messages on cell phones, tweets, blogs, updates on Facebook, YouTube videos, etc. To these genres, which all belong to the external crisis communication, we can add the genres used by organizations in their internal crisis communication: internal newsletters, dialogue meetings, emails, video letters, video conferences, updates on internal social media, etc..

One of the most popular genres in crisis communication is the press release (Frandsen & Johansen, 2004). The press release is written in a such a way that it can be absorbed by journalists when they transform the information into a news article. In order to live up to this, press releases usually apply so-called pre-formulation strategies (cf. Chapter 10). These strategies can also be examined as an instance of terminological control (cf. Chapter 5).

The press conference is a face-to-face event where actors representing the organization in crisis meet journalists representing the press. It is one of the most important genres at the onset of a crisis, and it often gives the first impression of the credibility of the organization in crisis. Statements are read, information and explanations aired, and the representatives answer questions from the journalists.

 Case example 8.1

Tiger Woods' apology

Press conferences are typically well prepared in an attempt to control audience perceptions. When American golfer Tiger Woods decided to hold a press conference on February 19, 2010, at Ponte Vedra Beach in Florida, to apologize for cheating on his wife, he decided himself how it was going to take place. According to the media, he handpicked 40 people

(Continued)

(Continued)

to be in the room, including a few journalists who were not allowed to ask questions. All the other journalists had to watch the event from a hotel half a mile away. His apology lasted more than 13 minutes and was staged in every aspect:

> Good morning, and thank you for joining me. Many of you in this room are my friends. Many of you have cheered for me or you've worked with me or you've supported me. Now, every one of you has good reason to be critical of me. I want to say to each of you, simply and directly, I am deeply sorry for my irresponsible and selfish behavior I engaged in ...
>
> I am also aware of the pain my behavior has caused to those of you in this room. I have let you down, and I have let down my fans ...
>
> I was wrong. I was foolish. I don't get to play by different rules. The same boundaries that apply to everyone apply to me. I brought this shame on myself. I hurt my wife, my kids, my mother, my wife's family, my friends, my foundation and kids all around the world who admired me. I've had a lot of time to think about what I've done. My failures have made me look at myself in a way I never wanted to before. It's now up to me to make amends and that starts by never repeating the mistakes I've made. It's up to me to start living a life of integrity ... Finally, there are many people in this room, and there are many people at home who believed in me. Today, I want to ask for your help. I ask you to find room in your heart to one day believe in me again. Thank you.

Sources: Newspaper articles, including video of his speech (February, 2010).

Text

The last parameter is *text*. Sometimes referred to as message, text can be defined as the product of a communication process. Text is a result of the sender's choice between and use of semiotic resources such as words, pictures, artifacts, and actions, also referred to as message strategies. However, a text first becomes a 'real' text when it has been communicated in a specific situation and interpreted by receivers (cf. this chapter). Terminological control theory is in fact a theory about text (cf. Chapter 5).

The crisis response strategies identified by Benoit (2015) and Coombs (2015) represent an important aspect of the crisis communication produced by organizations in crisis. However, they are applied as broad communicative functions that rarely are subjected to more detailed analysis. A denial, for example, can be expressed in various ways. It can be done in a very direct and explicit way: 'No, we have not done what you accuse us of!'; or more indirectly or implicitly: 'No comments!' In addition, a denial can be combined with other crisis response strategies in various ways, generating *tactical coherence* (Ihlen, 2002).

As we saw in Tiger Woods' press conference, an apology can be staged in various ways. In this case, Woods clearly used not just the spoken word in a specific way, but his statements were followed by a very orchestrated use of body language as well, and he ended his speech by embracing his mother before he left the room. It can all be considered part of his attempt to convince people about the sincerity of his apology.

In 1990, when a rumor spread in Denmark that using Proctor & Gamble's Wash & Go shampoo would lead to hair loss (Møller Jensen & Koed Madsen, 1992), a marketing director representing the American multinational corporation was sent to Copenhagen to get his hair washed with the new shampoo. This staged event took place on Danish public service television. This is not just an interesting case of ostensive communication where words, pictures, behaviour, and an artifact (the shampoo) are combined. It is also a specific crisis response strategy (a denial) in the shape of a ritual act which can be studied from an anthropological perspective: that is, an impure object (a product that may be defective) is made pure again as the representative of the corporation gets his hair washed in front of the Danish television audience (cf. Douglas's (1966) analysis of purity and danger; see also Chapter 10).

We have seen other examples of this use of artifacts in crisis communication. During the Coca-Cola crisis in Belgium in 1999 (see Chapter 7), the American CEO flew in from Atlanta, went on Belgian television, opened a can of Coca-Cola, drank from it, and declared that there was nothing wrong with the product. In relation to water supply pollution, we have also seen representatives from water utility and treatment companies drink their own product on television to convince people that there is nothing wrong with the water.

CASE STUDY 8.1

VOLKSWAGEN AND THE DIESELGATE SCANDAL

Volkswagen Group is a German automobile manufacturer headquartered in Wolfsburg, Germany. Founded in 1937, it sells automobiles under the Bentley, Bugatti, Lamborghini, Audi, SEAT, Skoda, and VW brands and commercial vehicles under the MAN, Scania, Neoplan, and VW brands. It is the largest car maker in Europe. The group does not have an official mission statement, but defines the company's goal as follows: 'The Group's goal is to offer attractive, safe and environmentally sound vehicles which can compete in an increasingly tough market and set world standards in their respective class' (Volkswagen.com, 2015). In 2015, the Reputation Institute listed VW second after BMW in its list of top German companies. The slogan of the Volkswagen Group is: Das Auto.

Dieselgate

On September 18, 2015, the US Environmental Protection Agency (EPA) issued a Notice of Violation of the Clean Air Act to Volkswagen Group alleging that approximately 480,000 VW and Audi automobiles equipped with two litre TDI engines sold in the United States between 2009 and 2015 had an emission-compliance 'defeat device' installed. According to the EPA, VW had intentionally programmed the cars so that US nitrogen oxide emissions standards were met only during laboratory emissions testing. Emissions during driving were up to 40 times higher.

(Continued)

(Continued)

The news media

The EPA's announcement quickly created a media storm (see Chapter 10). The first international headlines read as follows: 'VW is said to cheat on diesel emissions; U.S. to order big recall' (*New York Times*, September 18, 2015); 'Volkswagen under investigation over illegal software that masks emissions' (*Guardian*, September 20, 2015); 'EPA accuses VW of cheating on emission rules' (*CNN Money*, September 22, 2015). In Germany, the tabloid *Bild* claimed that the top management of VW had been aware of the existence of the illegal software as early as 2007. *Der Spiegel* followed *Bild*, claiming that some people knew about the manipulation as early as 2005 or 2006. However, as the scandal started escalating, there was one voice speaking in favor of VW. Renowned German business analyst Dirk Müller claimed that the media exaggerated the VW case – destroying VW's reputation as well as the 'Made in Germany' label. Some media such as the Clean Technica sustainable website responded to the crisis in a very provocative way: 'Hitler responds to the Volkswagen scandal' (video).

Investors

On September 21, the first business day after the breaking news, VW's stock price declined by 20 percent. The following day, the stock price declined another 17 percent.

Consumers and citizens

The reactions among consumers and citizens in and outside Germany were not only negative. According to a poll conducted for *Bild*, the majority of Germans (55 percent) still had 'great faith' in VW, with over three-quarters believing that other automobile manufacturers were equally guilty in manipulation.

The car industry

The Dieselgate scandal raised awareness about the higher levels of pollution being emitted by all vehicles built by a wide range of car makers. Companies, including Toyota, GM, Daimler-Benz, and Honda, issued press statements reaffirming their vehicles' compliance with all regulations and legislation for the markets in which they operate. The Society of Motor Manufacturers and Traders described the issue as affecting 'just one company', with no evidence that the whole industry might be involved.

The scandal also initiated a debate about the advantages and disadvantages of software-controlled machinery. A study conducted by ADAC and the International Council on Clean Transportation revealed the biggest deviations (real-world driving conditions vs. laboratory conditions) in vehicles from Volvo, Renault, Jeep, Hyundai, Citroën, and Fiat.

German politicians

At the end of October, German Chancellor Angela Merkel stated in one of her weekly podcasts that she did not believe the reputation of the 'Made in Germany' logo had been damaged by the Dieselgate scandal, but she warned against 'taking it lightly'. She also expressed confidence in the Volkswagen Group's response: 'I believe that VW is working on this with all of its powers'.

Volkswagen's crisis management and crisis communication

There were early warnings. In 2013, for example, the European Commission's Joint Research Centre Institute for Energy and Transport warned: 'Sensors and electronic components in modern light-duty vehicles are capable of "detecting" the start of an emissions test in the laboratory.'

On September 20, VW admitted deception and issued a public apology. Volkswagen Group CEO Martin Winterkorn declared: 'The Board of Management at Volkswagen AG takes these findings very seriously. I personally am deeply sorry that we have broken the trust of our customers and the public. We will cooperate fully with the responsible agencies … We do not and will not tolerate violations of any kind of our internal rules or of the law' (www.volkswagen-media-service.com). Three days later, on September 23, he resigned.

On September 29, Volkswagen Group of America CEO Michael Horn wrote a letter to customers: 'I am writing you today to offer a personal and profound apology. Volkswagen has violated your trust. I understand and fully appreciate your anger and frustration. I would like you to know that we take full responsibility and are cooperating with all responsible agencies.' On the same day, Volkswagen Group announced a plan to refit up to 11 million cars affected by the emissions-violation scandal.

Studying the rhetorical arena

(1) Macro component:

- List all the voices in the rhetorical arena that opens in September 2015 when the Dieselgate scandal breaks out, and then answer the following questions:

    o How do the voices communicate with each other? Do they communicate *to*, *with*, *against*, or *past* each other? Do the voices form sub-arenas?
    o What type of crisis are we dealing with? A product recall, a scandal, or a smoldering multi-crisis (see Chapter 2)?

(2) Micro component:

- Select a small sample of communication processes, for example the two press statements or letters from the two CEOs Martin Winterkorn and Michael Horn, and answer the following questions:

    o Describe the two messages using the four parameters: context, media, genre, and text.
    o Which crisis response strategies do Winterkorn and Horn apply?

Managing the rhetorical arena

- How would you manage the Dieselgate scandal if you were working as a crisis manager for Volkswagen Group?
- How would you manage the crisis if you were working as a crisis manager for the Society of Motor Manufacturers and Traders (trade association)?

Sources: Volkswagen Group website, newspaper articles.

CHAPTER SUMMARY

This chapter introduced a new theoretical framework: rhetorical arena theory and the multivocal approach to crisis communication. This framework focuses on the multiple voices that start communicating when a crisis occurs. The new approach is inspired by social science research in complexity, arenas, and communication. We redefined crisis communication, and the macro and micro components of the arena model were described. Crisis communication can no longer be reduced to a communication produced by the organization in crisis. We have to take into account all the other voices in the rhetorical arena. The next four chapters are devoted to *some* of these voices: consumers and citizens (Chapter 9), the news media (Chapter 10), trade associations (Chapter 11), and managers and employees (Chapter 12).

Further reading

Coombs, W. T., & Holladay, S. J. (2015). Digital naturals and crisis communication: Significant shifts of focus. In W. T. Coombs, J. Falkheimer, M. Heide, & P. Young (Eds.), *Strategic Communication, Social Media and Digital Naturals* (pp. 54–62). London: Routledge.

Frandsen, F., & Johansen, W. (2010). Crisis communication, complexity, and the Cartoon Affair: A case study. In W. T. Coombs & Holladay, S. J. (Eds.), *The Handbook of Crisis Communication* (pp. 425–448). Malden, MA: Wiley-Blackwell.

CONSUMERS AND CITIZENS: EMOTIONS AND SOCIAL MEDIA

9

CHAPTER OVERVIEW

This chapter explores the multiple voices of consumers and citizens and how they have been empowered by the Internet and social media. Today, consumers and citizens are more demanding than ever, and they can provoke a (para)crisis within hours. First, the chapter describes the socio-economic and technological transformations in society that have made this development possible. Then the concepts of social approval and the emotional stakeholder are introduced. The chapter draws together the threads in the last section on emotions, social media, and crisis communication.

INTRODUCTION

Where shall we begin? Which voice in the rhetorical arena is the most important during a crisis? If we put this question to the CEO of a private company, or to the mayor and the city council members in a municipality, they would probably answer 'Our customers' voice', or 'Our fellow citizens' voice'. Each year, private companies as well as municipalities invest large amounts of money, time, attention, and activities in their customers and citizens. Customers make it possible for companies to sell their products and to build up strong corporate brands. Citizens make it possible for local politicians to be elected and to create a favorable reputation in the public sector. Consumers and citizens provide both private and public organizations with legitimacy.

The aim of this chapter is to describe how the multiple voices of consumers and citizens have developed since the rise of the Internet and social media, and how this development has turned them into powerful actors in the rhetorical arena. We demonstrate that consumers and citizens interact and communicate not only with the organization in crisis, but also among one another. We also demonstrate that emotions – another area that has been neglected by many crisis communication researchers until recently – play a key role in turning stakeholders into supporters or enemies, sometimes called faith-holders or hate-holders. Finally, we introduce the new research on social media and crisis communication.

CONSUMERS AS CITIZENS/CITIZENS AS CONSUMERS?

Consumers and citizens are not what they used to be. It is possible to identify a series of transformations that have turned the mass consumers of the past into today's individualistic and claims-oriented actors who are more than willing to air their dissatisfaction and criticism on Facebook or Twitter and thereby start an online fire-storm or shitstorm.

First of all, the classical spheres of the liberal model of society seem to have conflated. In the liberal model of society, the private sphere was clearly separated from the public sphere, exactly as economics was clearly separated from politics. In the risk society, these spheres are blending (Table 9.1). Consumers behave more and more like citizens – but within the realm of the market. Citizens behave more and more like consumers – but within the realm of civil society and the state. In the private sector, consumerism – defined as the movement for the protection of consumers against, for example, dangerous products, misleading advertising, and unfair pricing – emerged in the 1960s. The political, ethical, or green consumer was born in the 1990s, at the same time as ecology and animal welfare became issues high on the political agenda. Consumers require companies to show corpo-rate citizenship and social responsibility. In the public sector, a new claims culture has emerged among citizens. The obedient citizen has been replaced by the con-sumerist citizen, one who follows a market logic asking for more choice regarding public services.

How can we explain this double process that turns consumers into 'citizens' and citizens into 'consumers'? It is all about a shift in rationale. In the private sector, companies have added a new vocabulary to the one already in use, redefining

Table 9.1 Drivers for the consumer–citizen and citizen–consumer

The development 1980-2015	Economics and ethics: separated The liberal society	Drivers
		(1) New understanding of risk
		(2) New ethical awareness
		(3) Claims culture
	The risk society Economics and ethics: conflated	(4) Empowerment through the Internet and social media

themselves as corporate citizens who focus on CSR, sustainability, and the triple bottom line. Similarly, in the public sector, organizations such as municipalities and universities have been subjected to what researchers label *company-ization* (Brunsson, 1994) or *corporatization* (Steck, 2003; Grossi & Reichard, 2008). The New Public Management wave that started in the 1990s and which made public organizations adopt the management and marketing understanding of large corporations can be seen as a step in the same direction.

Another important aspect is the new communication power balance. Today, most consumers and citizens have access to very powerful media; that is, they live in a network society, they are empowered by the Internet and social media, and they can express their dissatisfaction with the products and services delivered by private and public organizations wherever and whenever they want. There are no spatio-temporal barriers. There are no gatekeepers. Thereby, consumers and citizens become much more visible than before. However, this also applies to the crisis management activities of those organizations that are defending themselves against the attacks of angry consumers or citizens.

Coombs and Holladay (2012a) introduced the concept of paracrisis, which highlights that social media are used to pick up on crisis warning signs that 'mimic a crisis' when people air an online criticism toward an organization. And because the criticism is triggered online it is expected to be handled online. This means that the handling of the criticism is visible to all of the stakeholders of an organization. Before social media, crisis prevention activities were mostly hidden from public scrutiny, and handled internally.

A final important aspect is that consumers and citizens increasingly turn into activists, empowered by the Internet and social media as a global platform. In some cases, a single update followed by a few likes on Facebook morphs into a complete movement against a particular company or industry. In other cases, the activists themselves become an organization, and this newly formed organization itself then risks being hit by a crisis. In other words, consumers and citizens are able to campaign, whether or not they are formally supported by an activist or interest organization. However, research has demonstrated that citizens readily support a cause on the Internet without really committing themselves to the cause – a phenomenon sometimes called *slacktivism* (see Table 9.2).

Apart from these campaigns we have recently experienced newer and more sophisticated examples of what some scholars call *hijacking*. It is no longer about hijacking the product of a company (Wipperfürth, 2005), as in the case of the Norwegian company Helly Hansen, which had one of its high-quality jackets for sailors adopted by French street rappers in 1997 (Cova & Cova, 2001). Nor is it about the hijacking of the social media site of an organization, as in the case of the hijacking of Kraft's Facebook page by a blogger-activist in 2013 (Veil et al., 2014). It is about hostage taking or hijacking organizations in a conflict between an NGO and another organization (see Case example 9.1 on Greenpeace, LEGO, and Shell). Even though an organization is considered a victim of a hijacking or hostage-taking campaign, such crises can lead to reputational damage – for instance, if the cause gains support from citizens and consumers all over the world, as in the case of LEGO.

Table 9.2 Activist campaigning facilitated through social media

Art of action	Central features
Hijacking	To take over something (by force) and use it for a purpose that is different than originally intended
Brand hijacking	The consumers' act of commandeering a brand from the marketing professionals and driving its evolution (Wipperfürth, 2005) Serendipitous hijack: The act of consumers seizing control of a brand's ideology, use, and persona. It is most often practised by brand fanatics within subcultures, and is largely unanticipated by - and independent of - the brand's marketing department (ibid.)
Social media hijacking	Organized activists take over a corporation's social media page. A virtual 'sit-in' on an organization's social media site (Veil et al., 2014)
Hostage taking	The act of seizing or holding a person as security for the fulfillment of a condition
Brand hostage taking	Holding one brand hostage to target another brand Organized activists using the inter-organizational relations of corporations to fulfill their goal (Frandsen & Johansen, 2015a)
Slacktivism	A combination of slacker and activism used in connection with online activism Refers to the ease of retweeting, liking, or commenting on activist messages without truly being committed to the cause (Veil et al., 2014) The willingness to perform a relatively costless, token display of support for a social cause, with an accompanying lack of willingness to devote significant effort to enact meaningful change. (Kristofferson et al., 2014). Also named clicktivism

 ———— Case example 9.1 ————————————————

Citizens, activists, and hostage crisis

With the Internet, a potential political activist has been born, who on a permanent basis represents a threat to private or public organizations (Couldry, 2012, p. 128) When citizens and consumers care for a cause, some of them press the 'like' button and share the likes on social media, while others enter social movements or professional activist groups. In this way citizens get a more professional approach to critical actions and, not least, more resources.

Members of Greenpeace form an illustrative example of this. For many years, Greenpeace has conducted campaigns directed at specific companies in order to make these companies change behavior when it suited its cause. Social media have made it even easier to activate a large number of people - also non-members - for such causes. Lately, however, companies too, who are not themselves involved in activities damaging to the causes, have come into the line of fire. A matter of network communication thinking goes as follows: if we cannot get to the enemy itself, we can go behind the lines of the enemy, using one organization to target another. In the last three or four years we have seen several creative examples of this. Some call this kind of campaigning *hostage taking* or *hijacking*.

The 'Everything is NOT awesome' campaign of Greenpeace from 2014 is an example of such a campaign. It was created and triggered by Greenpeace to make Shell stop its plans for oil drilling activities in the Arctic, but supported by consumers and citizens from all over the world in a short amount of time.

On July 1, 2014, Greenpeace launched a campaign including a viral video, inspired by the animation film *The LEGO Movie*, asking people to 'tell LEGO to end its partnership with Shell' and to sign a petition. Greenpeace used LEGO to target Shell. Although Shell was the one being criticized, LEGO now faced a potential crisis. The first reaction from LEGO was to issue a press release on the launch date of the Greenpeace campaign, July 1, 2014:

> The Greenpeace campaign focuses on how Shell operates in a specific part of the world. We firmly believe that this matter must be handled between Shell and Greenpeace. We are saddened when the LEGO brand is used as a tool in any dispute between organizations. I would like to clarify that we intend to live up to our long-term contract with Shell, which we entered in 2011.

However, during the months of July to September more than 6.5 million views were recorded on YouTube, more than 1 million had signed the petition, and critical comments poured in through social media. This led to LEGO to issue a second press release, on October 8, 2014, seemingly using strategic ambiguity as a strategy:

> The Greenpeace campaign uses the LEGO brand to target Shell. As we have stated before, we think that Greenpeace ought to have a direct conversation with Shell … We want to clarify that as things stand we will not renew the co-promotion contract with Shell when the present contract ends. We do not want to be part of Greenpeace's campaign and we will not comment any further on the campaign. Our stakeholders have high expectations of how we operate. So do we. We do not agree with the tactics used by Greenpeace that may have created misunderstandings among our stakeholders about the way we operate.

Shell for its part tried to stay out of sight, but made the following statement:

> Recognizing the right of individuals to express their point of view, we only ask they do so in a manner that is lawful and does not place their safety or the safety of others at risk. (October 9, 2014)

This case illustrates that although a professional activist group generated the issue and targeted a seemingly 'innocent' second company, a number of citizens were more than willing to use the opportunity to vent and share their views on the matter. It seems to confirm that we are living in an age of hyper-connectivity and hyper-responsibility, where companies have to care not only for their own stakeholders, but also for the stakeholders of their stakeholders. In this age, inter-organizational relations have also been transformed into reputation risk areas.

Sources: Frandsen and Johansen (2015a), newspaper articles, www.lego.com.

DO I LIKE THIS ORGANIZATION? A THEORY OF SOCIAL APPROVAL

What makes people press the 'like' (or 'dislike') button on Facebook? Two sets of theories can shed light on this phenomenon.

We are living in a world where we make quick decisions. In order to understand people's judgments, choices, and biases of intuition, Professor of psychology, and winner of the Nobel Prize in Economics, Daniel Kahneman, distinguished between two fundamental ways of thinking in his book, *Thinking, Fast and Slow* (2011): (1) the automatic system that produces fast thinking and (2) the effortful system that produces slow thinking. System 1 is based on feelings, intuitive thinking, and is quick and easy, whereas system 2 is based on reasoning and conscious thinking – it is analytical, effortful, and slow. When a person is confronted with a problem, his or her mind will spontaneously search for intuitive solutions. However, in some cases, no solution comes to mind and he or she will then switch to a slower, more deliberate, and effortful way of thinking. This does not mean, however, that we always think straight when we are reasoning. It can be a matter of not knowing any better (2011, p. 415).

Bundy and Pfarrer (2015) have established a theory about social approval and external evaluators' general affinity toward an organization. They argue that social approval will serve either as a 'buffer or burden in influencing evaluators' crisis sense-making and attributions' (p. 345), especially at the onset of a crisis, because social approval plays a role in the perceptions and responses of evaluators and managers. Knowing how these socio-cognitive processes play out may help when choosing an appropriate response strategy.

Inspired by Kahneman's theory, Bundy and Pfarrer distinguish between two systems. System 1 is about the more intuitive and affective cognitive basis of social approval, and constitutes an answer to the question: Do I like this organization? System 2 is about the more deliberate and analytical evaluations related to reputation and legitimacy and forms an answer to the question: Does this organization create the expected value; does it live up to the expected norms? (See Chapter 3 for definitions of the concepts of reputation and legitimacy.)

The theory of social approval focuses on the perceptions and reactions of evaluators at the onset of a crisis, because at this point in a crisis there is a high degree of uncertainty. People typically do not know the causes of the crisis, explanations are ambiguous, and they do not have the required information about what is going on. This will make evaluators rely on heuristic and intuitive processes (feelings/emotions) and lead them to ask the spontaneous question: Do I like this organization? Here, the high or low level of social approval of an organization at the onset of the crisis plays an important role.

This phenomenon may explain the initial amount of likes and dislikes on Facebook when a crisis breaks out. However, as the crisis evolves, people get more information and more thorough explanations, and it may make them reason differently (triggering slow thinking). Sometimes they change their minds. This happened in the case of the giraffe Marius (see Chapter 7) and of Jensen's Steakhouse (see Case example 9.2 below). Once people learned more about the rationale behind the behavior of the organization, some of the intuitively emotional and condemning voices on social media gained more sympathy for the organization.

This theory about the role of social approval may, therefore, be useful as a theoretical framework for understanding the role of emotions and emotional stakeholders.

 Case example 9.2

Jensen's Steakhouse vs. Jensen's Seafood restaurant: From fast food to slow thinking

In 2014 Jensen was the commonest surname in Denmark (Statistics Denmark, 2016). This is the story about the conflict between two restaurants in Denmark, both with the name 'Jensen'.

In 2012, the Danish restaurant chain Jensen's Bøfhus (Jensen's Steakhouse), owned by Palle Jensen, sued a seafood restaurant named Jensen's Fiskerestaurant (JF), located in a small city in northern Denmark and owned by Jakob Jensen, for using the name Jensen. After a series of court battles, on September 19, 2014, the Danish Supreme Court handed down its judgment. The steakhouse won the patent case, and JF had to give up the name and domain of Jensen and pay DKK200,000 (US$30,000) to Jensen's Steakhouse for trademark violations.

Palle Jensen had created the first Jensen's Steakhouse in 1990 using his own name for the brand (inspired by companies like Heinz, McDonald's, and Anheuser-Busch). Today the Jensen's Steakhouse chain consists of 49 restaurants located in Denmark, Sweden, Norway, and Germany and has about 2,000 employees. To Jensen's Steakhouse, the case was about protecting the brand name, as the company had spent 25 years building up its branded restaurants.

The owner of the seafood restaurant, Jakob Jensen, had used the name of Jensen's Fiskerestaurant for 13 years, and had also put a great deal of work into building its brand up, but he did not understand the verdict. As he stated later, 'More than 95% of the sales in my restaurant is fish. No client has ever mistaken the fish restaurant for a steakhouse. I love to make good fish for my guests.' But the decision stood, and following the verdict the seafood restaurant's name was changed and is now known as Jakob's Fiskerestaurant.

In both traditional and social media the case was framed as a classic case of David vs. Goliath: the big chain bullying the small local restaurant. It triggered outrage on social media. Almost 110,000 people pressed the 'like' button on a 'boycott Jensen's Steakhouse' site that was immediately created on Facebook. First came the quick and angry reactions, then the boycott site. Next followed an attempt to sabotage the business of Jensen's Steakhouses when some of the angry voices started writing negative reviews of Jensen's Steakhouses on the online review site Trustpilot. Some of the critics apparently did this without having ever eaten at the restaurant, thus breaking Trustpilot's guidelines.

However, when Jensen Steakhouse's spokesperson on social media, a young employee, put out the following (humorous) message on the company's Facebook site, supporters started to come forward. The post read:

(Continued)

(Continued)

> The annual fall storm hit Denmark a little before usual time this year. It has made a really big impression on me and on all of us in the company. If you see a windproof jacket then please send me a private message. Mine has been worn a little thin lately ... but I am still here, if you need me, I hope that we can recreate a good atmosphere.

Palle Jensen also started telling about how awful it was to be met with all these angry and very unpleasant mails and phone calls. At the same time, he started communicating more details about the reasons for filing the lawsuit. Slowly, the public learned about the nuances of the conflict. It was not a problem that Jakob Jensen had a seafood restaurant in northern Denmark, but when he opened two new restaurants in other cities, it was seen as the start of a restaurant chain having the same brand name as Jensen's Steakhouses. This would create a situation akin to a McDonald's burger restaurant chain and a McDonald's taco chain, where consumers could easily believe the two were part of the same concern. At the same time, Jensen's Steakhouse also faced fights about the brand name with steakhouse chains in Norway.

These explanations led to a counter-reaction. Some voices apparently now started to consider Jensen's Steakhouse the victim, and showed an 'enough is enough' reaction. Positive and supportive voices (faith-holders) started telling about their positive experiences with the Steakhouse restaurants on Facebook, and some of them even offered the spokesperson a new warm, thick jacket. Traditional media started doing interviews with satisfied customers, and a television program held a double interview with Jensen and Jensen to get both points of view. This case shows the dynamics of the voices in the rhetorical arena. The spontaneous, intuitive, fast-thinking reactions eventually gave way to an effortful, more nuanced, and more slow-thinking approach (cf. Kahneman, 2011).

Sources: Newspaper articles and K-forum, TV2 September 20, 2014.

EMOTIONAL STAKEHOLDERS

Finnish public relations scholar Vilma Luamo-aho emphasizes the powerful nature of emotions in working with stakeholder communications. According to her, stakeholder theory must include emotional stakeholders. One just has to look at what is happening in social media, which clearly reflect the intensity of the emotional reactions of stakeholders. Strong, negative emotions such as anger and hate, especially, are often vented on social media, while satisfied stakeholders make less noise. Such negative voices often want specifically to make their criticism and anger known to the public, and this can be quite damaging to the social and symbolic capital of an organization. In contrast, positive voices can be central to maintaining the legitimacy of an organization. Luomo-aho (2010) has established a distinction between hate-holders and faith-holders that she has located at the extremes of a continuum. Hate-holders are 'formed when the distrust and negative emotion that stakeholders feel toward an organization are strong enough to hinder it' (p. 5). Faith-holders are 'formed when the trust and positive emotion they feel toward the organization is strong enough to be a beneficial resource' (p. 5).

Faith-holders embrace all kinds of fans and groups who like a brand or support it and are positively engaged with an organization. Hate-holders are negatively engaged and dislike – or even feel strong hate – toward the organization. However, not all negative experiences lead to this kind of negativity. Importantly, emotional stakeholders can easily be influenced and moved from one stance (positive) to another (negative) in relation to organizational incidents, accidents, misdeeds, or ethical dilemmas.

EMOTIONS AND CRISIS

By nature, crises call for emotional reactions, but these emotions also come in many colors. From practice as well as research we know that a variety of factors (crisis type, crisis origin, number of victims, severity, etc.) influence the kind of emotions that people feel when they are involved in, affected by, or responsible for a crisis. It is not necessarily all about negative emotions (e.g., anger, disgust, anxiety, fear, contempt, sadness, hate, sorrow, etc.). People may also experience positive emotions during a crisis (e.g., hope, relief, sympathy, surprise, happiness, love), and positive emotions can help them cope with a crisis.

Negative emotions and voices

Depending upon the crisis type, people react in different ways. According to an explorative study conducted by Coombs and Holladay (2005), crises from the victim crisis cluster produce the strongest feelings of sympathy, whereas crises within the preventable crisis cluster produce the strongest feelings of anger and *Schadenfreude*. When people are harmed or perceive others to be harmed wrongfully, moral outrage and anger are often the result. Outrage and anger can lead to various actions against an organization and damage its reputation, especially if the crisis is severe, and the stakeholders consider the organization to be responsible (Fediuk et al., 2010). Anger also drives negative secondary crisis communication, such as sharing or forwarding the crisis communication of the organization (Utz et al., 2013).

Another group of researchers has tried to map negative emotions during crises, emotions such as anger, anxiety, sadness, and fright (Jin et al., 2007, 2012) and to test the public's emotional strategies for coping with crises. The studies of these primary emotions have shown that publics are not just passive receivers who react to the information provided by organizations in crisis; they engage in various emotional coping strategies in an attempt to make sense of the crisis and to reduce stress (Jin, 2009). The dominant primary emotion depends upon the degrees of predictability and controllability (defined as the 'public's self-efficacy to take control of the crisis situation', (p. 310)). Anger is likely to be produced in controllable and predictable crises. Sadness appears when it is about predictable, but not controllable, crises, whereas fright is the primary emotion in non-controllable and non-predictable crises. Finally, concerning the fourth primary emotion, all publics seem to experience anxiety in a crisis situation.

Positive emotions and voices

Most research on emotions within crisis communication has concentrated on the negative voices and their reactions when they trigger or experience a crisis. Very little is known about the reactions, role, and importance of positive voices, or faith-holders, during a crisis. Apart from a few studies within organizational crisis communication (Coombs & Holladay, 2012b, Kim & Niederdeppe, 2013, Johansen et al., 2016), most studies about faith-holders take their starting point in research on sports fans.

Sports fans are typically very committed to their club and ready to defend it when the club or their idols are accused of wrongdoing. Brown and Billings (2013) have studied the reactions and communication strategies of fans on social media during the University of Miami athletics scandal in 2011. Brown and Billings discovered that fans were using new strategies that the university could not use without risk of a backlash. These included such things as diverting attention to the problems or crises of other similar institutions, or uniting University of Miami fans by organizing support hashtags and links. The fans' voices were also using traditional response strategies such as attack the accuser, reminder, and ingratiation.

Marketing research has focused on consumer relations to companies and brands, including studies of brand communities, brand love, fans, and customer loyalty. From this research we have learned that when consumers identify strongly with a company or a brand, it can create company loyalty and company promotion. In this case, consumers speak positively about the company and are willing to defend it and downplay negative information about the company or a product (Bhattacharya & Sen, 2003). This may explain the existence of faith-holders, for instance, in customer complaint crises.

Johansen et al. (2016) have studied the interactions of voices during a customer complaint crisis triggered on social media (see Case study 9.1 on Telenor). Their study confirms the findings of Brown and Billings. Faith-holders in this case defended the company using crisis communication strategies and tone-of-voice tactics that were different from what the company could legitimately do on its own. Interestingly the faith-holders also attacked the negative voices for their code of conduct on Facebook, reasoning that such hateful statements do not belong on Facebook. They used the divert attention strategy and they also used the well-known strategies found in the lists of response strategies of Benoit and Coombs (see Chapters 5 and 6). However, these strategies were applied in a slightly different way because they spoke mostly on behalf of the company, with the exception of when they described their own good experiences with the company in the past, which is an example of a bolstering or reminder strategy. As this study shows, faith-holders act as informal crisis communicators and can play an important role for the legitimacy of a company. They can be important to the strategic handling of a crisis. We have also seen examples of faith-holders not supporting top management, but instead blaming the employee or middle manager for the crisis. Finally, we have seen faith-holders who spent energy on supporting a brand only to be disappointed and disillusioned when their organization gave in to a critique, for instance, or an attack.

Thus, studies on emotional voices such as faith-holders and hate-holders add new perspectives to the inventories of the crisis response strategies established by Benoit (2015) and Coombs (2015).

Emotional voices of the organization

Research on emotions has concentrated on the emotions of the voices of consumers and citizens (publics) affected by a crisis. Little research has been conducted in relation to the emotions expressed by the organization in crisis. From Sturges (1994) and Coombs (2015) we learned that showing empathy and concern for the victims or people affected by the crisis helps them to cope psychologically. Communication of emotions has an impact on the crisis sensemaking of people. Van der Meer and Verhoeven (2014) have shown that the communication of negative emotions, such as shame or regret of the organization involved in a crisis, can have a positive impact on the perception of the organization and on reputation. By acting as a human, anger can be lowered, and the relationship with the stakeholders can be improved. In contrast, absence of emotions can easily make an organization appear distant, cold, and uninterested. However, the use of such emotional strategies will depend on the context, including crisis type, crisis consequences, and key stakeholder emotions.

DEFINING SOCIAL MEDIA

Kaplan and Haenlein (2010) define social media as 'a group of Internet-based applications that build on the technological foundations of Web 2.0, and that allow the creation and exchange of User-Generated Content' (p. 61). Based on key dimensions such as social presence, media richness, the degree of self-disclosure (conscious or unconscious revelation of personal information), and self-presentation (attempt to control the impressions other people form), Kaplan and Haenlein distinguish among collaborative projects, content communities, virtual games, blogs, social networking sites, and social worlds.

Social media have common characteristics such as interactivity, speed, global reach, convergence, lack of control (no gatekeeping), self-medium, mass self-communication, and cyberspace, and they constitute a new public sphere. Thus, they can be said to form a cornerstone within the network society. In relation to the triggering of a crisis they constitute a central part of what Moore and Seymour (2005) have named *cobra* technology, because they can suddenly strike an organization in its vital parts, just like a cobra snake. For instance, if a single critical voice starts spreading and gaining momentum across networking sites with important outreach it can lead to serious consequences for the organization.

SOCIAL MEDIA AND CRISIS COMMUNICATION

With the rise of the Internet, social structure in society has shifted from rigid vertical hierarchies to flexible horizontal networks, where consumers and citizens are sharing opinions between each other to a greater extent (Castells, 2009). They are expressing themselves more easily online, not because they are asked to do so, but because they want to do so. Thus, self-expression becomes one of the key drivers. It has become legitimate to express emotions (likes or dislikes) towards companies, products, and services. In principle, every individual can have a message going viral, and anybody can trigger a firestorm or shitstorm. Social media have become triggers and accelerators of organizational crises. Furthermore, they are facilitators of crises in so far as they constitute 'an additional channel for discussion of events that already occur in the real world' (González-Herrero & Smith, 2008, p. 145). If we follow this line of thought, companies' communication, including crisis communication, on social media with consumers and citizens as co-communicators can be said to be about risk, relationship, and network management.

BOX 9.1

ONLINE FIRESTORMS

Organizations being attacked or criticized on social media may suddenly find themselves in a *firestorm* or a *shitstorm*[1] when a criticism spontaneously spreads with enormous speed from one, or a few, critical voices to a significant number of angry voices.

Pfeffer et al. (2014) describe a firestorm as:

> the sudden discharge of large quantities of messages containing negative WOM and complaint behavior against a person, company, or group in social media networks. In these messages, intense indignation is often expressed, without pointing to an actual specific criticism … The essential feature is that the messages in a firestorm are predominantly opinion, not fact, thus having a high affective nature. (p. 118)

The extent of negativity and rudeness of the tone of voice in firestorms or shitstorms are typically shocking for the organization in the eye of the storm, and they put its staff under huge pressure. It is tough to face rude or hateful messages. How do you, for instance, deal with direct bodily threats or a voice that threatens to shoot your employees, as we saw in the case of the giraffe and Copenhagen Zoo (see Chapter 7)? Depending upon its nature and character, a firestorm is exhausting and constitutes a huge challenge to most organizations.

Further reading: Pfeffer et al. (2014).

Social media have an important impact on crisis management and attract a lot of attention from scholars, practitioners, and organizations. In academia, the study of crisis communication on social media is a vibrant field that has been growing quickly since the early years of this century (for overview see An & Cheng, 2010;

---

[1] The term *shitstorm* was recorded in German usage in 2010, referring to 'a widespread and vociferous outrage on the internet (social media platforms). It was voted Germany's Anglicism of the year in 2011' (*Guardian*, July 4, 2013). 'Shitstorm' has seemingly become the predominant term in a European context.

Avery et al., 2010; Valentini & Kruckeberg, 2016). Within practice, organizations and PR practitioners acknowledge that the Internet and social media have changed their way of operating (Fjeld & Molesworth, 2006).

Types of social media crises

Social media: friend or enemy? On the one hand, social media are useful to organizations during crises. Social media make it possible for an organization to quickly share crisis responses, instructions, and updates with stakeholders on both its corporate website and on stakeholders' networks (e.g., Facebook). Further, social media facilitate the spreading of messages from ambassadors (e.g., bloggers) and faith-holders communicating about the crisis in defense of the organization.

On the other hand, organizations are afraid of social media. They are afraid of shitstorms, and they are not happy when citizens, journalists, or citizen–journalists are the first to tell the story about a triggering crisis event. They dread the possibility that these stakeholders will post unpleasant pictures from an accident or an embarrassing situation on social media because they happened to be in the right place at the right time. On top of this, organizations risk triggering a crisis themselves on social media due to misuse or lack of social media competence.

Following the Coombs typology presented in Chapter 2, social media crises come in three types (see Table 9.3). While the organization itself triggers the first category of social media crises (organizational misuse), the organization's stakeholders (or professional activist voices) initiate complaints and challenge crises.

While this chapter's case study on Norwegian Telenor (see p. 174) is an example of a customer complaint crisis, the two previous case examples of the lawsuit crisis of Jensen's Steakhouse and the 'hostage-taking' campaign of Greenpeace vs. LEGO and Shell form very different examples of challenge crises.

Social-mediated crisis communication

Information source and form play a role in the way people search for and share information during a crisis and in how they react emotionally. Thus, it is important for organizations to match form and source on social media when they are communicating and responding to emotional voices.

Table 9.3 Crisis types on social media

Crisis type	Definition
Organizational misuse	When the organization itself misuses social media
Customer complaints	When customers are dissatisfied with products, services, or customer service of an organization
Challenge	When different stakeholders perceive an organization's behavior and/or policies to be unethical or inappropriate

Source: Coombs (2015).

A group of researchers has established what they call a social-mediated crisis communication (SMCC) model (Liu et al., 2011; Austin et al., 2012; Jin et al., 2014). The model was created in order to establish a framework for crisis communication and to understand how individuals and organizations use social media and offline interactions before, during, and after a crisis. Information form and source were found to be key factors here. In line with the views of Schultz et al. (2011) in their journal article 'Is the medium the message?', Austin et al. argue that 'information form may be as important as – or more important than – the actual crisis response message' (2012, p. 192).

The model consists of three sets of elements:

- For the *crisis information form*, the model operates with a distinction between crisis information in traditional media, on social media, and/or via off-line word-of-mouth communication (e.g., texting, conversation on phone or face-to-face).
- For the *crisis information source*, crisis information originates from three kinds of sources: the organization in crisis, journalists, and people creating content on social media. The model distinguishes further between three types of publics who have been identified in the social media literature and who are delimited by their role in either producing or consuming crisis information:

  o *Influential social media creators*: individuals or organizations who create crisis information for others to consume.
  o *Social media followers*: individuals or organizations who consume the social media crisis information of the social media creators.
  o *Social media inactives*: those who may consume crisis information indirectly through offline word-of-mouth communication with the social media followers, or traditional media who follow social media creators and/or followers.

- For the factors influencing the communication of the organization in crisis, the model includes five contextual factors: crisis origin, crisis type, infrastructure, message strategy, and message form.

The authors have tested the model several times and found interesting results in relation to the use of social media for information seeking and sharing during a crisis.

Why do people use media in general? The authors found that young adults (college students) were using social media in general for entertainment, relationship maintenance, and (professional) networking, whereas traditional media were used for education ('so I know what's going on in the world' (Austin et al., 2012, p. 196).

Why do people use media, especially social media, in crises? People use social media to get insider information and to correspond with family and friends, whereas they use traditional media for educational purposes (e.g., the news on TV). All participants in this study found traditional media to be more credible than social media for crisis information needs. Convenience was a key driver for their use of social media and/or traditional media in a crisis (Facebook, email, text messages, and random news articles) followed by involvement and personal recommendation (from friends, parents, and professors, for instance on Facebook). Specifically for social media, they also mentioned humorous appeal as a driver.

People were most likely to use the same type of media in which they heard about the crisis to seek more information later. If the initial information came from what the scholars have named third parties (being voices outside the organization), and especially voices on social media, people were likely to look for more information. For our understanding of third parties, see Chapter 8.

The most reported form of crisis communication was face-to-face communication, followed by TV, text messaging, phone calls, and Facebook. Twitter and blogs were used the least. For an organisation's approach to crisis communication, the authors conclude that traditional media should be used in combination with a deliberate approach to social media; key influencers should be identified; and organizations need to 'ensure that crisis communication information comes from other trusted sources of information, in addition to coming from the organization' (Austin et al., 2012, p. 203).

Another piece of research has shown that people react differently to an organization's response on social media, in traditional media, or via the corporate website, and that crises triggered online gain credibility offline when they transit to mainstream media (Pang et al., 2014).

PATTERNS OF INTERACTIONS IN THE RHETORICAL ARENA

The development described in the previous sections has consequences for the nature and content of the relations and interactions among voices, not only on social media, but also in the rhetorical arena as such. In fact, it is reasonable to conclude that social media networking sites such as Facebook allow us to get new insights into crisis communication and the complex interactions among voices in the rhetorical arena.

A crisis on social media triggers many *interactions among various voices*. At least three sets of patterns have been identified (Johansen et al., 2016). First, negative voices or hate-holders start attacking a company and invite other voices to support them and take consequential action. Thus, negative voices interact to support one another, to show empathy for victims, and/or to support the cause. This typically leads to the company defending itself in different ways depending on the situation and context. Then comes interactions between the negative and positive voices. Faith-holders or supporters typically appear, sometimes at the onset of the crises but typically as the crisis evolves, and interact with the negative voices or hate-holders. They defend the company, argue, and attack the critics. Third, other voices (third parties) not connected to the brand or the organization in crisis may appear, either to show solidarity and/or empathy for the negative voices or to profit from the crisis by positing their own agenda and/or drawing attention to their own cause. They all have an impact in the multivocal arena.

Another pattern in the rhetorical arena is the spillover from one media to another and the influence of form and source on the information-sharing and information-seeking behavior of the different voices (cf. the SMCC model). A crisis may spread from one social medium to another (e.g., from Facebook to Twitter or vice versa). However, crises on social media also have spillovers to traditional media when the newsworthiness is high enough, but will decline again when not fed with new insights. See Chapter 10 for the role of traditional media and the concept of newsworthiness during crises.

CASE STUDY 9.1

EMOTIONAL STAKEHOLDERS AND TELENOR'S CUSTOMER COMPLAINTS CRISIS ON FACEBOOK

When customers complain about a company on its corporate Facebook site a crisis can ensue, especially if fellow customers want to express sympathy for the dissatis-fied customers or have had the same experience themselves. This was, in fact, the case of the Norwegian telecommunications company, Telenor, who went through a customer complaints crisis in Denmark in August 2012 that was triggered on its Facebook site.

On August 2, 2012, a dissatisfied customer posted a farewell note to Telenor on Facebook. He had decided to end his relationship with Telenor because he had experienced too many problems. He had, for example, received payment reminders although he had not received any bills; he was told to pay fees because the payment system could not connect to his bank; and he wrote about how the company could not find his family contract when he asked for it. The shitstorm lasted three weeks. Within the first 24 hours more than 2,000 people had commented on his post. Many had faced similar problems or wanted to express sympathy. By August 25, more than 30,000 likes and 4,368 comments had been posted on the Telenor Facebook page. The many complaints on Facebook caused the crisis to transit to traditional media and, eventually, to the televised consumer advocacy program, *Kontant*. Thus, a post from one dissatisfied voice triggered the biggest public relations crisis for Telenor so far.

The dissatisfied customer's post on Facebook opened a multivocal rhetori-cal arena within which various voices started communicating and interacting with Telenor and with each other. Besides Telenor, its customers, previous customers, and customers from rival companies were to be found on the Telenor Facebook page. Many of the voices (hate-holders) were angry and dissatisfied customers or previous customers who had experienced similar problems with Telenor. Some were rude and even hateful: 'I hate Telenor', 'they deliberately cheat with the bills', 'I had to fight with them for more than six months', read some of the posts. Others suggested consequential actions such as 'boycott Telenor', 'change company', 'denounce them in the media', and so on. However, some Telenor customers supported it and acted as faith-holders. Finally, and interestingly, customers from rival telecommunications companies also interfered, although they were not related to Telenor, mostly inviting the Telenor customers to join their telecommunications service provider.

Telenor tried to communicate with these angry customers in an accommodative way through corrective action and bolstering strategies, but it was not until the company gave a full apology to all of its stakeholders that the crisis finally started to slow down. Surprisingly, Telenor was not alone in communicating to the dissatisfied customers. It was supported by an important number of positive voices or faith-holders (18 percent of the emotional voices) acting as informal crisis communicators or ambassadors. However, in contrast to Telenor, the faith-holders were almost exclusively using defensive strategies and appraisals. They made denials, telling the negative voices that they had never had problems or had always been offered good service at Telenor. Furthermore, they attacked the accusers, sometimes using the same rude language as the negative voices, 'You're awful complainers, crying and whining in front of your screens. Wake up and talk to them if you have problems', or they tried to establish a kind of code of conduct: 'Shame on you, all your filth doesn't belong on Facebook.' It meant that some of the hate-holders also had to defend themselves. During the same period, Telenor put up 10 small posts on its Facebook site.

As demonstrated in this example, a lot of interactions and dynamics were in play. Many voices were communicating, not only *to*, *with*, or *against* Telenor, but also *to*, *with*, or *against* each other. These voices all contributed to the interpretation of the crisis situation or issue.

Studying the rhetorical arena

Macro component

- Who are the voices in the rhetorical arena of Telenor? What does it reveal about voices acting in a customer complaint crisis?

Micro component

- Who is communicating to whom in this arena? What are the differences in the response strategies and language of the faith-holders compared to Telenor? How can these differences be explained?

Managing the rhetorical arena

- What is the role of the faith-holders in managing a crisis in general, and on social media in particular? Why do faith-holders intervene?

Source: Johansen and Weckesser (2013); Johansen et al. (2016).

CHAPTER SUMMARY

This chapter first described how the voices of multiple consumers and citizens have been empowered by the Internet, allowing them to interact and communicate in new ways on social media, and turning them into powerful actors in the rhetorical arena. Next, the chapter presented the theory of social approval and the theory of emotional faith-holders and hate-holders in an attempt to explain the emotional reactions of consumers and citizens that may lead to para(crisis) or firestorms in no time at all. In fact, very often both negative and positive voices are present and interacting in the rhetorical arena during a crisis. The chapter concluded by presenting key characteristics of social media and crisis communication, including a short overview of the social-mediated communication model, which has identified three types of social media publics and demonstrated how information source and form have an impact on the communication of the voices in a crisis situation.

Further reading

Bundy, J., & Pfarrer, M. C. (2015). A burden of responsibility: The role of social approval at the onset of a crisis. *Academy of Management Review*, 40(3), 345–369.

Jin, Y., Liu, B. F., & Austin, L. L. (2014). Examining the role of social media in effective crisis management: The effects of crisis origin, information form and source on publics' crisis responses. *Communication Research*, 41(1), 74–94.

NEWS MEDIA: MEDIATIZATION AND CRISIS JOURNALISM

10

⌐ CHAPTER OVERVIEW ⌐

This chapter explores the voice(s) of the news media, focusing on how the media coverage of crises has developed into a distinct type of news reporting: crisis journalism. A prerequisite for this development is mediatization, that is the process whereby a growing number of areas in society, including private and public organizations, adopt or accommodate the dominant media logic and media format. The first part of the chapter introduces the reader to the theory of mediatization. The second part describes various types of crisis journalism: from crisis news frames and crisis exploitation strategies to the interplay between the news media, organizations in crisis, and the public.

INTRODUCTION

In the previous chapter, we studied how the voices of *individual* customers and citizens interacted with an organization in crisis, and how they interacted among themselves as emotional stakeholders. We also examined how these multiple voices were supported by social media such as Facebook. In Chapters 10 and 11, we shall explore two *collective* voices.

The first is a voice we hear and listen to every day, in particular when a crisis breaks out. It is the voice of the news media. The news media play a key role before, during, and after a crisis. Journalists often 'break the news', writing front page articles in which serious allegations against an organization are made public for the first time. They cover how the crisis develops, and their investigative reporting sometimes contributes to an escalation of the crisis. The news media transform the crisis into a story where there are heroes and villains, plots and climaxes. Finally, the news media serve as a kind of institutional memory in society. When an organization is involved in a crisis, the media remind us about all the other crises in which the same organization has been involved (see also the concept of crisis history in Chapter 6). When all this is taken into account, it is no surprise that many consultants see the news media and their news coverage as part of the very definition of a crisis. In the mid-1990s, the Institute of Crisis Management (ICM), an American consulting firm founded by Robert Irvine in 1989, defined a crisis as a 'significant disruption which results in extensive news media coverage and public scrutiny' (Irvine & Millar, 1996).

The second voice is a voice we hardly notice, not even when a crisis breaks out. It is the voice of trade associations. By this we mean non-profit institutions that operate cooperatively for and among competitive, profit-making actors within an industry. They apply various types of strategies in their work. Among the internal strategies of action we find education and training, information sharing, research, certification, and accreditation. Among the external strategies of action we find lobbying and monitoring policy, public relations, and civic practices. Trade associations play a key role when one or more of their members, or the entire industry, is facing a (multi-) crisis (see case example 11.1).

These two voices are very different, but they have something in common: they both *mediate* between other voices. This means, first of all, that we will have to deal with a higher degree of complexity in the rhetorical arena. In Chapter 9, the interaction between Telenor and its (dis)satisfied customers was linear and direct. Each individual customer could present his or her complaint using the Norwegian telecommunications company's customer complaints management system or its Facebook site. The situation did not become complex until the customers started interacting among themselves. In this chapter and Chapter 11, the fact that the news media as well as trade associations mediate between the organization in crisis and the stakeholders an organization defines for itself complicates things. It increases the number of communicative interventions and interpretations of what is going on (see case study 11.1).

BOX 10.1

THE LIFE CYCLE OF A DISASTER: A FIELD GUIDE FOR JOURNALISTS

In 2001, Art Botterell, an American emergency management expert and journalist with four decades of experience, published a field guide for disaster and crisis journalists. Like most crisis management researchers, Botterell conceptualizes crises as cyclical processes going through a progression of a certain number of phases, in this case six: (1) preparation, (2) alert, (3) impact, (4) heroic, (5) disillusionment, and (6) recovery. However, his understanding of the life cycle of a crisis differs from the staged approaches introduced in Chapter 4. In his model, for example, the life cycle of a crisis ends with recovery and not with organizational learning. At the same time, he has added a *heroic phase* – the 'dramatic red-light-and-siren' phase of response. This addition reveals that he is writing for journalists and not for crisis managers.

Further reading: Crisis Journalism: A Handbook for Media Response. American Press Institute, 2002.

A THEORY OF MEDIATIZATION

Our world is a mediatized world. Every day, we spend several hours reading, listening to, and watching a growing number of newspapers, radio stations, television networks and, recently, online news companies providing us with news, information, advertising, entertainment, and other kinds of content. Reducing this diversity of media to the 'voice of the news media' may seem foolhardy. The truth is that it is more like a huge choir of voices.

In this mediatized world, the news media create 'pictures in our heads' (Lippmann, 1922), simplifying the complexity of the society in which we live and work and the crises we experience. 'Experience' is perhaps not the right word. Apart from the people who are directly involved in a crisis (members of the organization in crisis, customers, investors, etc.), we seldom 'face a crisis' as such. Most of us read about crises in the newspapers, hear about them on the radio, or follow them on television. For most of us, the experience is like that of the Englishmen, the Frenchmen, and the Germans who were all living together on an island in the ocean when World War I broke out in 1914 and that Walter Lippmann described in the famous opening chapter of *Public Opinion*.

The keyword is *mediatization*. If we want to understand the voice of the news media and the role they play in the rhetorical arena, we must first study the process of mediatization. In this section, we define what we mean by news media. Then we examine the consequences of the mediatization of society in general and the mediatization of organizations and organizational crises in particular.

Defining the news media

By media we mean print media (newspapers, news magazines), broadcast news (radio stations, television networks), and Internet publishers (online newspapers, news blogs) that are defined as *media organizations*.

What we understand by *news* depends on how we conceptualize the relationship between media, communication, and reality. The traditional way of defining news is based on an understanding of the media as transmitters of information that represent or reconstruct reality (meta-theoretical position: realism). According to this perspective, news exists 'out there'. The journalists just have to 'investigate' and 'dig deeper' to find what is new. This perspective lies behind the widespread idea among crisis communication researchers that the news media can serve as a reliable *data source*. An alternative way of defining news is to see the media as story makers that contribute to the construction of social reality (meta-theoretical position: constructivism). According to this perspective, news does not exist 'out there'. News is *produced* 'inside' the individual media organizations and/or in the (inter)national media systems based on specific news values or criteria, journalistic practices or cultures, and dominating media logics and formats.

The perspective on the news media that we find most coherent with rhetorical arena theory and the multivocal approach is the perspective where the media not only *cover* events, but also *intervene* in these events. As organizations, the news media also have their own reputation and can be hit by a crisis like every other organization.

Mediatization of society

Let us now turn to the concept of mediatization. It is a concept that has emerged among European media and communication scholars during the last 10 to 15 years. Basically, it is an attempt to understand how, and why, the media have become so omnipresent and powerful in today's society.

Hjarvard (2008) takes an institutional perspective when he defines mediatization as

> the process whereby society to an increasing degree is submitted to, or becomes dependent on, the media and their logic. This process is characterized by a duality in that the media become integrated into the operations of other social institutions, while they also have acquired the status of social institutions in their own right. As a consequence, social interaction – within the respective institutions, between institutions, and in society at large – takes place via the media. (p. 113)

(For alternative definitions, see Lundby, 2009, 2014; Couldry & Hepp, 2013.)

Hjarvard introduces a distinction between a direct (strong) and an indirect (weak) form of mediatization. In the strong form, a given activity is transformed from a 'real-life' activity, including face-to-face communication between two persons, to a mediatized activity where the interaction takes place directly through a medium. Internet banking is an example of such a transformation. In the weak form, a given activity is increasingly affected by symbols and mechanisms created by the media. The intertextual use of elements from popular Hollywood movies in corporate videos produced for a completely different audience is an example of this indirect form of mediatization.

Another keyword in this stream of research on mediatization is the concept of *media logic*, which refers to the assumptions and processes for constructing messages within a particular medium (Altheide & Snow, 1979). A media logic includes, among other things, a media format. And by media format, we mean the rules or 'codes' for defining, selecting, organizing, presenting, and recognizing information as one thing rather than another (e.g., 'an infotainment program on public service television' and not a 'news program' or a 'sit com', as in case study 10.1). Media culture is produced by the widespread application of media logics (Altheide, 2004).

How has this process unfolded historically? Strömbäck (2008) makes a distinction between four phases of mediatization of society. The first phase occurs when the news media in a specific society constitute the most important source of information. The picture of reality conveyed by the media starts to have an impact on how people perceive reality. This first phase is a prerequisite for the successive phases of mediatization. In the second phase of mediatization, the news media form an autonomous social institution. This institution begins to be governed by a media logic, and not by other logics in society, be they political, cultural, or commercial. Thus, the media logic becomes more important for those who wish to have an influence on the media and their content. In the third phase, the independence of the news media increases further and they are now so important that the other actors and institutions in society have to adapt to them – and not the other way around. The distinction between the media world – the pictures of reality produced by the media and shaped by the media logic – and the real world has lost its significance. Finally, in the fourth phase of mediatization, the other actors and institutions in society not only adapt to the media logic, but also internalize this logic.

Strömbäck's (2008) short history of mediatization has been criticized for being too linear and deterministic and for neglecting the micro-dynamics of mediatization (Pallas & Fredriksson, 2013; Pallas et al., 2014).

BOX 10.2

GATEKEEPING, NEWS VALUES, AND FOCUSING EVENTS

Why do disasters always make the headlines in the news media, even when they occur in remote places?

According to one of the most influential theories of news journalism, the gatekeeping theory, news does not exist 'out there'. News is produced by the media. Shoemaker and Vos (2009) explain: gatekeeping is the

> process of culling and crafting countless bits of information into the limited number of messages that reach people every day, and it is the center of the media's role in modern public life ... This process determines not only which information is selected, but also what the content and nature of the messages, such as news, will be.

The world is full of events. Every day, among all these events, journalists select those events that live up to a set of *news values*, including identification, familiarity, unexpectedness, and conflict. Notice that negativity also counts as a news value: 'Bad news is more newsworthy than good news.'

However, there seems to exist a category of events that do not need the media to be found newsworthy. These are the so-called *focusing events*. Birkland (1997) defines a focusing event as 'an event that is sudden, relatively

(Continued)

(Continued)

rare, can be reasonably defined as harmful or revealing the possibility of potentially future harms, inflicts harms or suggests potential harms that are or could be concentrated on a definable geographical area or community of interest, and that is known to policy makers and the public virtually simultaneously' (p. 22). According to Birkland (1997), there are three elements of focusing events that are most likely to induce media coverage of a focusing event: (1) the scope of the event, that is the number of people affected by the event; (2) the consequences of the event are visible and tangible; and (3) the event is rare and dramatic. Focusing events are also important from an agenda-setting perspective.

Fishman (1999) studied the crash of ValuJet Flight 592 using Birkland's theory of focusing events.

Further reading: Fishman (1999).

Mediatization of organizations

While the mediatization of politics, culture, and social issues has already been investigated from various analytical angles, the mediatization of organizations is still relatively under-researched. *Organizations and the Media: Organizing in a Mediatized World* (Pallas et al., 2014) is one of the few books on this topic.

Still, it is not difficult to verify how important the news media are to organizations. One just has to glance at the *attention* they devote to media coverage and the *resources* they spend on hiring press officers and practising media management or media relations (Ihlen & Pallas, 2014). Media coverage is vital to organizations for many different reasons. Organizations need the media to promote their products (advertising), to evaluate their performance (reputation rankings), to cultivate their status and celebrity (awards), to influence stakeholders' understanding of their position and values (public affairs), and to come across as a legitimate actor. Deephouse's (2000) concept of *media reputation*, defined as the overall evaluation of a firm presented in the media, can be seen as an attempt to understand the mediatization of organizations.

Inspired by the concept of institutional work within neo-institutional theory, Pallas and Fredriksson (2013) have introduced the concept of *corporate media work* in their study of the relations and interactions between the news media and private companies. They understand mediatization not as a linear and deterministic process where the media control and manage the companies' behavior and actions, but as a highly interactive process where the media and the companies are entangled with each other.

Jacobs' (1999) study of pre-formulation strategies in press releases is an excellent illustration of this micro-level perspective on the mediatization of organizations. This study, which started out as a research project on the pragmatics of a crisis, not only demonstrates how mediatization can be the result of sophisticated interactions between the media and organizations, but also shows that mediatization can come into play even at the textual micro-level where the media format is institutionalized in the shape of *text genres*.

In Chapter 8, we saw how the communicative processes inside the rhetorical arena formed specific patterns or chains when two or more processes were combined. A prime example is the *press release*, which is the written crisis communication genre par excellence and the cornerstone of many crisis communication plans (Frandsen & Johansen, 2004; Johansen et al., 2012). A press release usually represents the starting point of the following sequence of communicative processes:

- A private company facing a crisis issues a press release in the press room on its website and/or sends it to the news media to inform them about the crisis event and/or explain its part in the event.
- As an effect of their double role as both *gatekeepers* (Shoemaker, 1991; Shoemaker & Vos, 2009) and *agenda setters* (McCombs & Shaw, 1972; Dearing & Rogers, 1996; McCombs, 2004), the news media evaluate the content of the press release on the basis of a set of *news values*, and then recontextualize and interpret it by transforming the content (together with information from other sources) into a news article covering and/or intervening in the crisis.
- Readers, listeners, and viewers, on their side, recontextualize and interpret the news article, transforming it into a new text, for example a comment on Facebook showing a photo of the article, or a conversation, for example around the dinner table in the evening.

Jacobs (1999) calls such a chain of communicative processes a *history of discourse*. In the rhetorical arena, every text and every conversation is part of a short or long history of discourse.

Based on the analysis of a large corpus of press releases, including the press releases issued by the American multinational Exxon in the wake of the oil spill in Alaska, in 1989, Jacobs (1999) identified a series of so-called *pre-formulation strategies* applied by the sender. The purpose of these strategies is to 'enter the gate' of the news media, to be transformed into a news article, and to reach the audience. What makes press releases unique is that their only *raison d'être* is to be 'continued', but in such a manner that most of their original wording is kept throughout the process. Here it seems relevant to combine the study of pre-formulation strategies with terminological control theory (see Chapter 5). The pre-formulation strategies identified by Jacobs are presented in Table 10.1.

Exxon issued approximately 60 press releases in the first eight months following the accident on March 24, 1989. Only a few of these press releases contained 'hard news'. The bulk of the press releases were public relations efforts to restore Exxon's reputation by demonstrating the organization's commitment to clean up the oil spill. All of these press releases made use of one or more pre-formulation strategies. They were structured as newspaper articles. They used the third person in references, which made them seem more neutral and disinterested. They used self-quotation (president W. D. Stevens) which allowed Exxon to maintain control over the flow of information by offering a single, streamlined company viewpoint.

Table 10.1 Pre-formulating strategies in press releases

Pre-formulation strategy	Example: press releases issued by *Exxon* during the crisis (1989)
General structure of news article ('news pyramid'): the facts are presented in descending order of importance	**Lightering, oil spill cleanup efforts continue in Alaska** Houston, Texas - March 27, 1989 - The Exxon Valdez, a 987-foot tanker carrying 1.3 million barrels of crude oil, ran aground on Bligh Reef about 25 miles south of the Trans Alaska Pipeline Terminal at Valdez about 12:30 a.m. Alaska time on Friday, March 25, while maneuvering to avoid ice. There were no personnel injuries. However, the vessel ruptured a number of cargo tanks, and an oil spill estimated at 240,000 barrels occurred in Prince William Sound. Only five hours after word was received of the grounding, Exxon Shipping Company President Fransk Larossi and five specially qualified advisors were en route by air to Alaska ...
Self-reference (third person)	(Exxon Valdez, Alaska: August 30, 1989) *Exxon* has treated over 1,000 miles of affected shoreline in the Gulf of Alaska and Prince William Sound. With just over 70 miles remaining *the company* is confident that shoreline treatment work will be completed by mid-September
Self-quotation	**Exxon position on Alaska spill clean-up is unchanged** Houston, Texas - July 25, 1989 Exxon's schedule for oil spill related activities in Alaska is unchanged from the plans discussed by Exxon Company, U.S.A. president W. D. Stevens on July 20 before a Senate Subcommittee, the company said. '*Looking ahead, we plan to inspect the shoreline after the winter.*'
Semi-performative	(Exxon, Houston, Texas - July 12, 1989) *Exxon welcomes* the opportunity to present its position to the court.

And they used explicit semi-performatives that made it easy for the journalists to retell them verbatim. These pre-formulation strategies can be seen as a 'type of negotiation' (Jacobs, 1999, p. 303): the media manager is trying to influence the news makers and vice versa within the same media logic and format.

Mediatization of crises

Sometimes book covers can be revealing. Take for example *The Handbook of Crisis Communication*, edited by Coombs and Holladay in 2010. The cover of this comprehensive handbook shows the photo of a press conference, as if it was taken by the spokesperson just a few minutes before he or she starts briefing the audience about a crisis. The angle of the reader is exactly the same as the angle of the spokesperson.

However, what is most salient in the photo is not the audience but the enormous mass of microphones placed in the middle of the scene. The room is full of news reporters.

A group of Finnish researchers, including Johanna Sumiala and Salli Hakala, claim that we experience crises and disasters more and more through the media and in the media (see Sumiala & Hakala, 2010). The media have the power to influence how we as consumers and citizens, investors and employees, experience crises and communicate about crises, including their causes and consequences. The media also have the power to make organizations adopt or accommodate the dominant media logic as they try to manage a crisis.

Crises have increasingly been mediatized in at least four different ways. In the case of, for example, natural disasters and terrorist attacks, national emergency agencies use the news media to *inform* the citizens of the country about what has happened, about how to react, causes and consequences, public hearings and reports in the aftermath of the crisis, etc. Many news media contribute to the *dramatization* of crises. They amplify dangers and conflicts. As mentioned in Chapter 1, the news media also contribute to the transformation of certain crises into social icons. They serve as a kind of institutional *memory* reminding citizens of tragic events and situations.

Finally, the news media turn organizations, the places where people work and enact roles as employees and managers, into a stage for entertainment or infotainment. It started in 2008 with Donald Trump's *The Apprentice*, a reality game show broadcast by NBC, which then spread to other countries. This broad trend, which Altheide (2004) has declared a dominant media logic, and which Thussu (2007) has studied in detail, has now also reached the field of organizational crises. 'The Top 10 Crises of [the year]' form part of this logic. This also applies to case study 10.1, which is about the Danish consumer television program *Kontant*, which is also based on infotainment.

The theory of mediatization is an important supplement to older and more established theories such as the theory of the public sphere and the 'twin theories' of gatekeeping and agenda setting. It describes and explains how we have adopted and perhaps even internalized the dominant media logic in society, in politics and culture, as well as among organizations. This transformation also influences the way we think and talk about crises.

BOX 10.3

MEDIA STORM OR MEDIA HYPE

Organizations in crisis often find themselves in the midst of a media storm or media hype. The media coverage suddenly gets very intense and seems to develop a life of its own. This typically happens when a crisis breaks out, or when there is a turning point or a climax in the course of events.

(Continued)

(Continued)

Vasterman (2005) defines a media storm as a media-generated news wave, triggered by a specific event that receives more attention than usual and enlarged by self-reinforcing processes within the news production of the media, such as the journalists' search after 'newer news'. After a certain time, the news wave itself becomes news.

In their study of political media storms, Wien and Elmelund-Præstekær (2009) demonstrated that a media storm on average lasts three weeks and consists of three waves with decreasing intensity. In each wave, there seems to be a kind of 'speaking list': first the politicians, then the general public, then the experts.

A media storm is a very difficult and resource-demanding occurrence for an organization. The pressure is high and it is difficult to keep a logbook. During the Scandinavian Airlines Dash 8 Q400 crisis, from early September to late October 2007 (see Chapter 6), SAS experienced a media storm. The chief communication officer of SAS Denmark and her department received 453 phone calls from the media.

Further reading: Vasterman (2005).

CRISIS JOURNALISM

Crisis journalism is the study of those aspects of crisis reporting which turn the news media into a voice *sui generis* in the rhetorical arena. Gatekeeping and the use of news criteria or news values in crisis situations, journalistic genres, and styles are some examples of these aspects.

Recently, several researchers have emphasized the lack of research on crisis communication and the news media. Koerber (2015) claims that the intersection between media theory and crisis communication theory 'remains underdeveloped' and that crisis communication researchers generally have relegated media to a 'secondary or background position in studies of crises' (p. 91). According to Koerber, the role of the media – the processes of mediated meaning-making – is more fundamental than previously thought. Therefore, Koerber criticizes Sellnow and Seeger (2013) for reducing mediation to only one 'dimension' of crisis communication. This is, however, taking it one step too far. The news media represent a powerful and influential voice when a crisis breaks out and an arena opens up, but it is far from the only voice. Olsson and Nord (2015) also claim that there is a lack of research connecting media reporting to crisis communication. When the news media are included, they are studied as a 'platform for the communication efforts of crisis management actors' (Olsson et al., 2015, pp. 159–160).

It seems possible to identify at least three different approaches to crisis journalism within crisis communication research:

(1) The news media as *data source*. Many crisis communication researchers collect data for their research projects from the news media. It is, after all, easier to collect data (e.g., statements made by the spokesperson of the organization in crisis) from the news media than to collect data directly from the organization itself. Sometimes it is even the only solution. However, it is not always ideal. Theoretically speaking, this approach is problematic because it reduces the media to a simple *channel*. Methodologically speaking, this is problematic because the data collected is *recontextualized* and the risk involved has been framed and defined solely by the reporting journalists.

(2) The news media as a *stakeholder* (by proxy). Many crisis communication researchers see the news media as a stakeholder that produces media coverage of crises. The content of this media coverage (e.g., how the media frame a crisis) is viewed as an input (attribution of crisis responsibility) to the crisis management process of the organization in crisis (e.g., choice of the appropriate crisis response strategies).

(3) The news media as a *stage* for crisis exploitation.

Crisis news frames

Framing and frames are the two key concepts within a rich stream of research in the social sciences that investigate how people interpret, organize, and communicate about social reality. Framing and frames are studied within a wide range of social science disciplines, from sociology to psychology and from political science to media and communication studies. Gregory Bateson from the Palo Alto School in Communication Research was among the first to articulate the idea of framing at the beginning of the 1970s. The 1980s and 1990s saw the publication of many of the foundational texts. Today, framing and frames attract the attention of not only management and organization scholars (for an overview, see Cornelissen & Werner, 2014), but also researchers in public relations (Hallahan, 1999) and organizational communication (Fairhurst, 2010).

Entman (1993) defines framing in the following way: 'To frame is to select some aspects of a perceived reality and make them more salient in a communicating text, in such a way as to promote a particular problem definition, causal interpretation, moral evaluation, and/or treatment recommendation' (p. 52).

Crisis communication researchers have also become interested in studying the use of framing, in particular framing in the news media. An and Gower (2009) contributed a study of crisis news frames. They examined how the news media frame crises – that is, what *kinds of news frames* are used. They also examined how differently the news frames are used according to *crisis type* and *level of responsibility*. This last part of their study is based on the concept of level of responsibility established by Iyengar (1991) who identified two distinct news frames dealing with social issues: (1) the episodic news frame and (2) the thematic news frame. The former makes people attribute responsibility to individuals, while the latter makes them attribute responsibility to society (in our case: organizations).

Based on a content analysis of 247 newspaper articles (all published in American newspapers in 2006, before the financial crisis), a typology of five different news frames, and Coombs' crisis typology (see Chapters 2 and 4), An and Gower concluded that in the United States the attribution of responsibility frame was the most frequently used news frame in the media coverage of crises, and that the morality frame was less frequently used (see Table 10.2). That the economic news frame came in second is no surprise, given that the sample of the study came from the business press.

In general, the organizational level of responsibility was emphasized more often than the individual level in the media coverage of crises. However, if an executive of a company had caused the crisis, the news media tended to stress the individual level. If it was an employee who caused the crisis, the news media continued emphasizing the organizational level.

An and Gower's (2009) study demonstrates how the news media use news frames when they portray a crisis depending on crisis type and level of responsibility. They help us to understand better how the news media may influence attributions

Table 10.2 The most frequently used crisis news frames in American newspapers

Type of crisis news frame (definitions)	Comments concerning crisis type and level of responsibility (cf. Coombs' crisis typology)
(1) *Attribution of responsibility* Highlights the attribution of responsibility to an actor involved in the crisis Most frequently used crisis news frame	This frame was used more when the crisis type was in the preventable cluster
(2) *Economic frame* Highlights economic consequences of the crisis	The sample of this study came from the business crises area This frame was more likely to be used in conjunction with the organizational level of responsibility
(3) *Conflict frame* Highlights disagreement among actors involved in the crisis	Preventable crisis news stories were more likely to use this frame
(4) *Human interest frame* Highlights human or emotional perspective on the crisis	This frame was used more when the crisis type was in the victim cluster This frame was more likely to be used in conjunction with the individual level of responsibility
(5) *Morality frame* Highlights moral perspective on crisis Less frequently used crisis news frame	Preventable crisis news stories were more likely to use this frame

Source: An and Gower (2009)

of responsibility for a crisis – an insight that fits well with the SCCT framework (see Chapter 6). However, these types of studies suffer from a strong sender-oriented focus and do not view the communication of crisis news as a process of interpretive interaction among different voices.

The news media as a stage for crisis exploitation strategies

The theories of organizational crisis communication that we presented in Chapters 5 and 6 defined crises as a reputational threat to an organization – that is, as something purely negative. Consequently, the main purpose of crisis communication was to protect and/or repair the damaged reputation of the organization. The stream of research that we briefly touch upon now applies a different approach.

First, private and public organizations are replaced with politicians and political parties and their interactions with the news media. The researchers who first launched this approach – Arjen Boin, Paul 't Hart, and Allan McConnell – claim that 'crises are political at heart' (Boin et al., 2005, p. ix). Second, crises are seen not just as a threat to the organization but equally as a political opportunity. A crisis can also be understood as a 'calculated act where successful politicians manage to exploit crisis situations to their advantage by showing action, strengthening credibility and pushing through new policies' (Olsson & Nord, 2015). Third, crisis response strategies are replaced with *crisis exploitation strategies*. Boin et al. (2009) have developed a theory of crisis exploitation that they define as 'the purposeful utilization of crisis-type rhetoric to significantly alter levels of political support for public office-holders and public policies' (p. 83). Politicians and political parties engage in 'frame contests, that is, rhetorical battles between pro- and counter-frames' (p. 82).

Swedish crisis researcher Eva-Karin Olsson has focused our attention on the question: What is a crisis news event? Taking an insider perspective looking at how events are perceived by the journalists themselves, Olsson defines a crisis news event as a surprise event that challenges organizational values and demands a swift response (Olsson, 2010).

CASE STUDY 10.1

DARE YOU EAT YOUR OWN PRODUCT? CRISIS ENTERTAINMENT ON TELEVISION

Kontant (English translation: *In cash*) is a consumer television program that has been broadcast by the publicly funded station DR almost every week since 2001. The program presents itself as a 'consumer magazine that addresses important issues affecting Danes and their wallets' (www.dr.dk/Kontant). *Kontant* has a large audience with its critical approach, and it often generates articles in the newspapers after each broadcast. Many of the programs are based on complaints from customers of a particular company or industry. Every week, a spokesperson struggles to protect the

(Continued)

(Continued)

'good reputation' of a company in crisis. And, every week, viewers are witness to how a spokesperson inevitably loses the battle against the presenter. The ritual is almost the same from 'this week's crisis' to 'next week's crisis'. The best way to characterize the media format of *Kontant* is infotainment – that is, the combination of information and entertainment.

Until 2015, SuperBest was a chain of Danish supermarkets. In 2009, the year where the crisis described below took place, SuperBest had approximately 12,000 employees working in 220 supermarkets located all over the country. Originally established as a cooperative, SuperBest was initially created to gather the so-called 'free' groceries into a chain strong enough to compete with the big players such as Coop Denmark and Danish Supermarket Group. The organizational culture of SuperBest was characterized by autonomy and responsibility.

On September 29, 2009, the vigorous presenter of *Kontant*, Kåre Quist, introduced the topic of the evening: extensive fraud in Danish supermarkets in regard to relabelling packages of ground meat. Frank Sørensen, SuperBest CEO for more than a decade, had accepted the invitation from Kåre Quist to participate in the program. So had Karin Frøidt, quality manager of Coop Denmark.

In the weeks before the program's broadcast, *Kontant* visited 20 supermarkets in the Danish Supermarket Group, Coop, and SuperBest chains in the late afternoon. In each supermarket, packages with ground meat and fish on display in the cold counters were discreetly marked with a pen (and documented with photos). The following day *Kontant* returned to the supermarkets in order to find out if the same packages with meat or fish were still for sale. More often than not they were! SuperBest had the most egregious problems. In 8 out of 12 cases, the same packages were still for sale the day after they were packaged (in Denmark, it is illegal to store freshly ground meat in cold counters for more than 24 hours due to the risk of bacteria formation). Many of the supermarkets had circumvented the law, however, by covering the original packaging labels with new ones.

On September 24, the first SuperBest managers phoned the headquarters in Ringsted, not far from Copenhagen, and told the CEO that they had had visits from the public authorities who were accompanied by a camera crew from DR. On the very same day, the top management of SuperBest decided that the situation was serious enough that someone had to be held responsible. Seven butchers were fired and a press release was issued: 'All SuperBest supermarkets have received a letter that they have to sign. The letter confirms that you risk losing your job if you deliberately break the rules.' On September 28, just four days later, four more supermarkets were accused of relabelling packages with ground meat.

In the television program broadcast on September 29, the CEO of SuperBest and the quality manager from Coop were the last to be interviewed. Preceding them, a series of experts on food safety had explained to viewers the health risks related to eating old meat. Frank Sørensen said he felt ashamed and found it embarrassing that this had happened. Nevertheless, he emphasized that it was his responsibility. Presenter Kåre Quist and his crew had prepared one last surprise for each interviewee. Quist had asked two Danish chefs to prepare two dishes with old meat and old fish from SuperBest and Coop. At the end of their interviews, Frank Sørensen and Karin Frøidt were offered their own products served on a plate. Both refused to taste or eat the food.

Studying the rhetorical arena

(1) Macro component:

- List the voices in the rhetorical arena that opens up in September 2009. Do they form clusters or sub-arenas? How do the voices communicate with each other? What would have happened if the issue had spread to other news media?

(2) Micro component:

- How is infotainment used as a strategy?
- How would you describe and explain the two dishes prepared by the two chefs? Is it a kind of persuasive attack?

Managing the rhetorical arena

- How would you have managed the crisis?
- Would you have accepted the invitation to participate in *Kontant*? If so, would you also have eaten your own product?
- To what extent is the crisis triggered by the organizational culture of SuperBest?

CHAPTER SUMMARY

In this chapter, we have focused on two theories or streams of research: mediatization and crisis journalism. At first sight, these two fields seem quite separate, methodologically as well as theoretically. Mediatization is a product of media and communication research (perhaps more 'media' than 'communication'?). Crisis journalism, on the other hand, is a product of crisis communication research. To put it differently: while the study of media logics and media formats refers back to Chapter 1, the study of crisis news frames and crisis exploitation strategies refers back to Chapters 5 and 6 in this book. However, if we aim to understand the voice of the news media, we need to combine the two streams of research.

 Further reading

Olsson, E.-K. (2010). Defining crisis news events. *Nordicom Review*, 31(1), 87–101.

Pallas, J., Strannegård, L., & Jonsson, S. (Eds.) (2014). *Organizations and the Media: Organizing in a Mediatized World*. London: Routledge.

INTERMEDIARIES: TRADE ASSOCIATIONS

11

┌─ **CHAPTER OVERVIEW** ─┐

This chapter explores the voices of intermediaries, and in particular the voice of trade associations. The primary function of intermediaries is to *mediate* the relationship between an organization and its stakeholders, that is to represent either the organization or the stakeholders, and to intervene in their relationship by furthering or impeding their interests and activities. This function is crucial in a crisis situation. First, a general theory of intermediaries is briefly presented and illustrated. Second, the crisis communication of trade associations is investigated, focusing on the interplay of three levels of reputation (management): the corporate level, the industry level, and the trade association level.

INTRODUCTION

Trade associations are structured for studied consensus development with advocacy of their approved policy. They are not designed for crisis action. Crisis management, the antithesis of consensus management, is virtually unknown in the trade association field.

This is how Geraldine V. Cox, representing the Chemical Manufacturers Association (CMA), introduced her article entitled 'A trade association's role in crisis management', published in 1987, in *Industrial Crisis Quarterly*. It is a very pessimistic introduction in which the author, who served as CMA's spokesperson during the Bhopal crisis in December 1984, explains why trade associations have not been able to adopt crisis management in their organizations. However, she may be excused, since 1987 was in the very early days of the discipline of crisis management, a period when crisis-prone organizations clearly outnumbered crisis-prepared ones (Pauchant & Mitroff, 1992; see also the general introduction).

Today, the situation seems to have improved. A growing number of national and international trade associations, such as the American Association of Port Authorities (AAPA), adopt a strategic approach to crisis management, helping their members to implement crisis preparedness systems in their organizations. AAPA, for example, offers crisis webinars and workshops and best practice examples of crisis communication manuals to its members. A growing number of consulting firms, such as Black Swans Solutions, specialize in advising trade associations on how to handle crises. Unfortunately, as we shall see in the Bestseller multi-crisis case study at the end of this chapter, this development is still at its beginning. And what is perhaps worse, the type of crisis management that is now spreading among trade associations is very general and based on an approach that fits every type of organization. But trade associations are precisely not 'every type of organization'. They are very specific organizations operating under very specific internal and external conditions. The keywords are inter-organizational relations.

In this chapter we will concentrate on this inter-organizational dimension of crises, crisis management, and crisis communication. Berthod et al. (2013) define inter-organizational crisis management in the following way: 'Crisis management deserves the attribute "inter-organizational" when it is sensitive towards inter-organizational interdependencies (and the embeddedness of a focal organization in IORs more generally) and when it delves into the potential of these same inter-organizational relations to avert a crisis and/or counter its consequences' (p. 146). As we shall see, the interdependencies and embeddedness mentioned in this definition create a rhetorical arena that is more complex than the arenas we studied in Chapters 9 and 10, and where different levels of reputation and different types of reputation management are entangled.

A THEORY OF INTERMEDIARIES

The relationship between an organization and its stakeholders is seldom linear, direct, and dyadic. In fact, this relationship is often mediated by one or more *intermediaries* (Friedman & Miles, 2006; see also the network approach to stakeholder management in Chapter 4). Before we start focusing on the role of trade associations in crisis situations, we need to dwell a little on the concept of an intermediary. What is an intermediary? How can we describe and classify them? And what is their role and function in a crisis situation?

Intermediaries represent a very heterogeneous group of actors, including trade associations, trade unions, advocacy groups, government agencies, consulting firms, the media, etc. Frandsen and Johansen (2015b) define intermediaries as follows:

An intermediary is an actor, that is, an individual, a group of individuals, an organization, or a meta-organization, who belongs to a specific area in society (e.g., a specific industry, a specific organizational field and/or a specific sector), and whose primary function or mission is to mediate, that is, to represent an organization and/or a specific stakeholder group, and/or to intervene in the relationship between them either by furthering or by impeding the interests and activities of the organization in question and/or its stakeholders in a specific situation or over time. (p. 257)

Intermediaries can be described and classified according to a set of criteria. Here are four of these criteria (for the complete list, see Frandsen & Johansen, 2015b):

(1) *Areas of society in which the intermediary is active.* Like organizations and stakeholders, intermediaries operate in and across various societal and organizational contexts such as sectors, industries, and organizational fields. These contexts are structured in specific ways, forcing the actors to adopt specific behaviors. In case example 11.1, Tesla Denmark and the Danish Electric Vehicle Alliance form part of an organizational field where the government and political parties are important players (regulation).

(2) *Organizational form.* Intermediaries vary in size and may consist of everything from an individual, a group of individuals, and an organization (of individuals) to a meta-organization (of organizations). The Danish Electric Vehicle Alliance is a meta-organization consisting of more than 50 members, including private companies such as Arriva, Avis, BMW, and Bosch, educational institutions such as Aalborg University, and public organizations such as the municipality of Copenhagen

(3) *Status.* Intermediaries can be found on both sides of the relationship between an organization and its stakeholders. The organization has its own intermediaries, and so have the stakeholders. However, this is not merely an instance of symmetry. There will normally be important asymmetries too (e.g., differences in power and access to resources). Intermediaries are able to shift from acting as pure intermediaries to acting as stakeholders in their own right, with their own stakes and their own reputation. The membership of the Danish Electric Vehicle Alliance is very heterogeneous and looks more like a strategic alliance within an emergent market than a traditional trade association within an industry.

(4) *Representation.* Intermediaries can represent the organization and/or the stakeholders. Formal representation is the highest degree of representation (membership). The lowest degree of representation is when there is no formal or informal connection at all between the organization and/or the stakeholders and the intermediary. It is also important to distinguish between intermediaries that are elected by the organization and/or the stakeholders and intermediaries that are not elected, or that are self-elected or appointed by themselves. The Danish Electric Vehicle Alliance is based on formal representation. Tesla Denmark is a member.

Applying these criteria, a trade association can be described as a meta-organization with a high degree of formal representation (membership) that has been elected by the member organizations and that is on their side. Similarly, a trade union can be defined as an organization (of individuals) with a high degree of formal representation (membership) that has been elected by the employees and that is on their side. In the previous chapter, we claimed that the news media are intermediaries. However, they differ from both trade associations and trade unions in fundamental ways.

In a crisis situation, intermediaries serve many different functions: a trade association protects its members and the industry; a trade union protects its members and the profession; the government regulates; the news media intervene; etc. Each of these intermediaries interprets the course of events differently.

After this brief introduction to the general theory of intermediaries, we will in the remaining part of this chapter focus exclusively on one specific intermediary: trade associations and the role they play during a crisis.

BOX 11.1

THE BENEFITS OF TRADE ASSOCIATIONS

Companies and individuals should join trade associations because:

- in the long term it is in their financial interests to do so;
- associations are seen as the voice of their sector and able to represent all their members at every level;
- associations are trusted and central to their industry;
- enhancement of a company's reputation often follows the joining of a trade association.

The government should consult with trade associations because:

- they are representative of the interests of their members;
- they identify the effect of policy measures on their sector;
- they are the most effective way of establishing excellent lines of communication between the government and their represented sector.

Other parties should deal with members of trade associations because:

- many trade associations require their members to sign up to a code of practice;
- using trade association members means that there is somewhere to go for help in the event that things go wrong;
- trade association members are reputable businesses;
- some trade associations are TrustMark Licensed Operators.

Source: Trade Association Forum (UK).

TRADE ASSOCIATIONS

What is a trade association? Fifty years ago, Warner and Martin (1967) defined trade associations as non-profit institutions that operate cooperatively for and among competitive, profit-making actors within an industry (see also Aldrich & Staber, 1988).

This definition contains two keywords, *collaboration* and *competition*, that have been reformulated more recently in the context of reputation management. We shall return to these keywords later in this chapter.

Why do private companies become members of a trade association? What makes competitors engage in collective action? The promotional material *The Benefits of Trade Associations* distributed by the Trade Association Forum in the United Kingdom illustrates how organizations can benefit from being a member of a trade association. The material also clearly demonstrates that trade associations see themselves as intermediaries navigating between the member organizations, the government, and other parties (see Box 11.1). Applying a more systematic approach, we can make a distinction between internal and external strategies of action enacted by trade associations and from which their members can benefit. Among the most important internal strategies of action are: education and training, information sharing, research, certification, and accreditation. Among the most important external strategies of action are: lobbying, monitoring policy, public affairs, and civic practices.

There is one more good reason for becoming a member of a trade association, a reason which is not mentioned by the Trade Association Forum, and that is *crises*. It happens now and then that the reputation of an entire industry is challenged or damaged due to the wrongdoing of one of the companies operating within that industry. Here are three famous examples.

In 1989, the *Exxon Valdez*, an oil tanker bound for Long Beach, California, struck a reef in Prince William Sound in Alaska and spilled 11 to 38 million US gallons of crude oil over a short period. The *Exxon Valdez* oil spill was the largest ever at the time (until the Deepwater Horizon oil spill in 2010). It had a negative impact on the reputation of the oil industry for many years.

In 2001, Arthur Andersen, one of the 'Big Five' accounting firms in the world, was involved in the Enron scandal. This scandal brought the Andersen name into so much disrepute that it has not returned as a viable company. It also damaged the reputation of the accountancy industry.

In 2006 and in the years following, British confectionary subsidiary company Cadbury Schweppes had problems such as recalling chocolate bars due to labeling errors, salmonella infection, contamination with melamine (China), or traces of pork DNA (Malaysia). This damaged the reputation of the food industry.

What can companies within an industry do to protect their reputation, including the reputation of the industry, when they find themselves 'tarred by the same brush' as in the case of the *Exxon Valdez*, Arthur Andersen, and Cadbury Schweppes? They can become a member of a trade association and engage in collective reputation management.

 Case example 11.1

Tesla Denmark strikes back – supported by a trade association

It happens now and then that a trade association has to support one of its members in public, as in this case with Tesla Denmark and the Danish Electric Vehicle Alliance.

Tesla Motors, Inc. is an American company that designs, manufactures, and sells luxury electric cars. It was founded in 2003 and entered the Scandinavian car market in 2009.

The Danish Electric Vehicle Alliance is an independent trade association under the Danish Energy Association. The mission of the Alliance is to ensure Denmark is a pioneering country when it comes to the implementation of electric vehicles. This is also done by ensuring synergies between the energy sector and the industries involved in the introduction of electric vehicles.

For a number of years, electric vehicles have enjoyed tax exemptions in order to kickstart the market for these types of cars in Denmark. However, in October 2015, the Danish government, along with a broad coalition of political parties, decided to phase in taxes on electric vehicles from 2016 to 2020. From the beginning of 2016, expensive electric cars such as Tesla would be hit hard by the new taxes. According to the Danish Minister for Taxation, many people therefore had hoarded electric vehicles and stored them away in 2015 to avoid buying the more expensive cars in 2016. He claimed that no less than 2,500 license plates for expensive cars had been ordered in less than a month. This would lead to an income loss of about DKK 1 billion for the Danish state.

In a newspaper article headlined 'Tesla strikes back: Unworthy attack from the Minister for Taxation', published by the Danish business newspaper *Børsen* (November 17, 2015), Tesla Denmark defended itself against the attack from the Minister for Taxation. The company's spokesperson said, 'I am sure that the Minister made his statement on the basis of the information he has received. However, this information is not correct. Having said that, I find it problematic that a politician in public and on the basis of hurried conclusions accuses a named trademark of circumventing the law.'

In another newspaper article, published on the same day and by the same newspaper, the Danish Electric Vehicle Alliance supported Tesla Denmark. The trade association's brand manager declared: 'It is very unlikely that it has been possible to register so many cars within such a short period. So I don't think that the Ministry for Taxation has to be nervous.'

Source: Børsen (November 17, 2015).

However, as already suggested in the chapter overview, practising reputation management is more challenging for trade associations than for ordinary private companies. Why the difference? There are two explanations. First, trade associations are meta-organizations, that is 'organizations of organizations' driven by what Geraldine Cox from CMA referred to as consensus management (see the introduction to this chapter). It can turn decision making in crisis situations into a complicated activity. Second, trade associations have to take into consideration no less than three reputational levels: a corporate level, an industry level, and a trade association level. In crisis situations, this reputational complexity almost automatically prompts the questions: Which of these three types of reputation must be protected first? Or can all three of them be protected at the same time using a specific strategy, such as strategic ambiguity? In the following two sections, we will take a closer look at meta-organizations and collective reputation management.

Meta-organizations

The theory of meta-organizations was developed by two Swedish researchers, Göran Ahrne and Nils Brunsson. In their book *Meta-organizations* (2008), they apply the theory to explain how the growing number of meta-organizations has contributed to globalization and vice versa. We are interested in a different aspect of the theory: that is, if it can help us explain if the organizational design of trade associations has an impact on how they practise crisis management and crisis communication (see also Ahrne & Brunsson, 2005, 2012).

Ahrne and Brunsson (2008) define meta-organizations as 'organizations of organizations' (p. 2). Thus, all trade associations are meta-organizations. The general theory of meta-organizations is based on two arguments.

The first argument concerns the relationship between organization and environment. Every time a new meta-organization is created, part of what was before considered environment is transformed into organization. Before this transformation the individual organizations had to confront an unclear social context characterized by uncertainty and lack of control. After the transformation, when they have become a member of a meta-organization, they experience a new kind of social order

The second argument concerns the members of a meta-organization. As already mentioned, it is the character of the members that constitutes the difference between meta-organizations and individual-based organizations. On the one hand, organizations are free to become members of a meta-organization, and upon doing so they keep most of their autonomy and identity as independent organizations. On the other hand, there is a fundamental similarity between a meta-organization and its members. The members belong to the same industry, and in most cases it is an advantage for them to become members. Meta-organizations are heavily dependent on their members, both for their similarities and their differences.

Ahrne and Brunsson (2008) do not study what happens when a meta-organization or one or more of its members is facing a crisis. The closest they get to this topic is a chapter on conflicts and decision-making problems. According to the two Swedish scholars, 'meta-organizations harbour even more sources of conflict yet have more limited capacity to resolve conflict than do organizations comprising individuals' (p. 107). Although meta-organizations are based on a fundamental similarity, there will still be many differences between their members. The members may, for example, vary in their access to resources and in their motives for joining a meta-organization. When a conflict arises, meta-organizations have limited possibilities for solving the conflict. They can use their hierarchical authority; however, this authority is relatively weak, and this is the reason why meta-organizations often only aim at taking consensus decisions. They can also formulate controversial decisions as standards, but not as rules or directives. Or they can deliberately formulate their decisions in an ambiguous way, opening up a variety of interpretations among the members.

We expect that the organizational design of meta-organizations, which is also the design of trade associations, will have an impact on how they manage and communicate in crisis situations.

Collective reputation management

Let us return to Warner and Martin's (1967) old definition of trade associations including the two keywords: *collaboration* and *competition*. These two keywords have more recently been reformulated within the context of reputation management.

Winn et al. (2008) introduced a distinction between collaborative reputation management and competitive reputation management. By *collaborative reputation management*, they refer to 'all activities and behavior undertaken by members of a collective to deliberately alter judgements about the reputation of the collective' (p. 37). Trade associations were described as a 'primary vehicle of industry cooperation' (ibid.). By *competitive reputation management*, they refer to 'activities undertaken by a single firm to enhance its own reputation and competitive position *vis-à-vis* other members of the industry' (ibid.) (for a similar distinction, see Barnett, 2006).

This distinction between two types and levels of reputation (management), corresponding to the dynamic tension between collaboration and competition inside trade associations, is useful. It allows us to explain why some organizations decide to become members of a trade association and why others decide to cancel their membership.

It does not, however, account entirely for the complexity generated by a crisis situation that includes a specific industry, one or more companies operating within that industry, and one or more trade associations of which these companies are members (see case study 11.1). In order to study this complexity we need to add an extra reputational level: the trade association level. Or to put it differently, trade associations also have a reputation to protect. Thus, we end up with the following three levels.

(1) The corporate level of reputation

At the first level – the corporate level – we have the reputation of each individual company. Based on the idea of *a temporal context* (past vs. future), reputation is here conceptualized as the collective judgment by stakeholders of a particular organization and its performance over time within select areas. The evaluation of the behavior of a company in the past drives the stakeholders' expectations about how this company will behave in the future (Barnett & Hoffman, 2008). This understanding of reputation is in line with Fombrun's definition in Chapter 3. This is also how most crisis communication researchers understand reputation. A crisis represents a threat to the corporate reputation. The fact that a company's reputation also depends upon the actions of other companies is not taken into consideration.

(2) The industry level of reputation

At the second level – the industry level – we have the reputation of the industry inside which the companies operate. Based on the idea of a *comparative context*, reputation is here conceptualized as the collective judgment of a particular industry by stakeholders.

The concept of *reputation commons* is an attempt to understand the interdependent dimension of reputation at this level (King et al., 2002). Reputation commons refers to the fact that a company's reputation is tied to the reputation of other companies and that reputation may be a common resource shared by all members of an industry. As Barnett and Hoffman (2008) state a little paradoxically, 'The company you keep affects the company you keep' (p. 1).

The reputation commons of an industry must be managed strategically. Like natural resources, the reputation commons can be *overexploited*. A company may benefit from the favorable reputation of an industry even as it takes individual actions that may harm this shared reputation. A crisis is an example of overexploitation. When a crisis breaks out, stakeholders may punish not only the company in crisis, but the entire industry as well.

According to King et al. (2002), a reputation commons becomes a *reputation commons problem* when stakeholders are able to take action against companies and/or an industry. If stakeholders are sufficiently informed about the relative performance of the individual companies within an industry, then no reputation commons problem exists. However, if stakeholders are not sufficiently informed and, therefore, not able to differentiate the relative performance of the individual companies, then a reputation commons problem exists.

How can companies within an industry manage a reputation commons problem? According to King et al. (2002), they can either reduce the threat of stakeholder sanction, or 'privatize' the reputation commons. The first category includes four strategic responses: to improve collective performance (e.g., codes of conducts); to manage stakeholder perception (e.g., public relations campaigns); to lobby government (e.g. institutional barriers); and to co-opt threatening stakeholders (e.g., alliances with important stakeholder groups). The second category includes five strategic responses: to reveal individual performance (e.g., taking unilateral action to differentiate themselves from other companies); to team with credible stakeholders (e.g., working with a reputable NGO); to make credible investments, to adopt standardized reporting, and to form an elite club (e.g., an elite subgroup).

These strategic responses can be considered a kind of crisis response strategy.

(3) The trade association level of reputation

At the third level – the trade association level – we have the reputation of the trade association(s) that represents the given industry. Reputation is here conceptualized as the collective judgment of a particular trade association by stakeholders. Trade associations serve two reputation management functions.

First, they serve as what Tucker (2008) named 'industry reputation agents'. Tucker studied how trade associations manage their industries' reputations in order to identify success factors in the associations' role as reputation agents (e.g., self-regulation, collective response to consumer action, integrity, credibility, expertise in specific industry issues, speaking with a unified voice to the media, etc.). In this function, trade associations seem to act as pure intermediaries (cf. the theory of intermediaries).

Second, they serve as the managers of their own reputation. There may be more than one trade association representing the same industry. Some members may leave the trade association and create a new association if they are not satisfied with their membership benefits. In January 2016, five European airline companies – Air France KLM, easyJet, IAG, Lufthansa Group, and Ryanair – created Airlines for Europe (A4E) to improve lobbying of European aviation policy.

Table 11.1 provides an overview of the three levels of reputation, including the stakeholders who evaluate the companies, the industry, and the trade association. The corporate reputation of a company is constructed by, among others, its customers,

Table 11.1 Overview of the three reputation levels

Level of reputation	Stakeholders
Corporate level	Corporate-level stakeholders: • Customers • Investors • Competitors (other companies)
Industry level	Corporate-level stakeholders: • Customers • Investors • Competitors (other companies) Industry-level stakeholders: • Government • Trade unions • Media
Trade association level	Trade-association-level stakeholders: • Members • Competitors (other trade associations)

investors, and competitors. The industry reputation is constructed by the same stakeholders plus a series of specific industry-level stakeholders. Finally, the trade association reputation is constructed by a very small group of stakeholders: actual and potential members and competitors.

CASE STUDY 11.1

THE BESTSELLER MULTI-CRISIS

Bestseller is a family-owned clothing and accessories company founded in Denmark in 1975 by Merete Bech Povlsen and Troels Holch Povlsen. Bestseller employs more than 13,000 employees globally, 3,300 of whom work in Denmark. Bestseller's products are sold under brands such as Jack & Jones, Vero Moda, Only, Selected, and Name It. They are available online, in branded chain stores, and in multibrand and department stores. More than 30 years ago Troels Holch Povlsen, Bestseller's founder, phrased the ten basic principles of the company.

A multi-crisis

On July 7, 2011, www.business.dk, a business news portal owned by the Danish newspaper *Berlingske Tidende*, released an article entitled 'Children's clothing from Bestseller may cause cancer'. In this article, Bestseller was accused of two types of wrongdoing. First, it was accused of selling children's clothes (under the brand

(Continued)

(Continued)

of Name It) containing a high level of azo colors. Azo colors may cause bladder cancer and have been added to the EU list of prohibited chemical substances (Crisis I). Second, Bestseller was accused of failing to disseminate information about the discovery of azo colors in its products in an appropriate way. Instead of announcing a product recall in the mass media, as most Danish companies do, Bestseller had limited information to small notes informing customers about the recall that were hung inside its stores and put on its corporate website (Crisis II). Thus, the Danish company was facing a potential double crisis: a product crisis, overlapped by a management crisis; that is, the poor handling of the product recall (for a definition of double crisis, see Chapter 2).

In the following weeks and months, an impressive series of voices started communicating inside the rhetorical arena opened by the Bestseller crisis, which was soon to become a multi-crisis. Apart from the news media and a few public relations experts, the list of voices included the Danish Environmental Protection Agency, the Competition and Consumer Authority, trade associations such as Danish Fashion & Textile, Danish Detail, The Danish Chamber of Commerce and Danish Fashion Institute, competitors such as IC Companys and H&M, and, finally, of course, Bestseller itself.

Four trade associations

The crisis started in early July, and Bestseller was involved from the beginning. However, what seemed initially to be a Bestseller crisis transformed into a multi-crisis with a strong inter-organizational dimension when IC Companys, another large Danish clothing company, and the four trade associations listed below entered the arena later in the month. Here are the other organizations involved:

Danish Fashion & Textile is a non-profit organization which has about 350 members. Bestseller is not a member, but is considered a strategic partner. According to its statutes, Danish Fashion & Textile's aim is 'to operate across the textile and clothing industry, through organizational collaboration for the national and international interests of the members, including their competitiveness, productivity and reputation'.

Dansk Detail has about 2,300 members. According to its statutes, the purpose of this trade association is 'to create the best possible conditions where a common effort is of interest to members'.

The Danish Chamber of Commerce is not a trade association in the traditional sense of the word, but a large business organization representing about 17,000 companies and 100 trade associations. In its statutes it states that the organization's is 'to appear as the leading political representative and counselor of the business world, to make it attractive to run a business and create competitiveness among members' and 'to gain the highest possible influence on decisions concerning the conditions of the members through visibility and impact'.

Danish Fashion Institute (DAFI) is not a trade association in the traditional sense of the word either, but a 'network organization' with 130 members. Its statutes state that the purpose of DAFI is 'to strengthen and position Danish fashion through marketing, PR and dissemination of information'.

Bestseller and IC Companys' crisis communication

Bestseller was very inconsistent in its crisis communication from the outset, especially concerning Crisis II. First, on July 7, Bestseller denied that the product recall should have been handled differently, using minimalization as a crisis response strategy: 'It is only a matter of a very small lot of products compared to our total sales … Approximately 2,000 cardigans have been sold in all markets. If we had sold 100,000 pieces, we would perhaps have acted differently.' However, later the same day, Bestseller's CSR manager admitted that '[t]he discussion whether the homepage and the small notes inside the stores are enough has led us to reflect seriously on the matter'. The company also took corrective action: 'Should a similar situation occur in the future, we will advertise [product recalls] in the news media and inform the public authorities.'. However, when the company had to recall products again on July 23 and July 30 (bags and children's clothing), it did not advertise the product recall in the news media as promised, although this time customers who had signed up for Bestseller's SMS service were informed about the recall. Consequently, Bestseller was accused of a breach of faith, and *Berlingske Tidende* stated: 'The communication manager of Bestseller confirms that it has been decided not to publish the product recall in the press because it is not required by law.' Concerning Crisis I, Bestseller denied that it was its responsibility to 'account for everything that is going on in the supply chain'. Still, Bestseller applied a more accommodative approach by stating: 'We would of course like our suppliers to do business with a smaller number of suppliers, and right now we have started a dialogue with them [about this challenge].'

IC Companys did not enter the rhetorical arena until July 25. Just like Bestseller, IC Companys announced in relation to Crisis I that they were 'not able to guarantee that new matters will not arise', but that 'they have tightened the procedures to make sure to handle them in the right way in the future'. Regarding Crisis II, IC Companys admitted that they had not been informative enough, but when asked about how to proceed in the future, they stated that they 'have not decided whether they will inform through the news media or elsewhere, but that they will have a dialogue with the public authorities about this'. Furthermore, IC Companys refused to show pictures of the recalled products. However, on the following day, IC Companys changed their mind, announcing that they would advertise recalls in national news media including pictures of the recalled products.

The crisis communication of the four trade associations

Danish Fashion & Textile started intervening on July 26, only two days after the publication of IC Companys' press release and after the crisis had transformed into a multi-crisis. It was also just only one day after the announcement made by the Danish Minister of the Environment that the Danish Environmental Protection Agency would organize a meeting with representatives of the industry. The crisis had become so big, that both political and corporate voices were competing with each other in showing vigor. This also applies to the trade associations.

Danish Fashion & Textile expressed its concerns, warning the entire industry that it would end up with a trust crisis between clothing companies and consumers (leading to boycott and lower profit), if the revelations of dangerous clothing, the evasiveness, and the illegal behavior continued. This is an instance of what we call

(Continued)

(Continued)

a *second-order crisis response strategy*: that is, a crisis response strategy that is based on another crisis response strategy. The trade association announced that it would organize a series of dialogue meetings, establish a set of guidelines, and offer advice about how its members could inform consumers in the case of a product crisis. Danish Fashion & Textile claimed that the trustworthiness of the industry had not yet been damaged, although it recognized that parts of the industry were still not sufficiently open towards the environment – especially Bestseller, which had been accused by the news media of having an introverted organizational culture. Danish Fashion & Textile focused on the reputation of the industry and did not seem to make a clear distinction between the two crises.

The other trade associations did not start communicating until August 10, the very same day that the Danish Minister of the Environment was hosting a crisis meeting.

Dansk Detail started intervening on August 10, following revelations that Bestseller had also been selling leather bags containing exorbitant levels of azo colors without informing consumers of the danger. Apparently, this had taken place with the permission of the Danish Environmental Protection Agency. The Danish Consumer Council, one of the intermediaries fighting for the cause of the consumers, criticized the Environmental Protection Agency for having allowed this: 'It almost sounds like a blunder in the Environmental Protection Agency.' Dansk Detail, however, focused on the manufacturers: 'Whatever the law says, the provider is responsible for informing the consumers.' The existence of a law in this area was also emphasized: 'The law is the law, and it must be followed. If you are only allowed to drive 50 kilometers per hour, then you cannot drive 75 and claim that you did not know it was illegal', CEO Jens Birkeholm declared.

The Danish Fashion Institute also started intervening on August 10. Compared to the intervention made by Dansk Detail, however, the Danish Fashion Institute applied a different communication strategy: 'I have not heard about anything similar before; as a consumer I would like to know if I have bought a bag that is going to be destroyed because it is dangerous', said Eva Kruse, CEO of Danish Fashion Institute. It was not Bestseller that needed to be checked, but the law, she claimed: 'If the Environmental Protection Agency thinks that it isn't necessary to inform about a bag being considered dangerous waste, then it seems the rules need to be tightened.' Thus, Danish Fashion Institute indirectly attacked Bestseller concerning Crisis I, but at the same time it defended Bestseller concerning Crisis II. The so-called REACH Act, regulating chemicals in the EU beginning in 2009, was also included in the Danish Fashion Institute's criticism of the public authorities. 'In our organization, we have not been aware of REACH. We have not been informed about it by the authorities, and when we don't know anything about it, probably a lot of other organizations are not aware of it either', Eva Kruse declared.

The Danish Chamber of Commerce started intervening on August 11, the day after the crisis meeting organized by the Minister of the Environment. The participants ended up concluding that the law was good enough, but that the industry had difficulties in interpreting it. 'The industry agrees with the minister that the law is good enough within this area. However, there have been some problems concerning how to interpret the law. Consequently, we will now work together on common guidelines', said Jacob Zeuthen, Head of Environmental Policy at the Danish Chamber of Commerce.

August 11, 2011, was the last day where one or more of the four Danish trade associations intervened in the rhetorical arena. The Bestseller multi-crisis was later described as the worst crisis ever in the history of the Danish clothing industry.

Studying the rhetorical arena

(1) Macro component:

- List the voices in the rhetorical arena that opened in July 2011. Did they form clusters or sub-arenas? How did the voices communicate with each other?
- Do the trade associations behave as intermediaries and/or meta-organizations?

(2) Micro component:

- How would you describe Bestseller's crisis communication?
- Do the four trade associations use different strategies in their crisis communication? If so, how would you describe these strategies?

Managing the rhetorical arena

- If you were the crisis manager of Bestseller and/or IC Companys, how would you have managed the product recall?
- What is a multi-crisis? How can it be managed?
- If you were the crisis manager of one of the four trade associations, how would you manage a multi-crisis that may damage the reputation of the entire industry?
- Which trade association would you prefer to work for? Why?

Source: Frandsen and Johansen (2016a).

CHAPTER SUMMARY

The crisis communication of trade associations has been neglected by crisis communication researchers for a long time. In this chapter, we have studied the role and function of trade associations as intermediaries and meta-organizations in crisis situations. We have focused on reputation (management) at three different levels: the corporate level, the industry level, and the trade association level. These three levels are challenging our traditional understanding of reputation (management). They also add complexity to rhetorical arena theory and the multivocal approach.

 Further reading

Ham, C. D., Hong, H., & Cameron, G. T. (2012). Same crisis, different responses: Case studies of how multiple competing corporations responded to the same explosion-related crisis. *International Journal of Business and Social Sciences*, 3(20), 19–31.

King, A. A., Lenox, M. J., & Barnet, M. L. (2002). Strategic responses to the reputation commons problem. In A. Hoffman & M. J. Ventresca (Eds.), *Organizations, Policy, and the Natural Environment: Institutional and Strategic Perspectives* (pp. 393–406). Palo Alto, CA: Stanford University Press.

MANAGERS AND EMPLOYEES: INSIDE THE ORGANIZATION

12

CHAPTER OVERVIEW

This last chapter examines the internal dimension of organizational crises, crisis management, and crisis communication, focusing on the voices of top managers, middle managers, and employees. What happens inside an organization when a crisis occurs? How do managers and employees react? How do organizations manage the internal dimension of crises? This chapter provides answers to these questions. First, the internal voices are defined and various aspects of crisis-related employee behavior are described. Second, the chapter presents an integrative framework for the study of the many different types of internal crisis communication. The chapter concludes with the examination of the internal crisis management and crisis communication activities of private and public organizations, including internal whistleblower arrangements.

INTRODUCTION

In Chapter 6, we studied the Scandinavian Airlines Dash 8 Q400 crisis in the fall of 2007. Between September 9 and October 27, 2007, Danish newspapers published no less than 322 articles about Scandinavian Airlines, aircraft manufacturer Bombardier, and the three spectacular 'security landings'. In the communication department of SAS Denmark, the staff were more than busy throughout the period. The chief communication officer and her colleagues answered 453 telephone calls from the press. They organized four press conferences, including regular meetings with major customers and briefings of national and international media. They also distributed six letters to customers and updated www.sas.dk (the crisis-ready dark site) several times every day. But what was going on inside the organization during all this?

Inside SAS Denmark, the employees – pilots, crews, ground personnel, etc. – received nine special issues of the internal newsletter, *Radar*. They were invited to

20 dialogue meetings in the canteen at Kastrup Airport. They received five emails including three 'video letters' and a three-page long 'letter of concern' from the CEO, Susanne Larsen. The intranet portal was updated daily. Finally, an open house arrangement for employees and their spouses, children, and closest family was organized. All these internal crisis communication activities were important to the employees but remained invisible to the external observer.

The purpose of this last chapter is to introduce the reader to the internal voices of an organization in crisis. First, we define what we understand by internal voices. How do managers and employees differ from external voices such as customers? How do they serve as senders and receivers of internal crisis communication? And how internal is internal? Second, we examine how managers and employees react in crisis situations, including how they react emotionally to negative media coverage of their employer. Third, we study how organizations manage the internal dimension of crises. The chapter concludes with a section on the internal whistleblower arrangements that a growing number of private and public organizations have implemented as part of their formal crisis preparedness.

DEFINING THE INTERNAL VOICES OF AN ORGANIZATION

Who are the internal voices of an organization? By internal voices, we mean all the organization members, whom we divide into three categories: *employees*, *middle managers*, and *top management*. It is, of course, tempting to see these three categories of people as a homogeneous organizational entity, but nothing could be further from the truth. The employees, for example, will in most cases be divided into groups depending on their professional and functional subcultures, but also depending on their social networks inside the organization. An organization seldom speaks with one voice.

How do the internal voices differ from the external voices that we have investigated in this book? According to our previous work (cf. Frandsen & Johansen, 2011), employees have something in common that makes them different: (1) a specific type of relationship with the organization; (2) a specific set of stakes; (3) a specific identity and degree of identification with the organization; and (4) the role of the employees as both senders and receivers of internal (crisis) communication.

What characterizes *the relationship* between an organization and its employees? This relationship differs from the relationship between an organization and its external stakeholders. According to various stakeholder typologies, this relationship turns the employees into a *contractual stakeholder* who has a legal relationship with the organization, often materialized in the form of an employment contract. Employees have an employment relationship in the form of an economic relation, where a wage and salary earner is compensated for work and use of time. But they also have a formal relation based on a specific distribution of roles, tasks, and functions that may reflect the power structure of the organization. Some external stakeholders such as customers may also be described as contractual stakeholders, but their contract with the organization is quite different (and based on delivery of a product living up to certain promises and expectations). The relationship between an organization and its employees has an influence on how employees behave, what they are allowed to do and say in their everyday organizational life, as well as before, during, and after an organizational crisis.

So what are the *stakes* of the employees? As mentioned above, employees have stakes that differ from those of external stakeholders. Attempts have been made to describe some of these stakes by means of terms such as salary, job security, working hours and working conditions, degrees of freedom and autonomy versus control, and motivation and engagement. Stakes may vary from group to group depending on age, sex, seniority, educational background, private life, organizational functions and positions. These stakes affect the perceptions employees have of their own organization, as well as playing a role for how they interpret the external communication of the organization. Furthermore, one may assume – although it has not yet been demonstrated empirically – that employee stakes also have an influence on the responsibility that individual employees attribute to their own organization in a crisis situation (cf. Chapter 6).

Employees have an organizational *identity* and *identification* that make them different from other stakeholders. They typically feel a different sense of belonging and commitment to their job and workplace (unlike an external stakeholder who may have other kinds of interests in an organization). Research within the field of organizational identity (see, for instance, Ashforth & Mael, 1989; Pratt, 1998) has shown that the organizational membership of employees seems to constitute an integrated part of their personal identity and that this can explain the immediate sense of obligation to defend the organization from outside attacks, including attacks on the reputation of the organization. This kind of identity and identification may influence, for instance, the attitudes and emotions of employees, their self-esteem, and their sense of belonging or symbolic ownership.

Finally, employees can be mobilized in crisis communication, not only as receivers but also as senders, just as they can act proactively in a crisis situation within a rhetorical arena (and in the role of internal or external stakeholder). Not only do employees – in a crisis situation – talk about their feelings and attitudes towards their workplace with their colleagues, families, and friends, but some of them also give interviews or statements to the press or choose to express their own opinion, for instance through social media. Whether they act as negative or positive ambassadors can be very important to an organization in a crisis situation (see glassdoor.com).

In accordance with our previous work (cf. Frandsen & Johansen, 2011), we conclude that employees as internal stakeholders have a stronger and more *complex* psychological dimension than most other stakeholders (except perhaps investors who also form a kind of internal stakeholder group, and except customers who act as brand ambassadors). Employees are 'closer' to the organization. This psychological dimension is often characterized by specific emotional and cognitive reactions in a crisis situation.

INTEGRATIVE FRAMEWORK FOR THE STUDY OF INTERNAL CRISIS COMMUNICATION

Based on a staged approach, a simple distinction between employees and managers as either senders or receivers, and a set of organizational factors that may have a positive or negative influence, we have developed an integrative framework (cf. Frandsen and Johansen, 2011) for the study of many different types of formal and informal internal crisis communication (see Tables 12.1–12.4).

Crises create awareness across the entire organization. Consequently, crisis communication takes place not only up and down the line, but also across departments

Table 12.1   Receiver roles of employees

	Pre-crisis stage	Crisis stage	Post-crisis stage
Employees as receivers	Communication of risk, issues, and stakes	Communication of instructions and information	Communication of knowledge (learning and memory)
Management as senders	Communication strenghtening emotional crisis preparedness	Handling of employee reactions to crisis (sensegiving)	Communication of post-crisis changes
Voices outside the organization*	Communication of the CMP (policies and guidelines)	Protection and restoration of trust and credibility	Renewal discourse (see Chapter 6)
		Crisis auto-communication**	Memorials (monument, websites)

* By voices outside the organization, we mean not only the employees' family, friends, and neighbors, but also the news media (see later in this chapter).

** The term *crisis auto-communication* refers to the employees' interpretation of the crisis response strategies applied by their organization in its external crisis communication.

Source: inspired by Frandsen and Johansen (2011).

Table 12.2   Sender roles of employees

	Pre-crisis stage	Crisis stage	Post-crisis stage
Employees as senders	Negative upward communication	Communication of reactions to crisis	Organizational narratives
Management as receivers	Whistleblower arrangements	Positive and/or negative ambassadors*	
Voices outside the organization			

* The ambassador role can be formal and informal. In the first case, the ambassador function is applied strategically by the organization. In the second case, employees take the initiative to speak in favor of their workplace. In the Internal Crisis Management and Crisis Communication (ICMCC) survey, which we conducted in 2011 (see the last section of this chapter), almost 40 percent of the respondents answered that they deliberately involved employees as ambassadors *outside* the organization. Almost 50 percent said they deliberately involved employees as ambassadors *inside* the organization.

Source: inspired by Frandsen and Johansen (2011).

Table 12.3 Horizontal communication among organization members

	Pre-crisis stage	Crisis stage	Post-crisis stage
Horizontal communication	◄─────────── Crisis training ──────────►		
	◄──────── Knowledge sharing (coordination) ────────►		
	◄────── Informal communication in social networks ──────►		
	◄──────── Crisis sensemaking ────────►		

Source: inspired by Frandsen and Johansen (2011).

Table 12.4 Organizational factors that have a positive or negative influence

	Pre-crisis stage	Crisis stage	Post-crisis stage
Organizational factors	• Crisis history and type (see Chapter 2) • Cognitive, affective, and behavioral reactions, such as frustration, insecurity, need for information, and production of informal communication • Crisis culture (safety culture, psychological defense mechanisms, crisis perception, crisis memory, collective mindfulness, etc.) • Communication culture • Communication strategy		

Source: inspired by Frandsen and Johansen (2011).

and social networks. Organization members share knowledge, coordinate, and try to gather information to be able to cope with the crisis. They make use of their social networks in an attempt to make sense of what is going on.

As in Table 12.4, various factors, including the crisis culture and communication culture of an organization, have an impact on the way organization members communicate about crises during all the stages of the crisis life cycle. If the members are used to speaking up about irregularities or failures, they will talk about the crisis in the open as well, whereas if this has not been part of workplace talk, a full-blown crisis may create even more informal talk. The communication culture determines the internal crisis communication. If the employees are used to having an open dialogue, they will also expect managers to behave in this way during a crisis.

HOW INTERNAL IS INTERNAL?

Most of our knowledge about the internal voices of organizations is based on the personal experience of practitioners, in particular communication consultants. They are called upon when an organization in crisis does not have the necessary expertise or resources. In other words, they are present during the crisis and they cannot avoid noticing how both managers and employees are coping with the situation. Unfortunately, however, many of their insights are either not accessible or transformed into something generic, such as communication plans for internal crisis communication based on the same key questions as in every other communication plan (Frandsen & Johansen, 2011). They do not take us a step further in our understanding of the internal dimension. However, there are important exceptions to this rule.

In 2013, Steven Fink, the author of *Crisis Management* (1986), published a new book entitled *Crisis Communications: The Definitive Guide to Managing the Message*. In a short chapter on internal crisis communication, Fink pointed to some characteristics of employee behavior. Employees, for example, have unique vantage points that are not available to senior management. Chief communication officers tend to see themselves as the boundary spanners of organizations. This viewpoint is supported by the theory of excellent crisis public relations (cf. Chapter 5). But employees also talk to people in other organizations, and they often know more about what is going on than senior management. This challenges our traditional understanding of the concepts of *internal* and *external*. Instead of seeing organizations as watertight containers with a clear distinction between what is outside and what is inside, it would be better to define them as porous phenomena allowing informal communication to leach in and out.

CRISIS SENSEMAKING

Recently, a group of European crisis communication researchers from Italy (Alessandra Mazzei, Silvia Ravazzani), Germany (Sabine Einwiller, Christine Korn, Andreas Schwarz), Sweden (Mats Heide, Charlotte Simonsson) and Denmark (the authors of this book) lamented the lack of research on internal crisis management and crisis communication.

Heide (2013), one of these scholars, offers two explanations why organizational members have been ignored by researchers within the field. First, the majority of crisis communication scholars have an educational background in public relations, a discipline which by tradition has had a strong focus on external publics. Second, much crisis communication research is based on case studies *after* a crisis has occurred, and because, in many countries, it is difficult for scholars to get access to organizations, they are limited to investigating the external dimension of organizational crises.

Another relevant observation is that aspects of relevance to the study of internal crisis management and crisis communication are touched upon occasionally in the literature. Key examples of such aspects are decision making in crisis situations, psychological defense mechanisms, organizational learning, and the impact of organizational culture on an organization's ability to handle a crisis. However, this research has seldom been thematized explicitly as research in *internal* crisis management and crisis communication.

Karl Weick's theory of retrospective sensemaking, which often focuses on situations where organizational sensemaking processes break down (typically during change or crises), has so far been the most important and comprehensive contribution to the study of the internal dimension of organizational crises. Weick's studies of the Bhopal disaster in India and the Mann Gulch disaster in the United States have not only been regarded as paradigmatic examples of how to conduct a sensemaking study, but also initiated the stream of research known today as *crisis sensemaking* (for an overview, see Maitlis & Sonenshein, 2010; Maitlis & Christianson, 2014).

In Weick's first study, which draws on Shrivastava's (1987) analysis of the Bhopal disaster that took place in 1984, he investigated how 'action that is instrumental to understanding the crisis often intensifies the crisis' (Weick, 1988, p. 305). He demonstrated that crises in organizations are *enacted* rather than encountered by the organization members; that is, the organization members themselves 'co-create' the environment which constrains them. In the second study, Weick established his famous definition of crises as *cosmology episodes*: 'A cosmology episode occurs when people suddenly and deeply feel that the universe is no longer a rational, orderly system. What makes such an episode so shattering is that both the sense of what is occurring and the means to rebuild that sense collapse together' (1993, p. 105).

Unfortunately, neither Karl Weick himself nor crisis management and crisis communication researchers, as the majority, see him as a key contributor to the field, which is surprising given that he has formulated some of the most important questions pertaining to organizational crises. How do organization members make sense of crises? How do public hearings contribute to this sensemaking process in the post-crisis stage? How useful is a crisis management plan? An exception that proves the rule is the work of Seeger et al. (2003) and Sellnow and Seeger (2013) who consider Weick one of their sources of inspiration.

BOX 12.1

CRISIS COMMUNICATION AND STRATEGIC HUMAN RESOURCE DEVELOPMENT

Human resource management and development is traditionally defined as a management function that takes care of hiring and developing employees to the benefit of the organization. The HRM/HRD function (as it is often called) includes recruiting the right people for the job, orienting and training, managing wages and salaries, providing benefits and incentives, evaluating performance, resolving disputes, and communicating with all employees at all levels.

For almost a decade, researchers within HRM/HRD have made approaches to organizational crisis management. The aim of this academic maneuver is not only to introduce the field of crisis management to the HRM/HRD community, but also to demonstrate the value of HRM/HRD for managing crises.

Garavan's (2007) model of SHRD serves as the framework for how HRD can contribute to organizational crisis management. This framework includes three major constructs: (1) the context (including the global context; strategy, structure, culture, and leadership; the job context; and the individual context); (2) the HRD function (SHRD strategies); and (3) the stakeholder

(SHRD outcome). Strategic HRD can contribute to organizational crisis management when it comes to specific capability and learning issues.

Researchers such as Holly M. Hutchins have developed a specific 'HRD definition of crisis': 'A crisis is an unexpected, unlikely, yet high-impact event that may cause significant change in human knowledge and performance at the individual, group, organizational, and community levels' (2008, p. 302).

The Society of Human Resource Management Research has conducted surveys about the crisis preparedness of organizations – as reported by the *employees*, and not by the crisis manager or the CMT. In 2005, 60 percent of employees answered that their organization was not well prepared to effectively respond to a crisis (Fegley & Victor, 2005).

Source: Wang et al. (2009).

INTERNAL CRISIS MANAGEMENT AND CRISIS COMMUNICATION

How do employees react in a crisis situation? And how does negative media coverage affect their behavior during a crisis? How do organizations manage the internal dimension of organizational crises? Do they have internal spokespersons? Are parts of their crisis management plans devoted to employees? And which channels are used for internal crisis communication? To answer these questions and many more we conducted a large national survey – the so-called ICMCC survey – among private and public organizations in 2012. The respondents consisted of middle managers responsible for the crisis management and crisis communication function in their organization. A total of 237 respondents (166 out of 367 respondents from private companies, 45 percent) and 71 out of the total of 98 Danish municipalities (72 percent) answered the survey.

The ICMCC survey was part of a larger, publicly financed collaborative research project consisting of four subprojects: (1) a mapping study of how internal crisis management and crisis communication are practised by Danish organizations (the ICMCC survey); (2) a study of crisis perception and its impact on organizational crisis preparedness; (3) a study of organizational resilience; and (4) a study of how negative news media coverage affects employees (for an overview of the research project, see Johansen et al., 2012).

How do employees react in crisis situations?

In some of his most recent publications, Ian I. Mitroff examined the *emotional crisis preparedness* of organizations. He conducted detailed analyses of defense mechanisms such as denial, disavowal, idealization, grandiosity, projection, intellectualization, and compartmentalization. According to Mitroff (2005), one of 'the most striking and interesting features of crises is that, virtually without exception, they are experienced as major acts of betrayal ... because people need to have someone to blame for the crisis' (p. 39). Mitroff defines betrayal as the failure of a person or an organization to act and to behave in accordance with ways that they have promised or have led us to believe that they will. Betrayal is the violation of trust. Leaders or managers who betray their employees are demonized.

As part of the ICMCC survey, we asked respondents to report on their perceptions, from a managerial point of view, of how employees might react to crisis events. The respondents predicted that during a crisis employees would show higher levels of *frustration* and *insecurity*, and that they would have a greater *need for information* and produce more *informal communication*. At the same time, the likelihood of four reactions among employees were perceived as low: *panic*, *leaving the organization*, *feeling betrayed*, and *feeling ashamed*. The results showed that these feelings were perceived as being especially unlikely in private organizations. It is important to note that these perceptions did not differ based on size of the organization or whether the organization had a crisis management plan.

On the surface, the results of the survey could not confirm Mitroff's claim that crises are always experienced as an act of betrayal by employees. In fact, the contrary seems to be true: that betrayal is not perceived as a frequent employee reaction to crisis events.

German crisis communication researchers Christine Korn and Sabine Einwiller have also investigated how employees react in crisis situations, but in their case employee reactions to crisis events are mediated by *negative media coverage*. Korn and Einwiller's (2013) study was based on Kepplinger's (2007) *reciprocal effects model*, a theory of mass media effects. Data was collected by means of 15 interviews conducted with representatives from 14 organizations. Reciprocal effects are defined as 'the impact of the mass media on those who [are] depicted by the media – that is, the subjects of media coverage' (p. 3). Korn and Einwiller's findings demonstrated that employees were affected by negative media coverage about their employer. They also implied that employees with a strong organizational identification exhibit different reciprocal effects than those with a less strong or no identification.

BOX 12.2

IMPLICIT THEORIES ABOUT MANAGERS AND EMPLOYEES IN CRISIS SITUATIONS

In 2011, we conducted the ICMCC survey on internal crisis management and crisis communication among private and public organizations in Denmark and achieved a high response rate: 166 out of 367 private companies (45 percent) and 71 out of the 98 Danish municipalities (72 percent). The questionnaire consisted of 36 closed questions followed by a few open questions. The respondents made some interesting comments to the following two questions:

Question 15.1: *In which way does the organizational function and/or the educational background have an impact on how employees behave in a crisis situation?*

Question 16: *Are the causes of a crisis, the crisis event itself, and the consequences perceived differently by top management, the middle managers, and the employees? If yes, please specify.*

We say 'interesting' because many of the answers seemed to be based on preconceived notions, or what are sometimes referred to as implicit theories. *Implicit theories* (or naive theories or common-sense theories) are schema-like knowledge structures including assumptions about causes and effects. Implicit theories are based on different sources such as personal experience or observations, values, and training. They provide a sense of psychological control and create expectations regarding patterns of organizational behavior.

The respondents clearly had implicit theories about the impact of function and educational background. Most of them agreed that it also depended on factors such as the crisis type, how close you are to the problem, and level of information access.

According to the respondents, 'top managers have a better overview'; 'they put on a strategic helicopter perspective'; 'they have full knowledge about the incident'; and 'they take responsibility to get the company through the crisis'. Some of them also indicated that 'top-managers have difficulties in admitting their own part in a crisis'; 'they are in less contact with the consequences of the crisis'; they are 'cynical'; and 'they do not want to be involved personally'.

Employees were perceived to 'await reaction of their top manager'; 'search for information'; 'lack information'; 'are the last ones to be told'; 'have a focus on local area/problems'; and stress 'personal consequences: what's in it for me?'; also 'they often blame their superiors'; 'need to find a scapegoat'; 'are frustrated'; and 'feel afraid about their jobs'.

Middle managers were perceived to have 'reasonable knowledge'; 'a more practical approach to the problem'; and 'a victim role in solidarity with the employees'. And it was stressed that middle managers are under pressure from both sides in a crisis: 'The middle manager knows a little but not everything, and has to handle the pressure from below about more information, but also the pressure from above about handling the situation, without being allowed to tell the employees something that hasn't been approved by top management first'.

This is of course based on perceptions or implicit theories constructed by the respondents. It may reveal faulty rationalizations (cf. Pauchant & Mitroff, 1992). Nevertheless, it shows that they have a pre-understanding of differences in relation to the crisis perceptions of members of an organization.

Source: Frandsen and Johansen (2014).

How do private and public organizations practise internal crisis management and crisis communication?

As mentioned at the beginning of this chapter, it is difficult to get access to an organization during and/or after a crisis. This is the reason why the findings of the

ICMCC survey are so unique. For the first time we have been able to collect large amounts of authentic data from organizations across the private and public sectors. In this section, we cast a glance at how organizations practise internal crisis management and crisis communication – again, as perceived by the respondents.

Municipalities

Regarding the use of internal crisis management and crisis communication tools and activities, 73 percent of the municipalities had procedures for establishing an internal CMP; 56 percent had an internal spokesperson; 34 percent had organized crisis simulations with a specific focus on the internal dimension; and 31 percent had organized seminars on internal crisis management. However, only 6 percent of the municipalities had implemented an internal whistleblower arrangement. Regarding future needs, the municipalities emphasized the need for better internal coordination between departments and organizational levels (67 percent); integration of the internal dimension in CMPs (63 percent); and a stronger integration of external and internal communication (57 percent).

Private companies

Regarding the use of internal crisis management and crisis communication tools and activities, 57 percent of the companies had procedures for establishing an internal CMP; 68 percent had an internal spokesperson; 33 percent had organized crisis simulations with a specific focus on the internal dimension; and 22 percent had organized seminars on internal crisis management. However, more than 40 percent of the companies had implemented a whistleblower arrangement. Regarding future needs, the companies also emphasized the need for better internal coordination between departments and organizational levels (56 percent), and integration of the internal dimension in CMPs (50 percent), but they did not emphasize, to the same extent as the municipalities, a need for a stronger integration of external and internal communication (30 percent).

Communication channels

Figure 12.1 provides an overview of the use of communication channels for internal crisis communication in municipalities and private companies according to the ICMCC survey conducted in 2011.

Municipalities and private companies use almost the same channels. Face-to-face channels (joint meetings, meetings at department level) are the most important channels together with emails and an intranet. However, company magazines and newsletters are also used for crisis communication purposes. As we saw with Scandinavian Airlines (cf. the introduction to this chapter), additional newsletters can be a way to supply more detailed explanations of what is going on. Text messages are also used (e.g., for driving personnel) and represent a quick way to

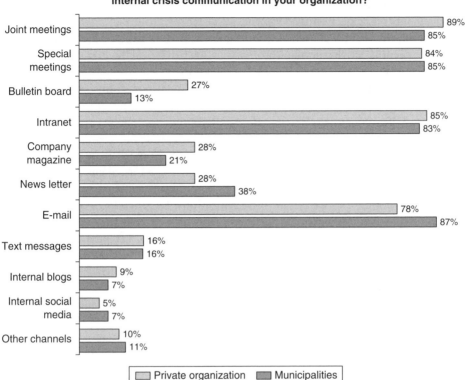

Figure 12.1 Use of internal crisis communication channels (ICMCC survey, 2011 in Johansen, Aggerholm & Frandsen, 2012)

contact employees. Finally, new media are only used internally to a small extent. However, we must not forget that the survey was conducted in 2011. More and more organizations are introducing social media for internal communication purposes (see Treem & Leonardi, 2012), but very little is known about the use of this platform in critical situations.

EMPLOYEES AS ACTIVE CRISIS COMMUNICATORS

In the previous section, we focused on employees as a group of people who react to crises in various ways, and who are managed by a crisis management team when a crisis occurs. To put it differently, the employees were seen as receivers. This is, in fact, a continuation of the traditional perspective on employees in crisis management. We often learn that having a communication plan to inform employees about the crisis is important. If employees first learn about the crisis from the news media before hearing about it from management, it will impair the credibility of top management (see, e.g., Barton, 1992).

However, the rhetorical arena forces us to redefine the roles of the internal voices and to see them as active communicators who often behave on their own – for better or worse. For instance, sometimes employees follow their own agendas, producing their own crisis messages. These messages are neither formal nor in line with the official strategy formulated by the board of directors or top management. It is in this category that we find the frequently referred to disgruntled employee who may trigger a crisis or scandal. Another example is seen in employees who support the agenda of their work-place, serving as ambassadors who respond to questions from family members, friends, and neighbors. This type of employee can be recruited in a formal and strategic way.

To understand these different patterns of communicative behavior, we can look for help in the literature on *dissent* in organizations. Kassing (1998) defines organizational dissent as '[e]xpressing disagreement or contradictory opinions about organizational practices, policies and operations' (p. 183). He puts the concept of organizational dissent together with perhaps seemingly similar, but in fact different, concepts: organizational conflict, upward influence, employee resistance, employee voice (and silence), and whistleblowing.

Whistleblowing can be defined as the 'disclosure by organization members (former and current) of illegal, immoral, or illegitimate practices under the control of their employers, to persons or organizations that may be able to effect action' (Near & Miceli, 1985, p. 4). Traditionally, whistleblowing involved only the disclosure of organizational wrongdoing or misconduct to audiences *outside* the organization, but today it has become usual to distinguish the following:

- Formal whistleblowing: through established channels, for example a whistleblower arrangement in an organization, or a public website or committee.
- Informal whistleblowing: through trusted colleagues in an organization, or the news media.
- Internal whistleblowing: to audiences inside the organization.
- External whistleblowing: to audiences outside the organization.

Whistleblowing does not necessarily begin with one or another of these four basic types. It is often a process that takes place in several steps, for example from a formal internal type to an informal external type.

Normally, whistleblowing (and whistleblower arrangements) are not seen as an area (and as a tool) within the field of crisis management and crisis communication. However, we suggest that whistleblowing could be looked upon as a type of signal detection located in the pre-crisis stage of the crisis life cycle.

Two issues are closely linked to the internal reporting of wrongdoing or misconduct in organizations. The first issue is ethical by nature: 'At its very core, whistleblowing involves making judgments about what is ethical' (Kassing, 2011, p. 50). Will employees and managers who are colleagues working for the same organization agree to denounce each other anonymously?

The second issue is more practical by nature and can be reduced to this short question: Is it effective? The answer is neither a clear 'yes' nor a clear 'no'. In their study of implicit voice theories, or taken-for-granted beliefs about when and why speaking up at work is risky or inappropriate, Detert and Edmondson (2011) identified five such theories that can explain important aspects of organizational silence, including important aspects of formal internal whistleblower arrangements (defined as internal, upward 'crisis communication'):

1. Managers, who by definition have a higher position in the organizational hierarchy, identify with the status quo, and will therefore interpret suggestions as personal criticism.
2. You need to know all the facts before it is safe to speak.
3. Don't bypass the manager upward.
4. Don't embarrass the manager in public.
5. Speaking up will have negative career consequences.

CASE STUDY 12.1

ODENSE WASTE MANAGEMENT COMPANY – WHEN WHISTLEBLOWING IS THE PROBLEM, NOT THE SOLUTION

While whistleblower arrangements have been in use in the United States since the mid-1970s, they are still considered an innovation in many European countries. In Denmark, Vestas Wind Systems was among the first private companies to implement a whistleblower arrangement in 2007. Public organizations such as municipalities have been far more hesitant and sceptical toward this new management tool to tackle fraud, crime, and unethical behavior.

Odense Waste Management Company in Denmark collects household refuse from 90,000 households. It operates eight recycling stations plus Odense Environmental Centre, a dumping ground with landfill, sorting, recycling, and composting activities as well as a training center. The company is publicly owned by the municipality of Odense and employs 167 people across seven divisions. It has an annual revenue of about DKr200 million (US$25 million). At the time the following events took place, the company had not yet implemented a whistleblower arrangement.

In the fall of 2011, it was revealed by a truck driver that a small group of employees working for Odense Waste Management Company had committed a fraud that earned them millions over the course of several years. These employees received secret payments from truck drivers who transported construction waste to the dumping ground at the Odense Environmental Centre. In return, the construction waste was classified as, for example, garden waste, and taxed at a considerably lower rate than normal construction waste. The profit was split between the employees and the truck drivers. On October 5, 2011, police carried out an operation that uncovered the fraud. The story made front page headlines for some time afterward. However, the company leadership expected to be able to continue while the trials were running. Then events took a new direction.

(Continued)

(Continued)

On January 16, 2012, several months after the police operation, the local newspaper ran an article headlined 'Revealed Fraud and Was Sacked!' The newspaper tells the story of a clerk at the Odense Environmental Centre who had identified by herself that something was wrong, and who apparently had been fired by top management. The reason why she was fired was that she did not contact top management with her knowledge about the fraud. First, she contacted a manager in the administration. Unfortunately, this person was also involved in the fraud and threatened to make her jointly responsible if she revealed anything. Then the clerk went to her trade union and was told to contact the local union representative. However, the representative was not sure whether he or the clerk should inform the CEO about the fraud, or whether it was better to keep the information secret.

The story about the clerk quickly spread to other media, including the national television networks. A media storm was building up. However, the CEO of Odense Waste Management Company declined to give interviews due to professional secrecy. The crisis did not abate until the company informed the public about the content of the accusations against the clerk.

On January 18, the Mayor of Odense, Anker Boye, suggested in the local newspaper that the municipality of Odense, the owner of Odense Waste Management Company, should implement an internal whistleblower arrangement as a consequence of the crisis.

Studying the rhetorical arena

- List all the voices that start communicating after the fraud has been uncovered and the clerk has been fired. How do they interact with each other?
- What kind of crisis is this?
- What kind of whistleblowing does the clerk apply?

Managing the rhetorical arena

- How would you manage the 'whistleblower crisis'?
- How would you communicate with the other employees working for Odense Waste Management Company during the crisis?
- If you invited them to a 'town hall meeting', what kind of questions would you expect them to ask? And what would your answers be?
- Would a formal internal whistleblower arrangement have solved the problem?

Source: Danish newspaper articles.

CHAPTER SUMMARY

This chapter explored the internal dimension of organizational crises, crisis management, and crisis communication, a dimension that has remained 'invisible' for a long time. First, we looked at how employees and managers differ from the external voices, and how they react emotionally and otherwise to critical situations.

Then we used the findings of the ICMCC survey to study how private and public organizations practise *internal* crisis management and crisis communication, including their use of communication channels. The chapter concluded with a section on organizational voice and silence and how internal whistleblower arrangements can serve as signal detection.

 **Further reading**

Heide, M., & Simonsson, C. (2014). Developing internal crisis communication: New roles and practices of communication professionals. *Corporate Communications: An International Journal*, 19(2), 126–146.

Mazzei, A., Kim, J.-N., & Dell'Oro, C. (2012). Strategic value of employee relationships and communicative actions: Overcoming corporate crisis with quality internal communication. *International Journal of Strategic Communication*, 6, 31–44.

EPILOGUE – THE FUTURE OF ORGANIZATIONAL CRISIS COMMUNICATION: AGENDAS FOR RESEARCH, EDUCATION, AND PRACTICE

INTRODUCTION

In the preface to this book, we started out on a personal note, telling the story of how we became crisis communication researchers thanks to the German automobile manufacturer Daimler-Benz and the Mercedes A-Class car in 1997. We would like to end this book on a similar note, intervening in a debate on the future of organizational crisis communication. This intervention will be followed by the presentation of three agendas: one for researchers, one for educators (and students), and one for practitioners. Each of these will be linked to rhetorical arena theory and the multivocal approach.

THOUGHT LEADERSHIP IN CRISIS COMMUNICATION

The expression *thought leader* is of American provenance and refers to a person or an organization that is regarded as an authority in a specific field ('What is a thought leader?', *Forbes*, March 16, 2012). It was used for the first time in 1887 but did not become popular until the 1990s. The idea of thought leadership has also spread to academia. The international journal *Management Communication Quarterly* introduced its 'Thought Leadership Series' in 2011. In his introduction, former Editor-in-Chief

James Barker formulated the aim of the new series as follows: 'Our new ... series will crystallize and articulate those areas in which our field holds thought leadership; that is, those areas in which we have specific expertise and knowledge of key organizational studies problems.'

In his article 'Increasing the impact of thought leadership in crisis communication', published by *Management Communication Quarterly* in 2012, American scholar Robert R. Ulmer claimed that it was time for the *academic discipline* of crisis management and crisis communication to move from a positive or analytical approach toward a normative approach to research in order to improve the *organizational practice* of crisis management and crisis communication (see the general introduction). Through a positive approach, researchers have documented how the majority of organizations struggle to communicate effectively during a crisis. As a result, Ulmer claimed, we are reaching our limits for a positive approach to crisis communication. Future thought leadership should focus more on producing normative theories that provide clear guidance to organizations and society about how to communicate effectively in crisis situations.

This claim was followed by what Ulmer regarded as the consequences of such a shift in focus and orientation. First of all, we need a new definition of crisis focusing not only on threats, but also on opportunities. Second, we need a new approach to crisis communication focusing not only on the protection of the image or reputation of an organization, but also on stakeholders and ethical communication practices. Finally, we need to take a cross-disciplinary perspective on crisis communication, eliminating the 'siloed academic disciplines' (p. 529).

We sympathize to a large extent with Ulmer's call. There are, however, several good reasons for maintaining a positive or analytical approach, including in a textbook. First, despite several years of intense research, the analytical approach to crisis communication is still at an early stage in its evolution. We are, in fact, talking about a period of less than 30 years. Second, an analytical approach may lead to important revisions of a normative theory. Third, who is going to benefit from the normative approach? The top management of the organization? The employees? Or society at large?

In the remaining part of this epilogue, we will present three agendas, one for researchers, one for educators (and students), and one for practitioners, based on or inspired by rhetorical arena theory and the multivocal approach to crisis communication.

AN AGENDA FOR RESEARCHERS

- Role model: the ideal researcher (or team of researchers) is one who investigates (1) what organizational crises are and/or how they are constructed, including their causes and consequences; (2) how private and public organizations manage crises and communicate in crisis situations; and (3) how stakeholders are affected by this. The ideal researcher is also someone who has acquired multidisciplinary competencies and who is driven by academic curiosity and practical caring.

- Task: crisis management and crisis communication research can best be conducted on the basis of (1) authentic data; (2) relevant combinations of quantitative and qualitative research designs and methods; and (3) relevant theories. The ideal researcher disseminates his or her knowledge to educators and practitioners, formulated in accessible language, and engages in an ongoing exchange of opinions in relevant forums (conferences, associations, etc.).
- Challenge: organizational crises, crisis management, and crisis communication can best be defined as a multidisciplinary field.
- Special mission: to describe and explain the many voices in the rhetorical arena, including the voices and types of interventions not covered by this book (e.g., activists, politicians, public relations experts, and third-party interventions).

We define the field of crises, crisis management, and crisis communication as a multidisciplinary field. By multidisciplinary, we mean the combination of two or more academic disciplines that helps explain a complex aspect of the world that would not be possible to understand within the limits of a single discipline (cf. the multidimensional approach in Part One).

There are individual and institutional barriers to conducting multidisciplinary research. Most researchers are trained within one and only one academic discipline. Similarly, most universities and business schools are organized in faculties and departments with strong mono-disciplinary identities. Many presidents and deans praise multidisciplinary research, but the fact is that this kind of research is seldom facilitated and rewarded. To conduct multidisciplinary research, especially in large research teams, you need to be able to see things from different perspectives – without giving up your own perspective (specialization).

Multidisciplinary research within the field of crises, crisis management, and crisis communication can be *developed in three steps*. The first step is the shortest and easiest to take. For example, to bring together some of the most important theories of crisis communication, such as image repair theory and situational crisis communication theory, and focus on their understanding of crisis response strategies. How can this understanding be developed further?

The second step is a little longer and more difficult to take. For example, to bring together crisis communication and crisis management researchers to discuss how they understand communication, organization, and management. This step is crucial. Falkheimer and Heide (2010) claimed that 'traditional crisis communication is based on an obsolete view of organization, communication, and society' (p. 512). By obsolete, they understand a rational view of organizations, positing that they can be controlled during crises; a transmission view of communication, positing that information can be disseminated without being interpreted; and a view of societies, positing that they are homogeneous entities between which only national cultural differences exist.

The third step is the longest, and a step where both crisis communication and crisis management scholars have to leave their academic 'comfort zone' in so far as they will encounter researchers working within other fields of study. To illustrate this last step, let's take three of the key concepts in the study of organizational crisis communication: *crisis*, *response*, and *reputation*. This small cluster of concepts has been applied in different ways within three different fields of study, but without researchers being aware of it, namely: (1) the field of public relations, including crisis communication theories, in which the protection and/or repair of the reputation of an organization in crisis is one of the strategic priorities (see Chapters 5 and 6); (2) the field of public administration, including bureaucratic reputation theory (Carpenter, 2001; Wæraas & Maor, 2015) and blame game theory (Hood, 2011); and (3) the field of business administration, including corporate reputation theory (Barnett et al. 2006), organizational perception management or event-based reputation management (Elsbach, 2006), new concepts such as reputation commons (problem), status, and stigma (King et al., 2002; Barnett & Pollock, 2012), and behavioral theories of reputation (Rhee & Kim, 2012).

In 1999, in the first edition of *Ongoing Crisis Communication*, W. Timothy Coombs made a call for more 'integrative efforts' within the field of crisis management and crisis communication. We see our agenda for research, in particular the definition of this field as a multidisciplinary field, as a response to this call.

AN AGENDA FOR EDUCATORS AND STUDENTS

- Role model: the ideal educator (or team of educators) is an educator who – through the usual communicative and personal qualities attributed by students – can establish optimal conditions for teaching and learning crisis management and crisis communication.
- Task: teaching crisis management and crisis communication can best be practised if based on (1) research-based knowledge *and* (but never *or*) personal experience; (2) relevant combinations of pedagogical methods and tools; and (3) ways that address the issue of multidisciplinary competencies (cf. the previous agenda).
- Challenge: crisis management and crisis communication must be taught as a course or unit in every study program with a strong focus on management and leadership in private and public organizations.
- Special mission: to teach students to be attentive to all the voices inside the rhetorical arena; that is, to avoid an organization-centric attitude.

Until the publication of the special issue of *Journal of Management Education* on 'Crisis management education' in 2013, the literature on how to teach students about crises had been meager. Within the field of public relations, Coombs (2001) offered some early advice on how to design a crisis management/communication course. He suggested the course could be built around nine objectives, which could then be divided into three categories: (1) how to approach crisis management (e.g., an ongoing approach), (2) understanding key concepts (e.g., the organization's crisis sensing mechanism), and (3) developing essential skills and abilities for crisis management (e.g., the ability to differentiate between different crisis types and to construct a CMP). Coombs also suggested that the structure of the course should follow a staged approach.

Almost 10 years later, Cirka and Corrigall (2010) demonstrated how metaphors could be used to overcome cognitive biases, helping students to 'imagine these often unimaginable crises' (p. 304). This article initiated a new stream of research in crisis management education, focusing on how (crisis) managers and leaders in organizations *think* about crises.

The special issue of *Journal of Management Education* from 2013 contained a series of articles approaching crisis management education from various angles. Space precludes us from presenting all of these articles, so we highlight only a few. Shrivastava, Mitroff and Alpaslan (2013) concluded their article with a short but important statement that every (crisis) management educator ought to read: 'Management educators need to integrate crisis analysis into their existing courses and develop stand-alone courses in crisis management. Education in crisis management needs to be socially and historically contextualized. It should go beyond abstract and cognitive understanding; it must be embodied and experiential, engaging participants as whole persons and responsible members of communities' (pp. 18–19). Lalonde and Roux-Dufort (2013) emphasized that the multidisciplinary nature of the field (cf. the previous agenda) must not only be seen as a disadvantage – due to a lack of integration or consistency across disciplines – but also as an advantage. It provides us with a conceptual toolbox composed of middle-range theories reflecting the complexity of today's society. Regarding pedagogical methods and tools, some of the articles mention the value of case studies, including student-constructed cases, and evidence-based management.

After the special issue of *Journal of Management Education*, Powley and Taylor (2014) presented two approaches – a personalized case study using a critical incident approach and a group poster session – designed for critical thinking skill development.

The study of crisis management and crisis communication education is still at its very beginning. However, the educational dimension of the field will become more and more important as the risk/crisis society develops.

AN AGENDA FOR PRACTITIONERS

- Role model: the ideal practitioner (or group of practitioners) is a reflective practitioner who has the capacity to reflect on action and engage in a process of continuous learning before, during, and after crisis.
- Task: practice can best be performed on the basis of (1) research-based knowledge, (2) education, and (3) personal experience. Research and education deliver the scientific infrastructure, and personal experience provides the contextualization of this infrastructure. The reflective practitioner is interested in an ongoing exchange of opinions with researchers and educators.
- Challenge: practitioners must avoid the field-specific version of the hero manager: the Crisis Commander. Practitioners must remain realistic in their understanding and approach to organizational crises. The reflective practitioner knows how to see through oversimplified viewpoints and models and how to identify temporal management fashions.
- Special mission: to apply rhetorical arena theory and the multivocal approach to crisis communication in practice.

Some scholars make a distinction between *reflexive* and *reflective*. According to Holmstrøm (2010), *reflexivity* is a first-order perspective that implies a narcissistic view from within. The organization reflects itself only in the environment, that is in a simplified, close-up context, as if it was a small mirror. *Reflection*, on the contrary, is a second-order perspective that implies a view from outside. The organization sees itself as part of a larger and more complex context. This distinction may be transferred to the organizational practice of crisis management and crisis communication. If so, reflection represents what we named the complex broad perspective in Chapter 3.

The marriage of rhetorical arena theory and the multivocal approach to crisis communication is an attempt to turn this perspective into a theoretical and practical model, one focused on the different voices that start communicating when a crisis occurs.

REFERENCES

Acquier, A., Gand, S., & Szpirglas, M. (2008). From stakeholder to stakesholder management in crisis episodes: A case study in a public transportation company. *Journal of Contingencies and Crisis Management*, 16(2), 101–113.

Ahrne, G., & Brunsson, N. (2005). Organizations and meta-organizations. *Scandinavian Journal of Management*, 21, 429–449.

Ahrne, G., & Brunsson, N. (2008). *Meta-organizations*. Cheltenham: Edward Elgar.

Ahrne, G., & Brunsson, N. (2012). How much do meta-organizations affect their members? In M. Koch (Ed.), *Weltorganisationen* [World Organizations] (pp. 57–70). Wiesbaden: Springer.

Aldrich, H. E., & Staber, U. H. (1988). Organizing business interests: Patterns of trade association foundings, transformations, and deaths. In G. R. Carroll (Ed.), *Ecological Models of Organizations* (pp. 111–126). Cambridge, MA: Ballinger.

Alpaslan, C. M., & Mitroff, I. I. (2011). *Swans, Swine, and Swindlers: Coping with the Growing Threat of Mega-Crises and Mega-Messes*. Stanford, CA: Stanford Business Books.

Alpaslan, C. M., Green, S. E., & Mitroff, I. I. (2009). Corporate governance in the context of crises: Towards a stakeholder theory of crisis management. *Journal of Contingencies and Crisis Management*, 17(1), 38–49.

Altheide, D. L. (2004). Mediatization and political communication. *Political Communication*, 21(3), 3–23.

Altheide, D. L., & Snow, R. P. (1979). *Media Logic*. Beverly Hills: Sage.

Alvarez, J. L. (Ed.) (1998). *The Diffusion and Consumption of Business Knowledge*. New York: St. Martin's Press.

Alvesson, M. (2013). *Understanding Organizational Culture*. London: Sage. Second edition.

An, S.-K., & Cheng, I.-H. (2010). Crisis communication research in public relations journals: Tracking research trends over thirty years. In W. T. Coombs & S. J. Holladay (Eds.), *The Handbook of Crisis Communication* (pp. 65–90). Malden, MA: Wiley-Blackwell.

An, S.-K., & Gower, K. K. (2009). How do the news media frame crises? A content analysis of crisis news coverage. *Public Relations Review*, 35, 107–112.

Andrews, R. V. (2005). Crisis communications and the Tylenol poisonings. In R. L. Heath (Ed.), *Encyclopedia of Public Relations, Vol. 1* (pp. 224–226). Thousand Oaks, CA: Sage.

Argyris, C., & Schön, D. A. (1978). *Organizational Learning: A Theory of Action Perspective*. Reading, MA: Addison-Wesley.

Ashforth, B. E., & Mael, F. (1989). Social identity theory and the organization. *Academy of Management Review*, 14(1), 20–39.

Austin, L., Liu, B. F., & Jin, Y. (2012). How audiences seek out crisis information: Exploring the Social Mediated Crisis Communication model. *Journal of Applied Communication*, 40(2), 188–207.

Avery, E. J., Lariscy, R. W., Kim, S., & Hocke, T. (2010). A quantitative review of crisis communication research in public relations from 1991 to 2009. *Public Relations Review*, 26(2), 190–192.

Barnett, M. L. (2006). Finding a working balance between competitive and communal strategies. *Journal of Management Studies*, 43(8), 1753–1773.

Barnett, M. L., & Hoffman, A. (2008). Beyond corporate reputation: Managing reputational interdependence. *Corporate Reputation Review*, 11(1), 1–9.

Barnett, M. L., & Pollock, T. G. (Eds.) (2012). *The Oxford Handbook of Corporate Reputation*. Oxford: Oxford University Press.

Barnett, M. L., Jermier, J. M., & Lafferty, B. A. (2006). Corporate reputation: The definitional landscape. *Corporate Reputation Review*, 9(1), 26–38.

Barton, L. (1992). *Crisis in Organizations: Managing and Communicating in the Heat of Chaos*. Cincinnati, Ohio: College Division South-Western Publishing Co.

Beck, U. (1992). *Risk Society: Towards a New Modernity*. London: Sage. German original, 1986.

Beck, U., & Holzer, B. (2007). Organizations in world risk society. In C. M. Pearson, C. Roux-Dufort, & J. A. Clair (Eds.), *International Handbook of Organizational Management* (pp. 3–24). Thousand Oaks, CA: Sage.

Benoit, W. L. (1995). *Accounts, Excuses, and Apologies: A Theory of Image Restoration Strategy*. Albany, NY: State University of New York.

Benoit, W. L. (1997). Image repair discourse and crisis communication. *Public Relations Review*, 23(2), 177–186.

Benoit, W. L. (2000). Another visit to the theory of image restoration strategies. *Communication Quarterly*, 48(1), 40–44.

Benoit, W. L. (2004). Image restoration discourse and crisis communication. In D. P. Millar & R. L. Heath (Eds.), *Responding to Crisis: A Rhetorical Approach to Crisis Communication* (pp. 263–280). Mahwah, NJ: Lawrence Erlbaum.

Benoit, W. L. (2015). *Accounts, Excuses, and Apologies: Image Repair Theory and Research*. Albany, NY: State University of New York. Second edition.

Benoit, W. L., & Lindsey, J. J. (1987). Argument strategies: Antidote to Tylenol's poisoned image. *Journal of the American Forensic Association*, 23, 136–146.

Benoit, W. L., & Dorries, B. (1996). Dateline NBC's persuasive attack on Wal-Mart. *Communication Quarterly*, 44(4), 463–477.

Bentele, G. (2005). Public sphere (*Öffentlichkeit*). In R. L. Heath (Ed.), *Encyclopedia of Public Relations, Vol. 2* (pp. 707–720). Los Angeles: Sage.

Bergeron, C. D., & Coreen, F. (2012). The collective framing of crisis management: A ventriloqual analysis of emergency operations centres. *Journal of Contingencies and Crisis Management*, 20(3), 120–137.

Bergin, T. (2012). *Spills and Spin: The Inside Story of BP*. London: Random House.

Berthod, O., Müller-Seitz, G., & Sydow, J. (2013). Interorganizational crisis management. In A. Thießen (Ed.), *Handbuch Krisenmanagement* [*Handbook of Crisis Management*] (pp. 139–152). Wiesbaden: Springer.

Bhattacharya, C. B., & Sen, S. (2003). Consumer-company identification: A framework for understanding consumers' relationships with companies. *Journal of Marketing*, 47(1), 76–88.

Billings, R. S., Milburn, T. W., & Schaalman, M. L. (1980). A model of crisis perception: A theoretical and empirical analysis. *Administrative Science Quarterly*, 25(2), 300–316.

Birkland, T. A. (1997). *After Disaster: Agenda Setting, Public Policy, and Focusing Events*. Washington, DC: Georgetown University Press.

Bitzer, L. F. (1968). The rhetorical situation. *Philosophy & Rhetoric*, 1, 1–14.

Black, E. (1965). *Rhetorical Criticism: A Study in Method*. New York: Macmillan.

Blaney, J. R., Lippert, L., & Smith, S. J. (Eds.) (2012). *Repairing the Athlete's Image: Studies in Sports Image Restoration*. Lanham, MD: Lexington Books.

Boin, A. (2009). The new world of crises and crisis management: Implications for policymaking and research. *Review of Policy Research*, 26(4), 367–377.

Boin, A., & Hart, P. 't (2005). The crisis approach. In H. Rodríguez, E. L. Quarantelli, & Dynes, R. R. (Eds.), *Handbook of Disaster Research* (pp. 42–54). New York: Springer.

Boin, A., Hart, P. 't, Stern, E., & Sundelius, B. (2005). *The Politics of Crisis Management: Public Leadership under Pressure*. Cambridge: Cambridge University Press.

Boin, A., McConnell, A., & Hart, P. 't (2009). Crisis exploitation: Political and policy impacts of framing contest. *Journal of European Public Policy*, 16(1), 81–106.

Bolden, R. (2004). *What is Leadership?* Leadership South West: Research Report 1. University of Exeter: Centre for Leadership Studies.

Botterell, A. (2001). The life cycle of a disaster: A field guide for journalists. Retrieved from www. victims.jrn.msu.edu.

Brown, N. A., & Billings, A. C. (2013). Sports fans as crisis communicators on social media websites. *Public Relations Review*, 39, 74–81.

Brunsson, N. (1994). Politicization and 'company-ization': On institutional affiliation and confusion in the organizational world. *Management Accounting Research*, 5, 323–335.

Bundy, J., & Pfarrer, M. C. (2015). A burden of responsibility: The role of social approval at the onset of a crisis. *Academy of Management Review*, 40(3), 345–369.

Burke, K. (1966). *Language as Symbolic Action: Essays on Life, Literature, Method*. Berkeley, CA: University of California Press.

Burke, K. (1970). *The Rhetoric of Religion*. Berkeley, CA: University of California Press.

Burns, J. P., & Bruner, M. S. (2000). Revisiting the theory of image restoration strategies. *Communication Quarterly*, 48(1), 27–39.

Cancel, A. E., Cameron, G. T., Sallot, L. M., & Mitrook, M. A. (1997). It depends: A contingency theory of accommodation in public relations. *Journal of Public Relations Research*, 9(1), 31–63.

Cancel, A. E., Mitrook, M. A., & Cameron, G. T. (1999). Testing the contingency theory of accommodation in public relations. *Public Relations Review*, 25(2), 171–197.

Carpenter, D. P. (2001). *The Forging of Bureaucratic Autonomy: Reputations, Networks, and Policy Innovation in Executive Agencies, 1862–1928*. Princeton, NJ: Princeton University Press.

Carroll, C. E. (Ed.) (2013). *The Handbook of Communication and Corporate Reputation*. Malden, MA: Wiley-Blackwell.

Castells, M. (2009). *Communication Power*. Oxford: Oxford University Press.

Champ, R. C. (1989). *Benchmarking: The Search for Industry Best Practices that Lead to Superior Performance*. Milwaukee, WI: ASQC Quality Press.

Chase, W. H. (1984). *Issue Management: Origins of the Future*. Stamford, CT: iap.

Cheney, G., Christensen, L. T., Conrad, C., & Lair, D. J. (2004). Corporate rhetoric as organizational discourse. In D. Grant, C. Hardy, C. Oswick, & L. Putnam (Eds.). *The Sage Handbook of Organizational Discourse* (pp. 79–103). Thousand Oaks, CA: Sage.

Cilliers, P. (1998). *Complexity & Postmodernism: Understanding Complex Systems*. London: Routledge.

Cirka, C. C., & Corrigall, E. A. (2010). Expanding possibilities through metaphor: Breaking biases to improve crisis management. *Journal of Management Education*, 34(2), 303–323.

Clarke, L. (1999). *Mission impossible: Using Fantasy Document to Tame Disasters*. Chicago: The University of Chicago Press.

Claeys, A. S., & Cauberghe, V. (2012). Crisis response and crisis timing strategies, two sides of the same coin? *Public Relations Review*, 38(1), 83–88.

Cloudman, R., & Hallahan, K. (2006). Crisis communications preparedness among U.S. organizations: Activities and assessments by public relations practitioners. *Public Relations Review*, 32, 367–376.

Coetzee, C., & Niekerk, D. van (2012). Tracking the evolution of the disaster management cycle: A general system theory approach. *Jamba: Journal of Disaster Risk Studies*, 4(1), 1–9.

Connerton, P. (1989). *How Societies Remember*. Cambridge: Cambridge University Press.

Coombs, W. T. (1995). Choosing the right words: The development of guidelines for the selection of the 'appropriate' crisis-response strategies. *Management Communication Quarterly*, 8(4), 447–476.

Coombs, W. T. (1998). An analytical framework for crisis situations: Better responses from a better understanding of the situation. *Journal of Public Relations Research*, 10(3), 177–191.

Coombs, W. T. (1999). *Ongoing Crisis Communication; Planning, Managing, and Responding*. Los Angeles: Sage.

Coombs, W. T. (2000). Crisis management: Advantages of a relational perspective. In Ledingham & S. D. Bruning (Eds.), *Public Relations as Relationship Management: A Relational Approach to the Study and Practice of Public Relations* (pp. 73–93). Mahwah, NJ: Lawrence Erlbaum.

Coombs, W. T. (2001). Teaching the crisis management/communication course. *Public Relations Review*, 27(1), 89–101.

Coombs, W. T. (2006a). Crisis management: A communicative approach. In C. H. Botan & V. Hazleton (Eds.), *Public Relations Theory II* (pp. 171–197). Mahwah, NJ: Lawrence Erlbaum.

Coombs, W. T. (2006b). The protective powers of crisis response strategies: Managing reputational assets during a crisis. *Journal of Promotion Management*, 12(3/4), 241–260.

Coombs, W. T. (2006c). *Code Red in the Boardroom: Crisis Management as Organizational DNA*. Westport, Connecticut: Praeger.

Coombs, W. T. (2007). *Crisis Management and Communications*. Institute for Public Relations: instituteforpr.org.

Coombs, W. T. (2010). Parameters for crisis communication. In W. T. Coombs & S. J. Holladay (Eds.), *The Handbook of Crisis Communication* (pp. 17–53). Malden, MA: Wiley-Blackwell.

Coombs, W. T. (2012). China and France. Olympic Torch protests in France. Reactions in China: Carrefour learns about international crises. In A. M. George & C. B. Pratt (Eds.), *Case Studies in Crisis Communication: International Perspectives on Hits and Misses* (pp. 152–170). New York: Routledge.

Coombs, W. T. (2014a). Introduction: Origins of crisis communication. In W. T. Coombs (Ed.), *Crisis Communication*, Vol. I, *Origins of Crisis Communication*. Los Angeles: Sage.

Coombs, W. T. (2014b). *Applied Crisis Communication and Crisis Management: Cases and Exercises*. Los Angeles: Sage.

Coombs, W. T. (Ed.) (2014c). *Crisis Communication, Vol. I–IV*. Los Angeles: Sage.

Coombs, W. T. (2015). *Ongoing Crisis Communication; Planning, Managing, and Responding*. Los Angeles: Sage. Fourth edition.

Coombs, W. T., & Holladay, S. J. (2001). An extended examination of the crisis situation: A fusion of the relational management and symbolic approaches. *Journal of Public Relations Research*, 13(4), 321–340.

Coombs, W. T., & Holladay, S. J. (2005). An exploratory study of stakeholder emotions: Affect and crises. In N. M. Ashkanasy, W. J. Zerbe, & C. E. J. Härtel (Eds.), *The Effect of Affect in Organizational Settings (Research on Emotion in Organizations, Vol. 1)* (pp. 263–280). Bingley: Emerald.

Coombs, W. T., & Holladay, S. J. (2006). Unpacking the halo effect: Reputation and crisis management. *Journal of Communication Management*, 10(2), 123–137.

Coombs, W. T., & Holladay, S. J. (Eds.) (2010). *The Handbook of Crisis Communication*. Malden, MA: Wiley-Blackwell.

Coombs, W. T., & Holladay, S. J. (2012a). The paracrisis: The challenges created by publicly managing crisis prevention. *Public Relations Review*, 38(3), 408–415.

Coombs, W. T., & Holladay, S. J. (2012b). Faith-holders as crisis managers: The Costa-Concordia Rhetorical Arena on Facebook, Conference paper, Euprera Congress, Istanbul, September 20–22 (retrieved from the conference proceedings).

Coombs, W. T., & Holladay, S. J. (2015). Digital naturals and crisis communication: Significant shifts of focus, In W. T. Coombs, J. Falkheimer, M. Heide, & P. Young (Eds.), *Strategic Communication, Social Media and Digital Naturals* (pp. 54–62). London: Routledge.

Cornelissen, J. P., & Kafouros, M. (2008). Metaphors and theory building in organization theory: What determines the impact of a metaphor on theory? *British Journal of Management*, 19, 365–379.

Cornelissen, J. P., & Werner, M. D. (2014). Putting framing in perspective: A review of framing and frame analysis across the management and organizational literature. *Academy of Management Annals*, 8(1), 181–235.

Couldry, N. (2012). *Media, Society, World: Social Theory and Digital Media Practice*. Cambridge: Polity Press.

Couldry, N., & Hepp, A. (2013). Conceptualizing mediatization: Contexts, traditions, arguments. *Communication Theory*, 23(3), 191–202.

Cova, B., & Cova, V. (2001). *Alternatives Marketing*. Paris: Dunod.

Covello, V. T. (2003). Best practices in public health risk and crisis communication. *Journal of Health Communication Research*, 8, 5–8.

Cox, G. V. (1987). A trade association's role in crisis management. *Industrial Crisis Quarterly*, 1(3), 4–13.

Craig, R. T. (2013). Constructing theories in communication research. In P. Cobley & P. J. Schultz (Eds.), *Theories and Models of Communication, Handbooks of Communication Science, Vol. 1*. (pp. 39–57). Göttingen: De Gruyter Mouton.

Cutlip, S. M., Center, A. H., & Broom, G. M. (1952). *Effective Public Relations*. Upper Saddle River, NJ: Prentice Hall.

Dardis, F., & Haigh, M. M. (2009). Prescribing versus describing: Testing image restoration strategies in a crisis situation. *Corporate Communications: An International Journal*, 14(1), 101–118.

Dearing, J. W., & Rogers, E. M. (1996). *Agenda-Setting*. Thousand Oaks, CA: Sage.

Deephouse, D. L. (2000). Media reputation as a strategic resource: An integration of mass communication and resource-based theories. *Journal of Management*, 26(6), 1091–1112.

DEMA (2009) *Comprehensive Preparedness Planning*. Available at: http://brs.dk/eng/emergency_management/Pages/emergency_management.aspx.

Detert, J. R., & Edmonson, A. C. (2011). Implicit voice theories: Taken-for-granted rules of self-censorship at work. *Academy of Management Journal*, 54(1), 461–488.

DiMaggio, P. J., & Powell, W. W. (1983). The iron cage revisited: Institutional isomorphism and collective rationality in organizational fields. *American Sociological Review*, 48(2), 147–160.

Donaldson, T., & Preston, L. E. (1995). The stakeholder theory of the corporation: Concepts, evidence, and implications. *Academy of Management Review*, 20(1), 65–91.

Douglas, M. (1966). *Purity and Danger: An Analysis of Pollution and Taboo*. London: Routledge.

Douglas, M., & Wildavsky, A. (1983). *Risk and Culture: An Essay on the Selection of Technological and Environmental Dangers*. Berkeley, CA: University of California Press.

Drennan, L. T., & McConnell, A. (2007). *Risk and Crisis Management in the Public Sector*. London: Routledge. Second edition, 2015.

Dreyfus, S. E., & Dreyfus, H. L. (1980). A five-stage model of the mental activities in directed skill acquisition. DTIC Document.

Dreyfus, H. L., & Dreyfus, S. E. (1986). *Mind over Machine: The Power of Human Intuition and Expertise in the Era of the Computer*. New York: Free Press.

DuBrin, A. J. (Ed.) (2013). *Handbook of Research on Crisis Leadership in Organizations*. Northampton, MA: Edward Elgar.

Elliott, D., Swartz, E., & Herbane, B. (2002). *Business Continuity Management: A Crisis Management Approach*. London: Routledge. Second edition, 2010.

Elsbach, K. D. (2006). *Organizational Perception Management*. Mahwah, NJ: Lawrence Erlbaum.

Entman, R. M. (1993). Framing: Toward clarification of a fractured paradigm. *Journal of Communication*, 43(4), 51–58.

Fairclough, N. (1992). *Discourse and Social Change*. Cambridge: Polity Press.

Fairclough, N. (1993). Critical discourse analysis and the marketization of public discourse: The universities. *Discourse & Society*, 4(2), 133–168.

Fairhurst, G. (2010). *The Power of Framing: Creating the Language of Leadership*. San Francisco: Jossey-Bass.

Falkheimer, J. (2013). Transboundary and cultural crisis communication. In A. Thiessen (Ed.), *Handbuch Krisenmanagement* [*Handbook of Crisis Management*] (pp. 211–223). Wiesbaden: Springer.

Falkheimer, J., & Heide, M. (2006). Multicultural crisis communication: Towards a social constructionist perspective. *Journal of Contingencies and Crisis Management*, 14(4), 180–189.

Falkheimer, J., & Heide, M. (2010). Crisis communicators in change: From plans to improvisation. In W. T. Coombs & S. J. Holladay (Eds.), *The Handbook of Crisis Communication* (pp. 510–525). Malden, MA: Wiley-Blackwell.

Fearn-Banks, K. (1996). *Crisis Communications: A Casebook Approach*. Mahwah, NJ: Lawrence Erlbaum. Fifth edition, 2015.

Fearn-Banks, K. (2001). Crisis communication: A review of some best practices. In R. L. Heath (Ed.), *Handbook of Public Relations* (pp. 479–486). Thousand Oaks, CA: Sage.

Fearn-Banks, K. (2011). *Crisis Communications: A Casebook Approach*. New York: Routledge. Fourth edition.

Fediuk, T., Coombs, W. T., & Botero, I. (2010). Exploring crisis from a receiver perspective: Understanding stakeholder reactions during crisis events. In W. T. Coombs & S. J. Holladay (Eds.), *The Handbook of Crisis Communication* (pp. 635–656). Malden, MA: Wiley-Blackwell.

Fegley, S., & Victor, J. (2005). *2005 Disaster Preparedness Survey Report*. Alexandria, VA: Society for Human Resource Management Research.

Fink, S. (1986). *Crisis Management: Planning for the Inevitable*. Lincoln, NE: An Authors Guild Backinprint.com Edition.

Fink, S. (2013). *Crisis Communications: The Definitive Guide to Managing the Message*. New York: McGraw-Hill.

Fishbein, M., & Ajzen, I. (2010). *Predicting and Changing Behavior: The Reasoned Action Approach*. New York: Psychology Press.

Fishman, D. A. (1999). ValuJet Flight 592: Crisis communication theory blended and extended. *Communication Quarterly*, 47(4), 345–375.

Fjeld, K., & Molesworth, M. (2006). PR practitioners' experiences of, and attitudes towards, the internet's contribution to external crisis communication. *Corporate Communications: An International Journal*, 11(4), 391–405.

Flyvbjerg, B. (2006). Five misunderstandings about case-study research. *Qualitative Inquiry*, 12(2), 219–245.

Fombrun, C. J. (2012). The building blocks of corporate reputation: Definitions, antecedents, consequences. In M. L. Barnett & T. G. Pollock (Eds.), *The Oxford Handbook of Corporate Reputation* (pp. 94–113). Oxford: Oxford University Press.

Foreman, P. O., Whetten, D. A., & Mackey, A. (2012). An identity-based view of reputation, image, and legitimacy: Clarifications and distinctions among related constructs. In M. L. Barnett & T. G. Pollock (Eds.), *The Oxford Handbook of Corporate Reputation* (pp. 179–200). Oxford: Oxford University Press.

Fösterling, F. (2001). *Attribution: An Introduction to Theories, Research and Applications*. Philadelphia, PA: Psychology Press.

Frandsen, F., & Johansen, W. (2004). *Hvor godt forberedte er de? En undersøgelse af danske virksomheders og myndigheders kriseberedskab anno 2003* [*How Prepared Are They? A Study of the Crisis Preparedness of Private Companies and Public Authorities in Denmark AD 2003*]. Aarhus School of Business: Reports from Centre for Corporate Communication.

Frandsen, F., & Johansen, W. (2007). The apology of a sports icon: Crisis communication and apologetic ethics. *Hermes: Journal of Language and Communication Studies*, 38, 85–104.

Frandsen, F., & Johansen, W. (2009a). Wash and communicate: Artifacts and actions in crisis communication. In L. Louhiala-Salminen & A. Kankaanranta (Eds.), *The Ascent of International Business Communication* (pp. 67–85). Helsinki: Helsinki School of Economics.

Frandsen, F., & Johansen, W. (2009b). Institutionalizing crisis communication in the public sector: An explorative study in Danish municipalities. *International Journal of Strategic Communication*, 3(2),102–115.

Frandsen, F., & Johansen, W. (2009c). Krisekommunikation. In J. Helder, T. Bredenlöw, & J. Lautrup Nørgaard (Eds.), *Kommunikationsteori – en grundbog [Communication Theory – An Introduction]* (pp. 329–363). Copenhagen: Hans Reitzels Forlag.

Frandsen, F., & Johansen, W. (2010a). Apologizing in a globalizing world: Crisis communication and apologetic ethics. *Corporate Communications: An International Journal*, 15(4), 350–364.

Frandsen, F., & Johansen, W. (2010b). Crisis communication, complexity and the cartoon affair: A case study. In W. T. Coombs & S. J. Holladay (Eds.), *The Handbook of Crisis Communication* (pp. 425–448). Malden, MA: Wiley-Blackwell.

Frandsen, F., & Johansen, W. (2010c). Corporate crisis communication across cultures. In A. Trosborg (Ed.), *Pragmatics across Languages and Cultures* (pp. 543–569). Berlin: De Gruyter Mouton.

Frandsen, F., & Johansen, W. (2011). The study of internal crisis communication: Towards an integrative framework. *Corporate Communications: An International Journal*, 16(4), 347–361.

Frandsen, F., & Johansen, W. (2013a). Public relations and the new institutionalism: In search of a theoretical framework. *Public Relations Inquiry*, 2(2), 205–221.

Frandsen, F., & Johansen, W. (2013b). Rhetorical arena (crisis theory). In R. L. Heath (Ed.), *Encyclopedia of Public Relations, Vol. II* (pp. 797–800). Thousand Oaks, CA: Sage.

Frandsen, F., & Johansen, W. (2014). When middle managers speculate about the behavior of employees in crisis situations: A study of the human factor in organizational crisis management. Paper presented at the 4th Annual International Crisis and Risk Communication (ICRC) Conference, Orlando, FL, University of Central Florida.

Frandsen, F., & Johansen, W. (2015a). Lego: Everything is not awesome. An emergent activist practice and inter-organizational relations. The case of Greenpeace, LEGO and Shell. Paper presented at 18th Annual International Public Relations Conference, IPPRC, March 4–8, 2015, Miami, FL.

Frandsen, F., & Johansen, W. (2015b). Organizations, stakeholders, and intermediaries: Towards a general theory. *International Journal of Strategic Communication*, (9)4, 253–271.

Frandsen, F., & Johansen, W. (2016a). Voices in conflict? The crisis communication of meta-organization. *Management Communication Quarterly*, In press.

Frandsen, F., & Johansen, W. (2016b). Crisis communication research in Northern Europe. In A. Schwarz, M. W. Seeger, & C. Auer (Eds.), *The Handbook of International Crisis Communication Research* (pp. 373–383). Malden, MA: Wiley-Blackwell.

Frandsen, F., Johansen, W., & Salomonsen, H. (2016). Responding to institutional complexity: Reputation and crisis management in Danish municipalities. *Scandinavian Journal of Public Administration*, 20(2), 69–100.

Freeman, R. E. (1984). *Strategic Management: A Stakeholder Approach*. Boston, MA: Pitman.

Friedman, A. L., & Miles, S. (2006). *Stakeholders: Theory and Practice*. Oxford: Oxford University Press.

Garavan, T. N. (2007). A strategic perspective on human resource management. *Advances in Developing Human Resources*, 9(1), 11–30.

Geertz, C. (1973). *The Interpretation of Cultures*. New York: Fontana.

George, A. M., & Pratt, C. B. (Eds.) (2012). *Case Studies in Crisis Communication: International Perspectives on Hits and Misses*. New York: Routledge.

Gerhard, J., & Neidhardt, F. (1990). Strukturen und Funktionen der moderner Öffentlichkeit: Fragestellungen und Ansätze [The structure and function of the modern public sphere: Questions and answers]. Working Paper, No. FS III, 90–101.

Giddens, A. (1990). *The Consequences of Modernity*. London: Polity Press.

Gilpin, D. R., & Murphy, P. J. (2006). Reframing crisis management through complexity. In C. H. Botan & V. Hazleton, (Eds.), *Public Relations Theory II* (pp. 375–392). Mahwah, NJ: Lawrence Erlbaum.

Gilpin, D. R., & Murphy, P. J. (2008). *Crisis Management in a Complex World*. New York: Oxford University Press.

Gilpin, D. R., & Murphy, P. J. (2010). Complexity and crises: A new paradigm. In W. T. Coombs & S. J. Holladay (Eds.), *The Handbook of Crisis Communication* (pp. 683–690). Malden, MA: Wiley-Blackwell.

Glaesser, D. (2006). *Crisis Management in the Tourism Industry*. London: Routledge.

Gleick, J. (1987). *Chaos: Making a New Science*. New York: Penguin.

Goetzee, C., & Niekerk, D. van (2012). Tracking the evolution of the crisis management cycle: A general system theory approach. *Journal of Disaster Risk Studies*, 4(1), 1–9.

González-Herrero, A., & Smith, S. (2008). Crisis communications management on the web: How internet-based technologies are changing the way public relations professionals handle business crises. *Journal of Contingencies and Crisis Management*, 16(3), 143–153.

Gray, R. H., Owens, D. L., & Adams, C. (1996). *Accounting and Accountability: Changes and Challenges in Corporate Social and Environmental Reporting*. Hemel Hempstead: Prentice Hall.

Grebe, S. K. (2013). Things can get worse: How mismanagement of a crisis response strategy can cause a secondary or double crisis: The example of the AWB corporate scandal. *Corporate Communications: An International Journal*, 18(1), 70–86.

Greenwood, R., Oliver, C., Sahlin, K., & Suddaby, R. (2008). Introduction. In R. Greenwood, C.. Oliver, K. Sahlin, & R. Suddaby (Eds.), *The SAGE Handbook of Organizational Institutionalism* (pp. 1–46). London: Sage.

Grossi, G., & Reichard, C. (2008). Municipal corporatization in Germany and Italy. *Public Management Review*, 10(5), 597–617.

Gundel, S. (2005). Towards a new typology of crises. *Journal of Contingencies and Crisis Management*, 13(3), 106–115.

Hallahan, K. (1999). Seven models of framing: Implications for public relations. *Journal of Public Relations Research*, 11(3), 205–242.

Ham, C. D., Hong, H., & Cameron, G. T. (2012). Same crisis, different responses: Case studies of how multiple competing corporations responded to the same explosion-related crises. *International Journal of Business and Social Sciences*, 3(20), 19–31.

Haruta, A., & Hallahan, K. (2003). Cultural issues in airline crisis communications: A Japan–US comparative study. *Asian Journal of Communication*, 13(2), 122–150.

Hearit, K. M. (1994). Apologies and public relations crises at Chrysler, Toshiba, and Volvo. *Public Relations Review*, 20(2), 113–125.

Hearit, K. M. (1995a). From 'We didn't do it' to 'It's not our fault': The use of apologia in public relations crises. In W. N. Elwood (Ed.), *Public Relations Inquiry as Rhetorical Criticism* (pp. 117–131). Westport, CT: Praeger.

Hearit, K. M. (1995b). 'Mistakes were made': Organizations, apologia, and crises of social legitimacy. *Communication Studies*, 46(1–2), 1–17.

Hearit, K. M. (2006). *Crisis Management by Apology: Corporate Responses to Allegations of Wrongdoing*. Mahwah, NJ: Lawrence Erlbaum.

Hearit, K. M., & Courtright, J. L. (2003). A social constructionist approach to crisis management: Allegations of sudden acceleration in the Audi 5000. *Communication Studies*, 54(1), 79–95.

Hearit, K. M., & Courtright, J. L. (2004). A symbolic approach to crisis management: Sear's defense of its auto repair policies. In D. P. Millar & R. L. Heath (Eds.), *Responding to Crisis: A Rhetorical Approach to Crisis Communication* (pp. 201–212). Mahwah, NJ: Lawrence Erlbaum.

Heath, R. L. (1997). *Strategic Issues Management: Organizations and Public Policy Challenges.* Thousand Oaks, CA: Sage.

Heath, R. L. (2006). Best practices in crisis communication: Evolution of practice through research. *Journal of Applied Communication Research,* 34(3), 245–248.

Heath, R. J., & Bryant, J. (1992), *Human Communication Theory and Research: Concepts, Contexts, & Challenges.* Hillsdale, NJ: Lawrence Erlbaum.

Heath, R. J., & Coombs, W: T. (2006). *Today's Public Relations: An Introduction.* Los Angeles: Sage.

Heath, R. L., & O'Hair, H. D. (Eds.) (2009). *Handbook of Risk and Crisis Communication.* New York: Routledge.

Heath, R. L., & Palenchar, M. J. (2009). *Strategic Issues Management: Organizations and Public Policy Challenges.* Los Angeles: Sage.

Heide, M. (2013). Internal crisis communication: The future of crisis management. In A. Thießen (Ed.), *Handbuch Krisenmanagement* [*Handbook of Crisis Management*] (pp. 195–209). Wiesbaden: Springer.

Heide, M., & Simonsson, C. (2014). Developing internal crisis communication: New roles and practices of communication professionals. *Corporate Communications: An International Journal,* 19(2), 126–146.

Henderson, J. C. (2006). *Managing Tourism Crisis: Causes, Consequences and Management.* New York: Routledge.

Herbane, B. (2010a). The evolution of business continuity management: A historical review of practices and drivers. *Business History,* 53(6), 978–1002.

Herbane, B. (2010b). Small business research: Time for a crisis-based view. *International Small Business Journal,* 28(1), 43–64.

Herbane, B. (2013). Exploring crisis management in UK small- and medium-sized enterprises. *Journal of Contingencies and Crisis Management,* 21(2), 82–85.

Hermann, C. F. (1963). Some consequences of crisis which limit the viability of organizations. *Administrative Science Quarterly,* 8, 61–82.

Hjarvard, S. (2008). The mediatization of society: a theory of the media as agents of social and cultural change. *Nordicom Review,* 29(2), 105–134.

Hjarvard, S. (2013). *The Mediatization of Culture and Society.* London: Routledge.

Hofstede, G. (1991). *Cultures and Organizations: Software of the Mind.* New York: McGraw-Hill.

Hofstede, G. (2001). *Culture's Consequences.* Beverly Hills, CA: Sage. Third edition.

Hofstede, G. (2002). Dimensions do not exist: A reply to Brendan McSweeney. *Human Relations,* 55(11), 1355–1361.

Holling, C. S. (1973). Resilience and stability of ecological systems. *Annual Review of Ecology and Systematics,* 4, 1–23.

Holmström, S. (2010). Reflective management: Seeing the organization as if from outside. In R. L. Heath (Ed.), *Handbook of Public Relations* (pp. 261–276). Thousand Oaks, CA: Sage.

Hood, C. (2011). *The Blame Game: Spin, Bureaucracy, and Self-Preservation in Government.* Princeton, NJ: Princeton University Press.

Huang, Y.-H., Lin, Y.-H., & Su, S.-H. (2005). Crisis communicative strategies in Taiwan: Category, continuum, and cultural implication. *Public Relations Review,* 31, 229–238.

Hutchins, H. M. (2008). What does HRD know about organizational crisis management? Not enough! Read on. *Advances in Developing Human Resources,* 10(3), 299–309.

Ihlen, Ø. (2002). Defending the Mercedes A-Class: Combining and changing crisis-response strategies. *Journal of Public Relations Research,* 14(3), 185–206.

Ihlen, Ø., & Pallas, J. (2014). Mediatization of corporations. In Lundby, K. (Ed.), *Mediatization of Communication* (Chapter 18). Handbook of Communication. Berlin: De Gruyter.

Irvine, R. B., & Millar, D. (1996). Debunking the stereotypes of crisis management: The nature of business crises in the 1990s. Paper presented at the 5th Annual Conference on Crisis Management, University of Nevada, Las Vegas (August 8, 1996).

Iyengar, S. (1991). *Is Anyone Responsible? How Television Frames Political Issues*. Chicago: University of Chicago Press.

Jacobs, G. (1999). *Preformulating the News: An Analysis of the Metapragmatics of Press Releases*. Amsterdam: John Benjamins.

Janis, I. L. (1972). *Groupthink: Psychological Studies of Policy Decisions and Fiascoes*. Boston: Houghton Mifflin.

James, R. K., & Gilliland, B. E. (2008). *Crisis Intervention Strategies*. Belmont, CA: Brooks/Cole.

Jaques, T. (2007). Issue management and crisis management: An integrated, non-linear, relational construct. *Public Relations Review*, 33(3), 147–157.

Jaques, T. (2009). Issue and crisis management: Quicksand in the definitional landscape. *Public Relations Review*, 35, 280–286.

Jaques, T. (2014). *Issue and Crisis Management: Exploring Issues, Crises, Risk and Reputation*. Sydney: Oxford University Press.

Jin, Y. (2009). The effects of public's cognitive appraisal of emotions in crises on crisis coping and strategy assessment. *Public Relations Review*, 35, 310–313.

Jin, Y., Pang, A., & Cameron, G. T. (2007). Integrated crisis mapping: Towards a public-based, emotion-driven conceptualization in crisis communication. *Sphera Publica*, 7, 81–96.

Jin, Y., Pang, A., & Cameron, G. T. (2012). Towards a public-based, emotion-driven conceptualization in crisis communication: Unearthing dominant emotions in multi-staged testing of the Integrated Crisis Mapping (ICM) Model. *Journal of Public Relations Research*, 24, 266–298.

Jin, Y., Liu, B. F., & Austin, L. L. (2014). Examining the role of social media in effective crisis management: The effects of crisis origin, information form and source on publics' crisis responses. *Communication Research*, 41(1), 74–94.

Johansen, B. F., & Weckesser, N. (2013). *Ven eller fjende: Emotionelle stakeholdere på Facebook. Om Telenors retoriske delarena på Facebook og emotionelle stakeholders betydning for krisekommunikation* [Friend or enemy: Emotional stakeholders on Facebook. The case of the Telenor Facebook sub-arena and the role of emotional stakeholders for crisis communication]. Master's Thesis, Aarhus University.

Johansen, B. F., Johansen, W., & Weckesser, N. (2016). Emotional stakeholders as 'crisis communicators' in social media: The case of the Telenor customer complaints crisis. *Corporate Communications: An International Journal*, 21(3), 289–308.

Johansen, W., & Frandsen, F. (2007). *Krisekommunikation: Når virksomhedens image og omdømme er truet* [Crisis Communication: When the Company's Image and Reputation Are under Threat]. Frederiksberg: Samfundslitteratur.

Johansen, W., Aggerholm, H. K., & Frandsen, F. (2012). Entering new territory: A study of internal crisis management and crisis communication in organizations. *Public Relations Review*, 38, 270–279.

Johnson, R. L. (2006). *Crisis Communication: Case Studies in Health Image Restoration*. Danvers, MD: Hcpro Inc.

Johnson, V., & Peppas, S. C. (2003). Crisis management in Belgium: The case of Coca-Cola. *Corporate Communications: An International Journal*, 8(1), 18–22.

Jones, B. L., & Chase, W. H. (1979). Managing public policy issues. *Public Relations Review*, 5(2), 3–23.

Journal of Contingencies and Crisis Management, 10(4), 2002. Special issue on 'Crisis management in France'.

Journal of Management Education, 37(1), 2013. Special issue on 'Crisis management education'.

Kahneman, D. (2011). *Thinking, Fast and Slow*. New York: Farrar, Straus & Giroux.

Kaplan, A. M., & Haenlein, M. (2010). Users of the world, unite! The challenges and opportunities of social media. *Business Horizons*, 53, 59–68.

Kaplan, R. S., & Norton, D. P. (1996). *The Balanced Scorecard: Translating Strategy into Action*. Boston, MA: Harvard Business School Press.

Kasperson, R. E., Renn, O., Slovic, P., Brown, H. S., Emel, J., Goble, R., Kasperson, J. X., & Ratick, S. J. (1988). The social amplification of risk: A conceptual framework. *Risk Analysis*, 8(2), 178–187.

Kassing, J. W. (1998). Development and validation of the Organizational Dissent Scale. *Management Communication Quarterly*, 12, 183–229.

Kassing, J. W. (2011). *Dissent in Organizations*. Malden, MA: Polity Press.

Kepplinger, H. M. (2007). Reciprocal effects: Towards a theory of mass media effects on decision makers. *Harvard International Journal of Press/Politics*, 12(2), 3–23.

Kim, H. K., & Niederdeppe, J. (2013). The role of emotional response during an H1N1 influenza pandemic on a college campus. *Journal of Public Relations Research*, 25, 30–50.

King, A. A., Lenox, M. J., & Barnett, M. L. (2002). Strategic responses to the reputation commons problem. In A. Hoffman & M. J. Ventresca (Eds.), *Organizations, Policy, and the Natural Environment: Institutional and Strategic Perspectives* (pp. 393–406). Palo Alto, CA: Stanford University Press.

Kivikuru, U., & Nord, L. (Eds.) (2009). *After the Tsunami: Crisis Communication in Finland and Sweden*. Gothenburg: Nordicom.

Knight, R. F., & Pretty, D. J. (1999). Corporate catastrophes, stock returns and trading volume. *Corporate Reputation Review*, 2(4), 363–378.

Koerber, D. (2015). Fundamental mediation: A classification of media in crisis communication research. *CMJS Fall 2015*.

Korn, C., & Einwiller, S. (2013). Media coverage about organisations in critical situations: Analysing the impact on employees. *Corporate Communications: An International Journal*, 18(4), 451–468.

Kristofferson, K., White, K., & Peloza, J. (2014). The nature of slacktivism: How the social observability of an initial act of token support affects subsequent prosocial action. *Journal of Consumer Research*, 40, 1149–1166.

Lagadec, P. (1980). *Le risque technologique majeur: Politique, risque et processus de développement* [*Major Technological Risk: An Assessment of Industrial Disasters*]. Paris: Pergamon.

Lagadec, P. (1981). *La civilisation du risque: Catastrophes technologiques et responsabilité sociale* [*The Risk Civilization: Technological Disasters and Social Responsibility*]. Paris: Le Seuil.

Lagadec, P. (2000). *Ruptures créatrices* [*Creative Breaks*]. Paris: Editions d'Organisation.

Lalonde, C., & Roux-Dufort, C. (2013). Challenges in teaching crisis management: Connecting theories, skills, and reflexivity. *Journal of Management Education*, 37(1), 21–50.

Lammers, J. C. (2011). How institutions communicate: Institutional messages, institutional logics, and organizational communication. *Management Communication Quarterly*, 25(1), 154–182.

Larkin, J. (2003). *Strategic Reputation Risk Management*. Houndmills: Palgrave Macmillan.

Larsson, L. (2010). Crisis and learning. In W. T. Coombs & S. J. Holladay (Eds.), *The Handbook of Crisis Communication* (pp. 713–718). Malden, MA: Wiley-Blackwell.

Lasswell, H. D. (1948). The structure and function of communication in society. In L. Bryson (Ed.), *The Communication of Ideas* (pp. 37–51). New York: Harper and Brothers.

Ledingham, J. A., & Bruning, S. D. (Eds.) (2000). *Public Relations as Relationship Management: A Relational Approach to the Study and Practice of Public Relations*. Mahwah, NJ: Lawrence Erlbaum.

Lee, B. K. (2004). Audience-oriented approach to crisis communication: A study of Hong Kong consumers' evaluation of an organizational crisis. *Communication Research*, 31(5), 600–618.

Lee, B. K. (2005a). Hong Kong consumers' evaluation in an airline crash: A path model analysis. *Journal of Public Relations Research*, 17(4), 363–391.

Lee, B. K. (2005b). Crisis, culture, community. In P. Kalbfleisch (Ed.), *Communication Yearbook 29* (pp. 275–309), New York: Routledge.

Lippmann, W. (1922). *Public Opinion*. New Brunswick, NJ: Transaction Publishers.

Lipshitz, R., Klein, G., Orasanu, J., & Salas, E. (2001). Taking stock of naturalistic decision making. *Journal of Behavioral Decision Making*, 14(5), 331–352.

Liu, B. F., Austin, L., & Jin, Y. (2011). How publics respond to crisis communication strategies: The interplay of information form and source. *Public Relations Review*, 37(4), 345–353.

Luhmann, N. (1993). *Risk: A Sociological Theory*. New York: Aldine de Gruyter.

Luhmann, N. (1995). *Social Systems*. Stanford, CA: Stanford University Press.

Lundby, K. (2009). *Mediatization: Concept, Changes, Consequences*. New York: Peter Lang.

Lundby, K. (Ed.) (2014). *Mediatization of Communication*. Handbooks of Communication Science. Berlin: De Gruyter.

Luoma-aho, V. (2010). Emotional stakeholders: A threat to organizational legitimacy? Conference paper for the 60th Annual Conference of the ICA, Singapore, June 22–26. www.academia.edu/245892/Emotional stakeholders (retrieved December 14, 2012).

Luoma-aho, V., & Vos, M. (2010). Towards a more dynamic stakeholder model: Acknowledging multiple issue arenas. *Corporate Communications: An International Journal*, 15(3), 315–331.

Lupton, D. (1999). *Risk*. London: Routledge.

Maguire, S., McKelvey, B., Mirabeau, L., & Öztas, N. (2006). Complexity science and organization studies. In S. R. Clegg, C. Hardy, T. B. Lawrence, & W. R. Nord (Eds.), *Handbook of Organization Studies* (2nd ed., pp. 165–214). London: Sage.

Maitlis, S., & Christianson, M. (2014). Sensemaking in organizations: Taking stock and moving forward. *Academy of Management Annals*, 8(1), 57–125.

Maitlis, S., & Sonenshein, S. (2010). Sensemaking in crisis and change: Inspiration and insights from Weick (1988). *Journal of Management Studies*, 47(3), 551–580.

Marcus, A. A., & Goodman, R. S. (1991). Victims and shareholders: The dilemmas of presenting corporate policy during a crisis. *Academy of Management Journal*, 34(2), 281–305.

March, J., & Simon, H. (1958). *Organizations*. Cambridge, MA: Wiley.

Marra, F. J. (1999). Crisis communication plans: Poor predictors of excellent crisis public relations. *Public Relations Review*, 24(4), 461–474.

Marra, F. J. (2004). Excellent crisis communication: Beyond crisis plans. In D. Millar & R. L. Heath (Eds.), *Responding to Crisis: A Rhetorical Approach to Crisis Communication* (pp. 311–325). Mahwah, NJ: Lawrence Erlbaum.

Martin, J. (2002). *Organizational Culture: Mapping the Terrain*. Thousand Oaks, CA: Sage.

Mazzei, A., & Ravazzani, S. (2011). Manager–employee communication during a crisis: The missing link? *Corporate Communications: An International Journal*, 16(3), 243–254.

Mazzei, A., Kim, J.-N., & Dell'Oro, C. (2012). Strategic value of employee relationships and communicative actions: Overcoming corporate crisis with quality internal communication. *International Journal of Strategic Communication*, 6, 31–44.

McCombs, M. (2004). *Setting the Agenda: The Mass Media and Public Opinion*. Malden, MA: Polity Press. Second edition, 2014.

McCombs, M., & Shaw, D. (1972). The agenda-setting function of mass media. *Public Opinion Quarterly*, 36, 176–187.

Merton, R. K. (1936). The unanticipated consequences of purposive social action. *American Sociological Review*, 1(6), 894–904.

Meyers, G. C. (1986). *When It Hits the Fan: Managing the Nine Crises of Business*. Boston, MA: New American Library.

Millar, F. E., & Beck, D. B. (2004). Metaphors of crisis. In D. P. Millar & R. L. Heath (Eds.), *Responding to Crisis: A Rhetorical Approach to Crisis Communication* (pp. 153–166). Mahwah, NJ: Lawrence Erlbaum.

Mitchell, R, K., Agle, B. R., & Wood, D. J. (1997). Toward a theory of stakeholder identification and salience: defining the principle of who and what really counts. *Academy of Management Review*, 22(4), 853–886.

Mitroff, I. I. (1994). Crisis management and environmentalism: A natural fit. *California Management Review*, 36(2), 101–113.

Mitroff, I. I. (2004). *Crisis Leadership: Planning for the Unthinkable*. Hoboken, NJ: Wiley.

Mitroff, I. I. (2005). *Why Some Companies Emerge Stronger and Better from a Crisis: 7 Essential Lessons for Surviving Disaster*. New York: Amacom.

Mitroff, I. I., & Kilman, R. H. (1984). *Corporate Tragedies: Product Tampering, Sabotage, and Other Catastrophes*. New York: Praeger.

Mitroff, I. I., Shrivastava, P., & Udwadia, F. E. (1987). Effective crisis management. *Academy of Management Executive*, 1(3), 291.

Moberg, T. (2015). *Må man dræbe en babygiraf? Om danske og udenlandske reaktioner på Københavns Zoos aflivning af giraffen Marius* [May one kill a baby giraffe? Danish and international reactions to Copenhagen Zoo's euthanasia of the giraffe Marius]. Master's Thesis, Aarhus University.

Moore, S., & Seymour, M. (2005). *Global Technology and Corporate Crisis: Strategies, Planning and Communication in the Information Age*. London: Routledge.

Murphy, P. (1996). Chaos theory as a model for managing issues and crisis. *Public Relations Review*, 22(2), 95–113.

Murphy, P. (2000). Symmetry, contingency, complexity: Accommodating uncertainty in public relations theory. *Public Relations Review*, 26(4), 447–462.

Mythen, G. (2004). *Ulrich Beck: A Critical Introduction to Risk Society*. London: Pluto Press.

Møller Jensen, J. & Koed Madsen, T. (1992). Analyse, klassifikation og behandling af negative rygter [Analysis, classification and management of negative rumors]. *Ledelse og Erhvervsøkonomi*, 56(1), 33–42.

Near, J. P., & Miceli, M. P. (1985). Organizational dissidence: The case of whistle-blowing. *Journal of Business Ethics*, 4, 1–16.

Nohrstedt, S. A. (2010). Threat society and the media. In S. A. Nohrstedt (Ed.), *Communicating Risk: Towards the Threat Society?* (pp. 17–51). Gothenburg: Nordicom.

Ogrizek, M., & Guillery, J.-M. (1997). *La communication de crise*. Paris: PUF. English translation: *Communicating in Crisis* (1999). New York: Aldine de Gruyter.

Olaniran, B. A., & Williams, D. E. (2001). Anticipatory model of crisis management: A vigilant response to technological crisis. In R. L. Heath & G. Vasquez (Eds.), *Handbook of Public Relations* (pp. 487–500). Thousand Oaks, CA: Sage.

Olaniran, B. A., Williams, D. E., & Coombs, W. T. (Eds.) (2012). *Pre-Crisis Planning, Communication, and Management: Preparing for the Inevitable*. New York: Peter Lang.

Oliveira, M. de F. (2013). Multicultural environments and their challenges to crisis communication. *Journal of Business Communication*, 50(3), 253–277.

Olsson, E.-K. (2010). Defining crisis news events. *Nordicom Review*, 31(1), 87–101.

Olsson, E.-K., & Nord, L. W. (2015). Paving the way for crisis exploitation: The role of journalistic styles and standards. *Journalism*, 16(3), 341–358.

Olsson, E.-K., Nord, L. W., & Falkheimer, J. (2015). Media coverage crisis exploitation characteristics: A case comparison study. *Journal of Public Relations Research*, 27, 158–174.

Pallas, J., & Fredriksson, M. (2013). Corporate media work and micro-dynamics of mediatization. *European Journal of Communication*, 28(4), 420–435.

Pallas, J., Strannegård, L., & Jonsson, S. (Eds.) (2014). *Organizations and the Media: Organizing in a Mediatized World*. London: Routledge.

Pang, A. (2006). *Conflict Positioning in Crisis Communication*. Doctoral Dissertation, University of Missouri–Columbia.

Pang, A., Jin, Y., & Cameron, G. T. (2010). Contingency theory of strategic conflict management: Directions for the practice of crisis communication from a decade of theory development, discovery, and dialogue. In W. T. Coombs & S. J. Holladay (Eds.), *The Handbook of Crisis Communication* (pp. 527–549). Malden, MA: Wiley-Blackwell.

Pang, A., Hassan, N. B. B. A., & Chong, A. C. Y. (2014). Negotiating crisis in the social media environment: Evolution of crises online, gaining credibility offline. *Corporate Communications: An International Journal*, 19(1), 96–118.

Parmar, B. L., Freeman, R. E., Harrison, J. S., Wicks, A. C., Purnell, L. & De Colle, S. (2010). Stakeholder theory: The state of the art. *The Academy of Management Annals*, 4(1), 403–445.

Pauchant, T. C., & Douville, R. (1993). Recent research in crisis management: A study of 24 authors' publications from 1986 to 1991. *Industrial & Environmental Quarterly*, 7(1), 43–66.

Pauchant, T., & Mitroff, I. I. (1992). *Transforming the Crisis-Prone Organization: Preventing Individual, Organizational, and Environmental Tragedies*. San Francisco: Jossey-Bass.

Pearson, C. M., & Clair, J. A. (1998). Reframing crisis management. *Academy of Management Review*, 23(1), 58–76.

Pearson, C. M., Roux-Dufort, C., & Clair, J. A. (Eds.) (2007). *International Handbook of Organizational Crisis Management*. Los Angeles: Sage.

Penrose, J. M. (2000). The role of perception in crisis planning. *Public Relations Review*, 26(2), 155–171.

Penuel, K. B., Statler, M., & Hagen, R. (Eds.) (2013). *Encyclopedia of Crisis Management*. New York: Sage.

Peretti-Watel, P. (2000). *Sociologie du risque [Risk Sociology]*. Paris: Armand Colin.

Peretti-Watel, P. (2001). *La société du risque [Risk Society]*. Paris: La Découverte.

Pergel, R., & Psychogios, A. G. (2013). Making sense of crisis: Cognitive barriers of learning in critical situations. *Management Dynamics in the Knowledge Economy*, 1(2), 179–205.

Perrow, C. (1984). *Normal Accidents: Living with High-Risk Technologies*. Princeton, NJ: Princeton University Press.

Peters, H. P. (1990). Risiko-Kommunikation: Kernenergie [Risk Communication: Nuclear energy]. In H. Jungermann, B. Rohrmann, & P. M. Wiedemann (Eds.), *Risiko-Konzepte, Risiko-Konflikte, Risiko Kommunikation* (pp. 59–148). Monograph Series of the Research Center Jülich. Vol. 3.

Pfeffer, J., & Sutton, R. I. (2006). *Hard Facts, Dangerous Half-Truths & Total Nonsense*. Boston, MA: Harvard Business School Press.

Pfeffer, J., Zorbach, T., & Carley, K. M. (2014). Understanding online firestorms: Negative word-of-mouth dynamics in social media networks. *Journal of Marketing Communications*, 20(1–2), 117–128.

Pinsdorf, M. K. (1991). Flying different skies: How cultures respond to airline disasters. *Public Relations Review*, 17(1), 37–56.

Pinsdorf, M. K. (2004). *All Crises Are Global: Managing to Escape Chaos*. New York: Fordham University Press.

Portal, T., & Roux-Dufort, C. (2013). *Prévenir les crises: Ces Cassandres qu'il faut savoir écouter [Preventing Crises]*. Paris: Armand Colin.

Power, M. (2004). *The Risk Management of Everything*. London: Demos.

Power, M. (2007). *Organized Uncertainty: Designing a World of Risk Management*. Oxford: Oxford University Press.

Powley, E. H., & Taylor, S. N. (2014). Pedagogical approaches to develop critical thinking and crisis leadership. *Journal of Management Education*, 38(4), 560–585.

Prince, S. H. (1920). *Catastrophe and Social Change*. New York: Columbia University Press.

Pratt, M. G. (1998). To be or not to be? Central questions in organizational identification. In D. A. Whetten & P. C. Godfrey (Eds.), *Identity in Organizations: Building Theory through Conversations* (pp. 171–208). Thousand Oaks, CA: Sage.

Prigogine, I., & Stengers, I. (1984). *Order Out of Chaos: Man's New Dialogue with Nature*. New York: Bantam.

Pugh, D. S. (Eds.) (1973). *Organization Theory: Selected Classic Readings*. London: Penguin.

Putnam, L. L., & Boys, S. (2006). Revisiting metaphors of organizational communication. In S. R. Clegg, C. Hardy, T. B. Lawrence, & W. R. Nord (Eds.), *Handbook of Organization Studies* (2nd ed., pp. 165–214). London: Sage.

Putnam, L. L., Phillips, N., & Chapman, P. (1996). Metaphors of communication and organization. In S. R. Clegg, C. Hardy, & W. R. Nord (Eds.), *Handbook of Organization Studies* (pp. 375–408). London: Sage.

Quarantelli, E. L. (Ed.) (1998). *What is a Disaster? Perspectives on the Question*. London: Routledge.

Quarantelli, E. L. (Ed.) (2005). *What is a Disaster? New Answers to Old Questions*. Philadelphia, PA: Xlibris.

Ray, S. J. (1999). *Strategic Communication in Crisis Management: Lessons from the Airline Industry*. Westport, CT: Quorum Books.

Renn, O. (1992). The social arena concept of risk debates. In S. Krimsky & D. Golding (Eds.), *Social Theories of Risk* (pp. 179–197). Westport, CT: Praeger.

Rhee, M., & Kim, T. (2012). After the collapse: A behavioral theory of reputation repair. In M. L. Barnett & T. G. Pollock (Eds.), *The Oxford Handbook of Corporate Reputation* (pp. 446–465). Oxford: Oxford University Press.

Robert, B., & Lajtha, C. (2002). A new approach to crisis management. *Journal of Contingencies and Crisis Management*, 10(4), 181–191.

Robert, B., & Lajtha, C. (2007). Crisis management simulations. In C. M. Pearson, C. Roux-Dufort & J. A. Clair (Eds.), *International Handbook of Organizational Management* (pp. 315–325). Los Angeles: Sage.

Rodrígez, H., Quarantelli, E. L., & Dynes, R. R. (Eds.) (2007). *Handbook of Disaster Research*. New York: Springer.

Rosenthal, U., Charles, M. T. & Hart, P. (Eds.) (1989). *Coping with Crises: The Management of Disasters, Riots and Terrorism*. Springfield, IL: Charles C. Thomas.

Rosenthal, U., Hart, P. 't, Van Duin, M.-J., Boin, R. A., Kroon, M. B. R., Otten, M. H. P., & Overdijk, W. I. E. (1994). *Complexity in Urban Crisis Management: Amsterdam's Response to the Bijlmer Air Disaster*. London: James & James.

Rosenthal, U., Boin, A., & Bos, C. J. (2001a). Shifting identities: The reconstructive mode of the Bijlmer plane crash. In U. Rosenthal, R. A. Boin, & L. K. Comfort (Eds.), *Managing Crises: Threats, Dilemmas, Opportunities* (pp. 200–215). Springfield, IL: Charles C. Thomas.

Rosenthal, U., Boin, R. A., & Comfort, L. K. (Eds.) (2001b). *Managing Crises: Threats, Dilemmas, Opportunities*. Springfield, IL: Charles C. Thomas.

Rothenbuhler, E. W. (1998). *Ritual Communication: From Everyday Conversation to Mediated Ceremony*. Los Angeles: Sage.

Rousseau, D. M. (2006). Is there such a thing as 'evidence-based management'? *Academy of Management Review*, 31(2), 256–269.

Roux-Dufort, C. (1999). Why organizations don't learn from crisis: The perverse power of normalization. *Review of Business*, 21(3/4), 25–30.

Roux-Dufort, C. (2000). *Gérer et décider en situation de crise: Outils de diagnostic, de prévention et de décision*. [Management and Decision-making in Crisis Situations]. Paris: Dunod.

Roux-Dufort, C., & Vidaillet, B. (2003). The difficulties of improvising in a crisis situation: A case study. *International Studies of Management and Organization*, 33(1), 86–115.

Ryan, H. R. (1982). *Kategoria* and *apologia*: On their rhetorical criticism as a speech set. *Quarterly Journal of Speech*, 68, 256–261.

Schannon, M. (2006). Risk, issue and crisis management: Ten observations on impediments to effectiveness and what can be done about them. *Journal of Promotion Management*, 12(3/4), 7–38.

Schultz, F., Utz, S., & Görit, A. (2011). Is the medium the message? Perceptions of and reactions to crisis communication via Twitter, blogs and traditional media. *Public Relations Review*, 37(1), 20–27.

Schwarz, A., Seeger, M. W., & Auer, C. (Eds.) (2016). *Handbook of International Crisis Communication Research*. Hoboken, NJ: Wiley-Blackwell.

Scott, M. H., & Lyman, S. M. (1968). Accounts. *American Sociological Review*, 33, 46–62.

Scott, W. R. (2008). *Institutions and Organizations: Ideas and Interests*. Thousand Oaks, CA: Sage.

Seeger, M. W. (2006). Best practices in crisis communication: An expert panel process. *Journal of Applied Communication Research*, 34(3), 232–244.

Seeger, M. W., Sellnow, T. L., & Ulmer, R. R. (2003). *Communication and Organizational Crisis*. Westport, CT: Praeger.

Seeger, M. W., Sellnow, T. L., & Ulmer, R. R. (2010). Expanding the parameters of crisis communication: From chaos to renewal. In R. L. Heath (Ed.), *Handbook of Public Relations* (pp. 489–499). Thousand Oaks, CA: Sage. Second edition.

Selart, M., Johansen, S. T., & Nesse, S. (2013). Employee reactions to leader-initiated crisis preparation: Core dimensions. *Journal of Business Ethics*, 116, 99–106.

Sellnow, T. L., & Seeger, M. W. (2013). *Theorizing Crisis Communication*. Malden, MA: Wiley-Blackwell.

Sethi, S. P. (1977). *Advocacy Advertising and Large Corporations: Social Conflict, Big Business Image, the News Media, and Public Policy*. Lexington, MA: Lexington Books.

Shoemaker, P. J. (1991). *Gatekeeping*. Newbury Park, CA: Sage.

Shoemaker, P. J., & Vos, T. P. (2009). *Gatekeeping Theory*. London: Routledge.

Shrivastava, P. (1987). *Bhopal: Anatomy of a Crisis*. Cambridge, MA: Ballinger.

Shrivastava, P., & Mitroff, I. I. (1987). Strategic management of corporate crises. *Columbia Journal of World Business*, 22(1), 5–11.

Shrivastava, P., Mitroff, I. I., & Alpaslan, C. M. (2013). Imagining an education in crisis management. *Journal of Management Education*, 37(1), 6–20.

Simonsen, D. M. (2014). *Organisatorisk resiliens fra et kommunikativt perspektiv: Meningsskabelse og organisering i krise* [Organizational Resilience from a Communicative Perspective: Sensemaking and Organizing in Crisis]. Doctoral dissertation, Aarhus University.

Smith, D., & Elliott, D. (Eds.) (2006). *Key Readings in Crisis Management: Systems and Structures for Prevention and Recovery*. London. Routledge.

Smith, D., & Elliott, D. (2007). Exploring the barriers to learning from crisis: Organizational learning and crisis. *Management Learning*, 38(5), 519–538.

Sørensen, M., & Christiansen, A. (2014). *Ulrich Beck: An Introduction to the Theory of Second Modernity and the Risk Society*. London: Routledge.

Statistics Denmark (2016). Nielsen har slået Jensen af pinden. January 14. www.dst.dk/da/Statistik/emner/navne (retrieved on February 4, 2016).

Steck, H. (2003). Corporatization of the university: Seeking conceptual clarity. *The Annals of the American Academy*, 585, 66–83.

Stoddard, E. R. (1968). *Conceptual Models of Human Behavior in Disasters*. El Paso, TX: Texas Western Press.

Strömbäck, J. (2008). Four phases of mediatization: An analysis of the mediatization of politics. *International Journal of Press/Politics*, 13(3), 228–246.

Sturges, D. L. (1994). Communicating through crisis: A strategy for organizational survival. *Management Communication Quarterly*, 7(3), 297–316.

Suchman, M. (1995). Managing legitimacy: Strategic and institutional approaches. *Academy of Management Review*, 20(3), 571–610.

Sumiala, J., & Hakala, S. (2010). Crisis: Mediatization of disaster in the Nordic media sphere. In P. Broddason, U. Kivikuru, B. Tufte, L. Weibull, & H. Østbye (Eds.), *Norden och världen: Perspektiv från forskningen om medier och kommunikation* [The Nordic Countries and the World: Perspectives from Research on Media and Communication] (pp. 361–378). Gothenburg: Nordicom.

Swales, J. M. (1990). *Genre Analysis: English in Academic and Research Settings*. Cambridge: Cambridge University Press.

Taylor, M. (2000). Cultural variance as a challenge to global public relations: A case study of the Coca-Cola scare in Europe. *Public Relations Review*, 26(3), 277–293.

Thießen, A. (Ed.) (2013). *Handbuch Krisenmanagement* [*Handbook of Crisis Management*]. Wiesbaden: Springer.

Thompson, J. B. (2000). *Political Scandal: Power and Visibility in the Media Age*. Cambridge: Polity Press.

Thussu, D. K. (2007). *News as Entertainment: The Rise of Global Infotainment*. Los Angeles: Sage.

Tierney, K. (2007). From the margins to the mainstream? Disaster research at the crossroads. *Annual Review of Sociology*, 33, 503–523.

Tierney, K. (2014). *The Social Roots of Risk: Producing Disasters, Promoting Resilience*. Stanford, CA: Stanford Business Books.

Toth, E. (2010). Reflections on the field. In R. L. Heath (Ed.), *The SAGE Handbook of Public Relations* (pp. 711–722). Thousand Oaks, CA: Sage.

Towner, E. B. (2009). Apologies, image repair, and reconciliation: The application, limitations, and future directions of apologetic rhetoric. In C. S. Beck (Ed.), *Communication Yearbook 33* (pp. 431–468). New York: Routledge.

Treem, J. W., & Leonardi, P. M. (2012). Social media use in organizations: Exploring the affordances of visibility, editability, persistence, and association. *Communication Yearbook 36* (pp. 143–189). New York: Routledge.

Tucker, A. (2008). Trade associations as industry reputation agents: A model of reputational trust. *Business and Politics*, 10(1), 1–26.

Turner, B. A. (1978). *Man-made Disasters*. Oxford: Butterworth-Heinemann.

Turner, B. A., & Pidgeon, N. F. (1997). *Man-made Disasters*. Oxford: Butterworth–Heinemann. Second edition.

Ulmer, R. R. (2012). Increasing the impact of thought leadership in crisis communication. *Management Communication Quarterly*, 26(4), 523–542.

Ulmer, R. R., & Sellnow, T. L. (2002). Crisis management and the discourse of renewal: Understanding the potential for positive outcomes of crisis. *Public Relations Review*, 28(4), 361–365.

Ulmer, R. R., Sellnow, T. L., & Seeger, M. W. (2007). *Effective Crisis Communication*. Thousand Oaks, CA: Sage. Second edition, 2011.

Utz, S., Schultz, F., & Glocka, S. (2013). Crisis communication online: How medium, crisis type and emotions affected public reactions in the Fukushima Daiichi nuclear disaster. *Public Relations Review*, 39(1), 40–46.

Valentini, C., & Kruckeberg, D. (2016). The future role of social media in international crisis communication. In A. Schwarz, M. W. Seeger, & C. Auer (Eds.), *Handbook of International Crisis Communication Research*. Hoboken, NJ: Wiley-Blackwell.

van der Meer, T. G. L. A., & Verhoeven, J. W. M. (2014). Emotional crisis communication. *Public Relations Review*, 40, 526–536.

Vasterman, P. L. M. (2005). Media-hype: Self-reinforcing news waves, journalistic standards and the construction of social problems. *European Journal of Communication*, 20(4), 508–530.

Veil, S. R., Sellnow, T. L., & Heald, M. (2011). Memoralizing crisis: The Oklahoma City National Memorial as renewal discourse. *Journal of Applied Communication Research*, 39(2), 164–183.

Veil, S. R., Reno, J., Freihaut, R., & Oldham, J. (2014). Online activists vs. Kraft Foods: A case of social media hijacking. Paper presented at the 2014 Conference of the ICA, May 22–26, 2014, Seattle, WA.

Verhoeven, P., Tench, R., Zerfass, A., & Moreno, A. (2014). Crisis? What crisis? How European professionals handle crises and crisis communication. *Public Relations Review*, 40, 107–109.

Vigsø, O. (2010). Naming is framing: Swine flu, new flu, and A(H1N1). *Observatorio Journal*, 4(3), 241.

Vos, M., Lund, R., Reich, Z., & Harro-Loit, H. (Eds.) (2011). *Developing a Crisis Communication Scorecard: Outcomes of an International Research Project 2008–2011.* Jyväskylä University.

Vos, M., Schoemaker, H., & Luoma-aho, V. L. (2013). Setting the agenda for research on issue arenas. *Corporate Communications: An International Journal,* 19(2), 200–215.

Waldrop, M. M. (1992). *Complexity: The Emerging Science at the Edge of Order and Chaos.* New York: Simon and Schuster.

Wang, J., Hutchins, H. M., & Garavan, T. N. (2009). Exploring the strategic role of human resource development in organizational crisis management. *Human Resource Development Review,* 8(1), 22–53.

Ware, B. L., & Linkugel, W. A. (1973). They spoke in defense of themselves: On the generic criticism of *apologia. Quarterly Journal of Speech,* 59, 273–283.

Waring, A., & Glendon, A. I. (1998). *Managing Risk: Critical Issues for Survival and Success into the 21st Century.* London: Thomson.

Warner, W. L., & Martin, D. (1967). Big trade and business associations. In W. L. Warner (Ed.), *The Emergent American Society, Vol. 1* (pp. 314–346). New Haven, CT: Yale University Press.

Watson, W. (Ed.) (2001). *Crisis Journalism: A Handbook of Media Response.* New York: The American Press Institute.

Weick, K. E. (1988). Enacted sensemaking in crisis situations. *Journal of Management Studies,* 25(4), 305–317.

Weick, K. E. (1993). The collapse of sensemaking in organizations: The Mann Gulch disaster. *Administrative Science Quarterly,* 38, 628–652.

Weick, K. E., & Sutcliffe, K. M. (2001). *Managing the Unexpected: Assuring High Performance in an Age of Complexity.* San Francisco: Jossey-Bass.

Weick, K. E., & Sutcliffe, K. M. (2007). *Managing the Unexpected: Resilient Performance in an Age of Uncertainty.* San Francisco: Jossey-Bass. Second edition

West, M. D. (2006). *Secrets, Sex, and Spectacle: The Rules of Scandal in Japan and the United States.* Chicago: The University of Chicago Press.

Wicks, D. (2001). Institutionalized mindsets of invulnerability: Differentiated institutional fields and the antecedents of organizational crisis. *Organization Studies,* 22(4), 659–692.

Wien, C., & Elmelund-Præstekær, C. (2009). An anatomy of media hypes: Developing a model for the dynamics and structure of intense media coverage of single issues. *European Journal of Communication,* 24(2), 183–201.

Wildavsky, A. (1988). *Searching for Safety.* New Brunswick, NJ: Transaction Publishers.

Winn, M. I., MacDonald, P., & Zietsma, C. (2008). Managing industry reputation: The dynamic tension between collective and competitive reputation management strategies. *Corporate Reputation Review,* 11(1), 35–55.

Wipperfürth, A. (2005). *Brand Hijack: Marketing without Marketing.* New York: Portfolio.

Wise, K. (2003). The Oxford incident: Organizational culture's role in an anthrax crisis. *Public Relations Review,* 29, 461–472.

Wæraas, A., & Maor, M. (Eds.) (2015). *Organizational Reputation in the Public Sector.* London: Routledge.

Zdziarski, E. L., Dunkel, N. W., & Rollo, J. M. (2007). *Campus Crisis Management.* Hoboken, NJ: Wiley.

INDEX